# THE BRAZILIAN ECONOMY:
## STRUCTURE AND PERFORMANCE
## IN RECENT DECADES

Edited by

Maria J.F. Willumsen and
Eduardo Giannetti da Fonseca

North·South Center Press
UNIVERSITY OF MIAMI

The publisher of this book is the North-South Center Press at the University of Miami.

The mission of the North-South Center is to promote better relations and serve as a catalyst for change among the United States, Canada, and the nations of Latin America and the Caribbean by advancing knowledge and understanding of the major political, social, economic, and cultural issues affecting the nations and peoples of the Western Hemisphere.

All copyright inquiries should be addressed to the publisher: North-South Center Press, 1500 Monza Avenue, Coral Gables, Florida 33146-3027, U.S.A., phone 305-284-8914, fax 305-284-5089, or e-mail mvega@nsc.msmail.miami.edu.

To order or to return books, contact Lynne Rienner Publishers, Inc., 1800 30th Street, Suite 314, Boulder, CO 80301-1026, 303-444-6684, fax 303-444-0824.

**Library of Congress Cataloging-in-Publication Data**

Economia brasileira. English

The Brazilian economy: structure and performance in recent decades / edited by Maria J.F. Willumsen and Eduardo Giannetti da Fonseca

      p. cm.

Includes bibliographical references and index.

ISBN 0-935501-98-3 (pbk.: alk. paper)

    1. Brazil—Economic conditions—1985-    I. Willumsen, Maria José Fernandes.    II. Fonseca. Eduardo Giannetti da.

III. Title.

HC187.E2313 1996                          95-49723

                                                CIP

Printed in the United States of America/T-S

02 01 00 99 98 97   6 5 4 3 2 1

# Contents

# Acknowledgments

Several institutions contributed to the success of this project. The University of Miami North-South Center provided the financial support that commissioned the articles for this book and funded a seminar that served as a forum for debate on the topics examined here. The University of São Paulo's School of Economics, Administration, and Accounting (Faculdade de Economia, Administração e Contabilidade da Universidade de São Paulo), the Institute of Economic Research Foundation (Fundação Instituto de Pesquisas Econômicas, FIPE), and Florida International University — all institutions to which the editors are affiliated — provided the logistical support necessary for the development and successful completion of this work. The authors are greatly appreciative of these institutions and their support.

Our gratitude also goes out to several individuals who contributed to the success of this project. Antônio E. Comune, Guilherme Leite da S. Dias, Juan H. Moldau, and Paulo de Tarso André read preliminary versions of the chapters and provided valuable suggestions. They also participated as discussants in the seminar held in São Paulo. Sandra W. Joice helped with the translation of articles from Portuguese to English. Special thanks go to the North-South Center's Editorial and Publications Departments. Joseph Domask very competently edited the text. His suggestions for improving the English and making the text more accessible to readers were invaluable. Editorial Research Coordinator Mary D'León also assisted with proofreading and reconciling the English version with the Portuguese. Senior Editor Jayne Weisblatt further edited the text, and Editorial Director Kathleen Hamman supervised the editing process. Graphic Arts Consultant Stephanie True Moss formatted and indexed the book and designed the cover. Associate Director of Publications Susan Holler entered final edits and prepared final text. Finally, we also express our most sincere gratitude to our families for their understanding and support.

*Maria J.F. Willumsen*
*Eduardo Giannetti da Fonseca*

# Introduction

This volume presents a collection of articles that investigate the performance of the Brazilian economy in recent decades and analyze the prospects for the country at a moment when it is in search of economic stabilization and greater insertion into the international economy. The articles, commissioned by the North-South Center of the University of Miami and discussed at a conference held at the University of São Paulo in 1993, analyze current topics that are of great interest to anyone who is concerned about the Brazilian economy.

The first two articles discuss the state's role as a dynamic element in the development of the Brazilian economy. Roberto Macedo and Fábio Barbosa present a retrospective look at the macroeconomic policies adopted in Brazil and analyze the difficulties the country will have to face before it can achieve economic growth with stability. Carlos Alberto Longo explores the importance of the state in Brazil's development and designs a model for a modern state that can draw Brazil into a more active participation in the world economy.

The following four chapters focus on the performance of the country's main economic sectors. Hélio Nogueira da Cruz and Marcos Eugênio da Silva discuss the development of Brazilian industry and technology, emphasizing the challenges imposed by international competition. The ensuing chapter by Fernando Homem de Melo examines the country's agricultural sector, illustrates the detrimental effects of Brazil's macroeconomic policies on this sector during the period of analysis, and identifies a new horizon for growth. The importance of the energy sector and the challenges presented by environmentally sound economic recovery are the topics of the chapter by Eli Roberto Pelin. Simão Davi Silber presents an evaluation of recent Brazilian trade policies, investigates the role of the external sector, and discusses the implications of the external debt problem on foreign trade. His conclusion points to particular niches in the world economy that could be occupied by Brazil. Alvaro Antônio Zini, Jr. complements the analysis of the external sector with an evaluation of the country's exchange rate policy and an examination of alternative proposals for reforming the exchange rate regime and the likely consequences of such reforms.

The next chapters are devoted to themes concerned with the labor market, human capital formation, and income distribution. José Paulo Zeetano Chahad examines the evolution of Brazil's population and the consequences of urbanization on the labor market and on the generation of employment opportunities. Eduardo Giannetti da Fonseca's article focuses on the evolution of the national education system, its relationship to the prevailing levels of poverty in the country, and the challenges facing the development of human capital. Maria Cristina Cacciamali analyzes income distribution in Brazil, stressing the exacerbation of inequalities and their origins and suggesting long-term economic policies that could help alleviate such disparities. Maria J.F. Willumsen focuses on economic and social inequalities from a spatial perspective, examining various forms of regional disparities across the nation. She argues that the elimination of such disparities depends on the design and implementation of a development project that explicitly contemplates policies aimed at inducing economic integration of Brazil's geographic territory.

*Maria J.F. Willumsen*
*Eduardo Giannetti da Fonseca*

# Brazil: Instability and Macroeconomic Policies

## Roberto Macedo
## Fábio Barbosa

The objective of this chapter is to present an overview of the Brazilian macroeconomic scene while explaining the main obstacles to growth and price stability. Persistent fiscal crises are identified as the main determining factors in the stagflationary process faced by the Brazilian economy in recent years. Given the size and nature of the Brazilian public sector, extending beyond the typical activities of the state and encompassing the ownership of large enterprises, the term "fiscal" must be interpreted broadly as a concept that covers the public sector as a whole.

The second section of this chapter presents a summary of the recent crisis from its beginnings to the early 1990s, at which time the possibility of a hyperinflationary economic breakdown became evident. The third section looks at several attempts to stabilize the economy after 1986 and points out the reasons for their failure or partial success. Emphasis is placed on the recent administration headed by Fernando Collor de Mello because its policies represented effective attempts to bring about stability through fiscal and monetary measures and to prepare the economy to resume growth via structural reforms. The fourth section analyzes economic measures adopted by the administration of Itamar Franco and evaluates their prospects for success. The fifth and final section of the chapter focuses on the relationship between price instability and economic stagnation, stressing the importance of stabilization in the growth process. Some concluding remarks also are offered in this section.

## The State: From Locomotive to Derailer of Growth[1]

In the current debate, most economists agree that the Brazilian economic crisis is linked closely to the chronic public finance imbalance that has become the greatest obstacle to macroeconomic stabilization — a fundamental precondition for long-term growth.

The public sector has played a crucial role in Brazil's economic development, notably by adopting a model of industrialization based on import substitution. In its initial stages in the 1930s, government intervention in the economy was primarily indirect; protectionist tariffs, credit and exchange subsidies, fiscal incentives, and economic subsidies were implemented to protect infant industries.

In 1942, however, the installation of the state-run steel industry, Companhia Siderúrgica Nacional (CSN), marked the beginning of more direct government intervention in the production structure. Intervention was based primarily on the creation of state-owned enterprises that produced basic inputs. These enterprises promoted the growth and diversification of Brazilian industry, in addition to other stimuli to private accumulation and efforts to attract foreign capital.

It should be mentioned that the inflation accompanying these state efforts did not reach high enough levels to compromise economic growth. A more aggressive policy of economic development was adopted during the second half of the 1950s during the Juscelino Kubitschek term, a period marked by incentives to the national and foreign private sectors and by large infrastructural investments, such as the construction of Brasília. Each action contributed to more serious inflation. As a result, Brazil experienced economic stagnation in the early 1960s that, in combination with political problems, brought about a period fraught with difficulties, eventually leading to the overthrow of the government in 1964 and a period of military rule that would extend until 1985.

During its initial phase, military rule produced great economic successes. It implemented a stabilization and adjustment program that accelerated growth between 1967 and 1973. Again, the government took the lead role in economic development by undertaking infrastructure projects, enlarging the realm of state-owned enterprises, and stimulating private initiatives through credit and fiscal incentives.

Until 1973, interventionist strategy did not compromise the finances of the public sector, nor did it seriously affect macroeconomic stability. Successful results were obtained through the expansion and rationalization of public sector financing mechanisms — notably toward a more effective tax structure and more effective domestic financing. Improvements were made possible through the implementation of compulsory savings mechanisms, such as the Time-Service Guarantee Fund (Fundo de Garantia por Tempo de Serviço — FGTS) and the Social Integration Program (Programa de Integração Social — PIS/PASEP), through monetary adjustments, and through expansion of production that generated resources needed to finance growth.

However, the first oil shock in 1973 — when oil prices increased fourfold — reduced potential consumption and investment. Events surrounding the oil shock foretold the end of an expansionist cycle that had lasted three decades without any major interruptions.

Anticipating decreasing levels of national income resulting from a deterioration in Brazil's terms of trade, the Brazilian government adopted a strategy that attempted to avoid decreases in consumption and in domestic investment. It adjusted the productive structure through an ample import substitution program in the capital and intermediate goods sectors. These sectors either received strong fiscal and credit incentives, as was the case of the capital goods sector, or became the target of massive investment by state-owned enterprises, as were the cases of the energy, steel, and telecommunications sectors.

Despite adverse international conditions that unfavorably affected growth rates in developed countries, Brazil was able to maintain high growth rates during the second half of the 1970s. Such positive results primarily were the product of the degree of government intervention, which reversed prospects for stagnation and increased the availability of external credit, thereby permitting the continued inflow of necessary resources to finance investments.

In spite of accelerating inflation, economic policies were relatively successful at diversifying the productive structure. Their implementation, however, resulted in an enormous increase in foreign debt. Though much of the debt was initially accumulated by the private sector, the public sector was especially hard hit since it had to accept the foreign obligations that gradually resulted from these policies. The repercussions of decisions adopted during the period also translated into an increase in the domestic public debt. In retrospect, it is possible to identify these policy decisions as the root of the imbalance still felt by the Brazilian public sector. Decisions reached later in the decade must be added as they were a response to new oil shocks and the growing burden imposed by foreign debt interest payments.

At the onset of the second oil shock, the Brazilian economy, already extremely vulnerable to changes in external conditions, was subjected to drastic increases in international interest rates derived from the new restrictions of U.S. monetary policy. Enhanced by higher external debt servicing obligations, largely taken on by the central government and state-owned enterprises, the initial impacts created more problems for an already unstable public finance sector. Later, accelerated inflation would worsen these conditions even more. Financing for public and private sectors was adversely affected in light of doubts about the future health of the country's economy. The resulting process of stagnation would contaminate the entire decade to follow — a period that would become known as the "lost decade."

Despite changes in international economic conditions, contractionary policies at the beginning of the 1980s again went unpursued except in those areas affected by a reduction in available financing. In fact, it was clear that politicians, businesspeople, workers, and society in general resisted the implementation of a strategy that could help resolve the persistent disequilibrium felt in external and public accounts.

In 1980, the Brazilian government enacted policies that seemed to run counter to what was needed for balancing accounts. The government specifically opted for the implementation of expansionist policies, accompanied by predetermined interest and exchange rates, an increase in the level of wage indexation, and the maintenance of high levels of investment in segments of the productive sector controlled by state-owned enterprises. Taken as a whole, these policies resulted in new and significant increases in the foreign debt and a strong acceleration of inflation. By 1981, the policies were abandoned and replaced by a policy based on high internal interest rates designed to encourage the inflow of foreign capital; however, an economic recession was the result.

In 1982, Mexico's declaration of a moratorium on its debt payments marked the beginning of a drastic reduction in the availability of foreign capital to developing countries. In the years to follow, developing countries could no longer count on external flows to finance the disequilibrium in the current account of their balance of payments or their public deficit. This "definancing" corresponded with a reorientation in the Brazilian economy toward the generation of a positive trade balance that would allow the government to honor its external commitments. In fact, in 1983 an adjustment program was undertaken to reduce internal demand through the implementation of changes in relative prices (exchange rate devaluation and control of nominal wage adjustments) and public expenditures.

Several measures were adopted simultaneously to preserve the productive structure developed in the previous period, including the creation of an exchange hedge for companies with external debt. This strategy, however, presupposed new internal and external commitments by the Central Bank, without the creation of mechanisms capable of assuring long-term equilibrium in public finances.[2]

As a matter of fact, gross tax expenditure fell from a level of 26 percent of gross domestic product (GDP) between 1970 and 1975 to 23 percent of GDP during the 1984-1989 period. One of the factors contributing to this decrease was the structural narrowing of the fiscal base, resulting from an increase in exports and incentives designed to assist in the import substitution process.

Some authors attribute this reduction in tax revenues to the continuous increase in the participation of states and municipal governments in total taxes, a process reinforced after 1985 by the Passos Porto Amendment and passed into law by the 1988 Constitution.[3] The argument holds that the increase in constitutional federal transfers has discouraged state and local governments, especially small municipalities, from pursuing effective tax collection strategies by guaranteeing resources at zero cost (even from a political perspective).

The proponents of these arguments, however, cannot ignore the fact that average annual growth rates during the 1980s (2.2 percent) suffered a marked decrease from the rates registered in the 1970s (8.6 percent) that had brought about a more than proportional reduction in tax revenue growth. Additionally, the acceleration of inflation, caused by macroeconomic disequilibrium, reinforced a tendency toward loss of tax revenue; real tax revenues were eroded by the inflationary process through the so-called "Tanzi effect," which occurs when inflation and real interest rates are high, and taxpayers have the incentive to delay paying taxes as long as possible, thereby reducing the real value of tax collections when ultimately received by the government.

In the late 1980s, there was increasing evidence of tax evasion, not only as a result of an increasingly complex taxation structure, but also because of deterioration of enforcement mechanisms and "informalization" of several segments of the productive structure, processes largely associated with the stagnation of the Brazilian economy.

In addition to an unfavorable revenue situation, current expenditures increased dramatically, climbing from 9.9 percent of the GDP in 1980 to 14.3 percent in 1989. Personnel expenditures in the same period increased from 7 percent of the GDP to 9.7 percent. Sixty percent of this increase occurred at the state and local government levels due to a restructuring of the distribution of federal revenue in the 1980s.

The country also experienced during the same period an increase in the government's financial commitments. Total expenditures jumped from 0.63 percent of GDP in the 1970-1978 period to 3.5 percent in 1988-1989, largely as a result of the domestic and foreign debt accumulation. The inevitable consequence was the draining of government savings as a source of investment financing and, consequently, the exhaustion of economic growth. In fact, government savings fell significantly over the years (and especially during the latter half of the 1980s) from 7 percent of GDP in the early 1970s to negative values in the 1987-1989 period.

The growing scarcity of government and foreign savings was accompanied by an equivalent reduction in total investment in the country. Total investment dropped from 26 percent of GDP in the mid-1970s to 18 percent by 1979. This adjustment was particularly visible in expenditures with gross capital formation of the public sector and its enterprises, which dropped from 12 percent of GDP in the 1970s to 6 or 7 percent in recent years. However, the contraction in investment expenditures was nearly offset by an increase in other expenditures.

There was also a significant shift in the composition of expenditures, a drastic decrease in expenditures for investment, and significant increases in expenditures for personnel and financial obligations.

Despite cuts, the public sector continued to experience operational deficits on the order of 5 percent of GDP annually. If, for the sake of comparison, this percentage were applied to today's GDP (approximately US$400 billion), these values would signify that the public debt grew by at least an additional US$180 billion between 1981 and 1989. In fact, this never occurred. A part of the deficit was financed by monetary expansion through forced reductions in government liabilities, as will be seen in the latter portion of this chapter.

In addition to inadequate financing for the needed public sector resources, there was a substantial loss in the "quality" of federal spending due to changes in its composition. The government had ceased to invest in order to cover expenditures that did not generate economic returns and were of questionable social value.

There is no doubt that the economy's capacity for future growth was compromised by limitations on expansion and modernization of the productive structure and a reduction in relative competitiveness and efficiency. At least two factors were identified as contributing to this situation. First, the drastic reorientation of the public sector away from its previous role as direct investment inducer created a gap that the private sector could not fill. Second, a significant public debt and successive interventions in the pricing mechanism and financial assets through the so-called "heterodox plans" prompted high levels of uncertainty that would further limit investments.

Because of internal difficulties and drastic reductions in external financing after 1982, the process by which domestic savings compensated for fiscal disequilibriums started to show signs of ineffectiveness. Lending terms were reduced, and real interest rates required, *ex ante*, to roll over the ever-expanding public sector debt began to show consistent increases.

There was a sustained and increasingly common perception that the public sector would face liquidity constraints in the short run and structural insolvency in the long run. According to Fabio Barbosa and Carlos Mussi (1991):

> ... in flow terms, the fiscal hiatus necessary to cover the (public) sector's commitments grew. Likewise, the principal on the debt was accumulating as a result of past deficits, and the fiscal adjustment became an increasingly apparent solution.... From a passive government activity, fiscal policy became the country's most important instrument of macroeconomic policy by the end of the 1980s. The possibility of a hyper-inflationary process reflected this situation.[4]

Indeed, at the beginning of the 1990s, the nonfinancial component of the public sector registered an operational deficit estimated at 9 percent of GDP. Since the economy was recession-bound and showed a monthly inflation rate of 100 percent, there were no prospects for noninflationary financing. The public sector's continuous structural disequilibrium and the interruption of its financing pattern were clearly at the core of inflation and the overall stagnation of economic production.

## The Worsening of Inflation and Heterodox Attempts at Stabilizing the Economy: 1986-1992

This section examines in greater detail the growth of inflation occurring after 1985, continuing stagnation, and policies adopted to contain the inflationary process between 1986 and 1992.

In order to understand the turn of events after 1985, it is important to recognize the serious changes that took place in the political arena. After two decades, governmental power was relinquished by the military and turned over to civilian rule. Tancredo Neves had negotiated the transition of power to full democracy successfully and was elected president by the National Congress in 1985. He died, however, before being inaugurated, and José Sarney, his vice president, was sworn in as the new president. Sarney brought with him a past association with the military regime and weak leadership skills. The coalition government had the ability to distribute patronage and to protect populist interests but lacked leadership. It was unable ultimately to obtain the support necessary to solve the country's dire problems.

The economic policy of the Sarney administration that ended in 1990 suffered from an inherited political fragility aggravated by difficulties in implementing measures required for economic stabilization, many of which were inevitably unpopular. All stabilization policies adopted during this administration failed primarily because of an absence of public sector structural adjustment and a restrictive monetary policy.

Ironically, the most valuable contribution of Sarney's administration — though only a perception — was the recognition that no stabilization plan would succeed unless the fiscal crisis itself were resolved. Today, there is virtual consensus concerning the reasons for the failures of the various stabilization plans.

Aside from this "positive result," changes in indexation rules imposed by Sarney's price freeze policies, associated with the volatility of inflation rates in the very short run, had a serious effect on the expectations of economic agents. From the public sector's viewpoint, the government's successive devaluation of liabilities based on drastic changes in the "rules of the game" further eroded the credibility of treasury bonds and made their transactions more difficult to carry out.

To present a better analysis of the topics covered in this section, certain developments in the macroeconomic analysis of particular countries with prolonged processes of high inflation, as well as in other economic policies, should be taken into consideration. Several Brazilian and foreign research centers believed that confronting chronic inflationary processes through the usual restrictive monetary and fiscal policies had become more complicated due to the presence of "inertial inflation," or inflationary memory as it is also called. There existed, accordingly, a process that tended to be perpetuated by the actions and beliefs of economic agents, particularly through the widespread adoption of formal and informal indexation of prices and contracts. In such an environment, the adoption of policies aimed at limiting aggregate demand became more complicated because of the existence of this inflationary inertia. The insistence on implementing such policies also exacted high social costs; an increase in restrictive policies was required to halt inflation and eradicate the inertia inherited from the past.

Notions concerning inertial inflation led to the launching of "heterodox" policies. In addition to adopting fundamental fiscal and monetary policies, the idea was also to adopt a set of measures that would embrace other policies aimed specifically at containing inflationary inertia. Included among these were the de-indexation of the economy, temporary price freezes, and the use of income policies to coordinate prices in the economy as an initial step toward stabilization. These ideas were greatly bolstered after Israel successfully adopted a similar plan in 1985. The Israeli case was widely publicized not only as a result of its impact *per se*, but also because many of Israel's economists are well-known internationally.[5]

It is important to keep in mind that these heterodox plans do not essentially constitute the antithesis of traditional anti-inflationary policies. On the contrary, they emphasize that the fundamentals of a stabilization plan, fiscal or monetary, must be in place before additional measures targeting expectations and price coordination that comprise the accessory component of the plan are adopted. These policies are ancillary because they cannot be sustained in the absence of fiscal and monetary fundamentals.

In Brazil, economists had extended and elaborated upon these ideas. However, their implementation by a fragile government that was incapable of assuring the maintenance of required fundamental measures resulted in many failures. There existed a series of stabilization plans believed to be heterodox. With the exception of a few measures adopted by the Collor government, these plans could not attack the fundamental issue of public sector fiscal disequilibrium, as financing the public sector ultimately led to inflationary pressures derived from its monetary impact. Since fiscal and monetary issues were not adequately addressed, policies implemented during the Sarney administration were only instrumental in bringing about temporary reductions in the inflation rate through a series of price freezes. Once price freezes were removed, the inability of the plans to tackle fiscal issues caused inflation to reach even higher levels.

For an illustration of the ephemeral impact of these policies, see Graph 1, which indicates the rate of inflation from 1985 to date and shows the periods during which each plan was adopted. The Cruzado Plan, the first of many, was perhaps the most frustrating. Because of Brazilian society's belief in the plan, it brought great relief to the economy, although for a brief period, and represented a favorable moment for the adoption of fundamental fiscal and monetary measures. President Sarney and other politicians around him, however, were so euphoric about the popularity and success of the Cruzado Plan that they ignored the warnings of economic advisers and others who had participated in the debate. Lacking the necessary fundamental measures, the plan ultimately failed. The effects of the Bresser Plan, next adopted in the midst of greater skepticism, were fleeting. It failed due to a lack of political support for implementation of fundamental measures. Later during Sarney's term, a Summer Plan was also implemented that was basically an attempt at keeping things under control. It was already clear that further drastic measures could not be adopted so late in Sarney's term of office.

Under the Collor administration, plans were considered that were incapable of stabilizing the economy (see Graph 1) but had basically different results. Inflation never returned to the formerly higher rates of the previous administration and, on the contrary, experienced a decrease.

Graph 2 helps to show why Sarney's plans failed and why Collor's were relatively successful. The difference between these graphs is that the rates of inflation displayed in Graph 1 are presented on an annual basis in Graph 2. Graph 2 also shows the operational balance of the public sector, a concept typically used to characterize financial disequilibrium in the sector. The operational balance shown in the graph as a percentage of the GDP refers to the public sector as a whole and includes federal, state, and local governments as well as state-owned enterprises.

Graph 2 shows that the stabilization plans of Sarney's administration were limited to their ancillary component. In other words, they were limited to the interruption of inflationary inertia through price freezes, de-indexation, and "monetary reforms," measures that were restricted to the creation of new currencies by means of the elimination of digits off the old currency. These measures and the creation of new currencies are often essential in Brazil since high levels of inflation result in excessively high (and difficult to manage)

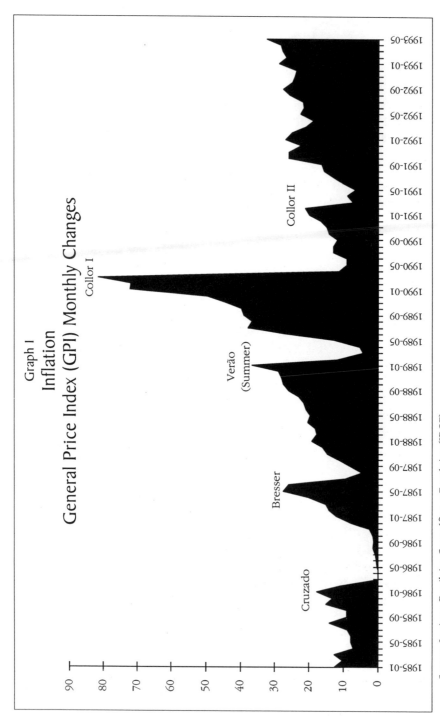

Graph 1
Inflation
General Price Index (GPI) Monthly Changes

Source: Instituto Brasileiro Geográfico e Estatístico (IBGE).

nominal values in common economic transactions, especially in the financial sector.

Graph 2 also makes it clear that past promises to address fundamental issues, particularly the issue of public debt, were nothing more than empty words. The fact that disequilibrium was permanently intensified shows that promises were not honored. Besides a worsening of the economy during the period 1986 to 1989 (shown in Graph 2), it was also understood that if nothing was done, the public sector deficit for 1990 could reach 9 percent of the GDP. After 1990, the operational deficit suffered a significant decline. The Collor government had reoriented its economic policy in terms of formulation as well as of implementation.

When Collor was inaugurated, the country's economic and financial situation was in a state of chaos, and the economy faced imminent hyperinflation. A large part of the growing public deficit was financed through an expansion of the money supply. Transactions were performed at increasingly shorter intervals because of uncertainties permeating the market. Shortly after Collor's inauguration, the new administration adopted drastic measures, including taxation and a freeze on financial assets to reduce the economy's liquidity and generate resources for the budget. Prices were frozen, indexation mechanisms were attenuated, and the government attempted to reduce the number of employees through administrative reform. The sale of public assets through patrimonial reform was contemplated in order to reduce the deficit. Other measures aimed at deregulating the economy were also implemented, including a tighter control on expenditures in terms of operational expenditures and in terms of personnel costs in particular. All of these measures were part of Collor Plan I.

As Graph 2 illustrates, these measures completely eliminated the public deficit as well as reversed it into a surplus in the federal budget in 1990 and 1991. Although positive, the results stemmed from short-term adjustments that failed to address some additionally important problems. Furthermore, many administrative aspects in the implementation and enforcement of new measures were extremely problematic.

The government was soon faced with strong pressure against the withholding of financial assets. Policies were therefore relaxed, which resulted in weaker monetary control. In addition, the government could not effectively control state-owned enterprises. Due to political pressures exerted around the time of the senatorial and gubernatorial elections in 1990, state banks, for example, extended credit operations above and beyond permissible levels. Patrimonial and administrative reforms were also discontinued. Expectations were high because economic agents knew that the fiscal adjustment had not been consolidated. A large portion of adjustments had been implemented exclusively on that one occasion only and would not be repeated.

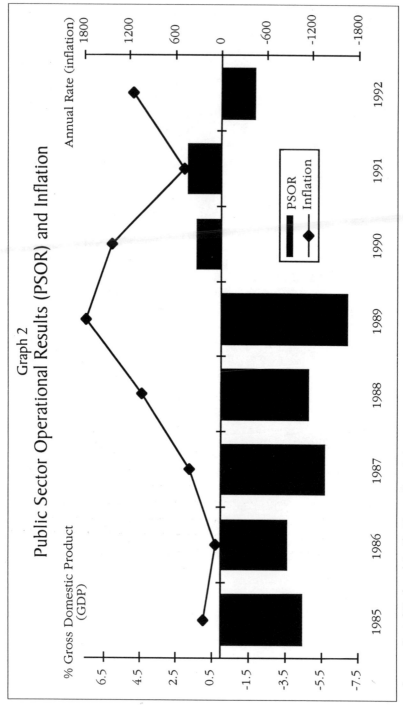

Graph 2

Public Sector Operational Results (PSOR) and Inflation

Sources: Central Bank and Getúlio Vargas Foundation.

By the end of 1990, expectations and the inertia behind fiscal and liquidity pressures had driven inflation once again on an upward course. Rising inflation rates sparked a renewal of government measures, including price freezes, containment of liquidity, and the creation of specific short-term funds. The economy entered 1991 with prices frozen and without any clear-cut indication that the basic factors causing the inflationary process were being effectively eliminated. The failure of Collor Plan II, together with several other problems, discredited the administration's team of economic advisers and forced them to leave office in May 1991.

The basic policy orientation taken by the country's new Minister of Economics, Marcílio Marques Moreira, was to unfreeze prices, take effective steps toward liberalizing the economy, renegotiate foreign debt, and proceed with structural reforms. Emphasis was given, for example, to the privatization of state-owned enterprises and fiscal reform that would aid the consolidation of prior adjustments made by the Collor administration. Prior to the consolidation of these adjustments, the government focused on expenditure control and monetary policy, both of which played particularly important roles in bridging the prevailing conditions with future conditions after fiscal adjustments were consolidated.

Despite opposing pressures and despite predictions made by the press and economic agents that the new team of economic advisers would resort to price freezes because they lacked alternatives, the policy was pursued persistently during the course of one year, from May 1991 to May 1992, and a series of measures were adopted that represented tangible advances toward stability and structural reform.

Collor's new team of economic advisers initiated a privatization program, established mechanisms that allowed for the financing of a larger agricultural supply, adopted several measures to reduce the bureaucratization of the economy, and advanced trade liberalization and negotiations of sectoral agreements aimed at increasing the economy's productivity and competitiveness. Also addressed were foreign debt problems. Agreements were obtained with the International Monetary Fund (IMF) and the Paris Club and negotiations established with private banks. The team of economic advisers advanced the reformulation of insurance systems and adopted a new wage policy that reduced the previous policy's impact on public finance, especially on social security. A policy was implemented to attenuate the disequilibrium and contain expenditures on the fiscal side, while supporting high interest rates that maintained financial assets invested as such.

Although the high interest rate policy and the contraction of expenditures were agenda items, it was recognized that their effects would be limited since high interest rates would eventually compromise fiscal equilibrium by reinforcing a growth in the debt. High interest rates also generated a large influx of foreign resources that affected the economy in two ways: the country's supply of foreign currency increased, while the Central Bank had to negotiate bonds at higher interest rates in order to contain the liquidity resulting from that same influx of foreign currency. The monetary control mechanism was, therefore, only partially effective because, accompanied by a return of withheld *cruzados*, a large inflow of foreign capital, and substantial trade surpluses, it acted only as a conduit that would eventually lead to needed fiscal adjustments.

Congress began to negotiate projects aimed at bringing about fiscal reforms that were seen as crucial in gaining economic agents' confidence in the government's financial situation. With their trust, it would be possible to pursue lower interest rate policies that would, in turn, stimulate the economy and generate demand for external resources that could be covered by accumulated reserves.

According to Graph 1, once prices were liberated, inflation reached a monthly rate of approximately 25 percent toward the end of 1991. Prices decreased during a period before April 1992, except for a seasonal increase observed in January. As demonstrated by the price indices, various indicators showed that inflation fell to 20 percent monthly in April 1992. According to the team of economic advisers, this signified that success was indeed possible if fiscal reforms were to consolidate the progress that had already been made and if problematic monetary factors were successfully removed.

At this time the government had undergone an extensive ministerial reform. Discredited ministers were replaced by ministers with national recognition, resulting in an improved Collor administration vis-à-vis its political supporters in Congress. Reform helped the administration to obtain approval for a new wage policy and various important projects, such as port reform and public service concessions.

In mid-1992, however, this path was challenged when accusations of corruption against President Collor surfaced. Forced to step down in October 1992, Collor was impeached in December 1992. The fiscal adjustment debate already before Congress was interrupted, and no subsequent projects were approved. During this period, two factions emerged within the Collor administration. On the one side, the economic team continued to press forward and insisted that expenditures needed to be contained and that fiscal reform was still necessary. On the other side, factions tried to use public sector resources as a way to obtain support for their campaign to prevent the president's impeachment.

The internal dispute between the economic and political sectors of government did not compromise public finances significantly. However, given the pessimistic atmosphere and growing public disbelief in the ability of the government to promote fiscal reform, prices increased again to levels of 25 percent per month. Recession intensified as entrepreneurial and consumer confidence plummeted even further because of the proliferation of negative press reports. Amid these conditions Itamar Franco was sworn in as provisional president of the country in October 1992.

## Measures Adopted by the Itamar Franco Administration and the Current Economic Status

In order to understand the economic policies of the Itamar Franco administration, it is necessary to remember that his government came in under forces that differed from Collor's on economic policy. As a result, one faction within his government was willing to make greater fiscal concessions, wanted to see the immediate recovery of economic growth, and proposed nominal wage increases. Another segment wanted fiscal reform and supported economic policies that were more in line with those of the previous government. The president himself espoused a conflicting position. Based on his own words, one can easily conclude that controlling inflation was not his top priority. He was more concerned with achieving economic growth, lowering interest rates, and attacking poverty. Franco's philosophy on the nation's modernization and the role of the government differed from the previous administration and was more in line with an interventionist approach.

During the provisionary period, from October to December 1992, the Franco administration divided up the Ministry of the Economy. The ministry previously encompassed the ministries of planning, finance, and industry and had been able to control economic policy in a unified manner. The Ministry of the Economy was also responsible for wage policies. Once the division was made effective, economic policy was conducted by the segment willing to make concessions, particularly the Ministry of Labor. Such concessions were made as a result of the conflicting forces in the area of wage policy: the government increased bimonthly adjustments, extended the adjustments to include a wider range of salaries and social security benefits, and expedited settlements in pending labor cases.

Together with a rise in positive consumer expectations after Collor's impeachment, measures sparked an increase in economic activity that led to greater demand for money and placed pressure on prices. By February 1993, the inflation rate had increased to 30 percent monthly from a previous rate of 25 percent.

On the fiscal side, the government was unable to pass the strongest measures (originally proposed by the previous government) through Congress. The only measures passed were some minor modifications in the corporate income tax structure adopted in 1992. Moreover, Congress, during a first reading, had already approved a new tax on financial transactions (Imposto

Provisório sobre Movimentações Financeiras — IPMF), proposed during the Marcílio Marques Moreira period. Marques Moreira had proposed that the IPMF be a social contribution that would substitute for other taxes and not an object of earmarked expenditures. As approved, the IPMF includes a provision that 38 percent of its revenues be spent on education and housing. Additionally, it was not substituted for any other taxes. The modified version of the tax would pass a second reading and become effective as of the second half of 1993. With these changes, however, the public's lack of confidence in the government's ability to implement any effective fiscal adjustment was reinforced. Discussions of fiscal reform would apparently be postponed until the end of the year, at which time Congress would address the issue of constitutional reform.

In terms of structural reform, the privatization process was redefined, thereby causing the government to lose its credibility to follow through on its commitments. On a more positive note, however, the port reform proposed by the previous administration was approved, resulting in the adoption of a more liberal posture vis-à-vis private investment in port development and personnel hiring policies. The port reform involved such substantial reform that not even a military administration was able to adopt it.

Regardless of its positive accomplishments, the Franco administration was unlikely to succeed in implementing an effective solution to Brazil's fiscal problems without overcoming contradictory forces within the federal government and without clearly defining an anti-inflationary policy. Franco's mandate was short and culminated in congressional, senatorial, gubernatorial, and presidential elections in 1994. Franco's provisional government was not likely to stabilize the economy in such a short period of time unless it succeeded in carrying out a profound reorientation.

The situation could have led to two alternative scenarios. Although not committed to combating inflation, the government, on the one hand, might have refrained from engaging in destabilizing policies. The Franco administration did inherit certain favorable conditions from the Collor administration (a smaller deficit, reduced internal debt, and larger international reserves) and did have a viable set of stabilizing policy options. There was a possibility of correcting, *ex post*, the short-term public debt. This was carried out *ex ante*, generating uncertainties that increased interest rates and debt service payments. Since the country held a surplus of foreign currency, another policy option at its disposal was to adjust exchange rates. In a second scenario, the government might have opted for expansionary policies in an effort to resume growth. Here the administration risked the possibility of pushing the economy onto the recurring inflationary path that plagued the Sarney administration.

The first of these two scenarios depended heavily on the approval of the IPMF and on constitutional reforms scheduled for the end of 1992.

## Inflation and Stagnation

Graph 3 shows Brazil's real GDP per capita for the 1970s and 1980s and indicates the presence of a sharp contrast between the two: strong growth in the first decade and stagnation, with the exception of a small and brief growth spurt, in the second decade. Graph 4 demonstrates that underlying the decrease in GDP is an expected decrease in the country's investment rate. Inflation and policies adopted to attack it in Brazil clearly are strongly related to stagnation. In its initial stages, inflation was a disease that the economy could cope with; the implementation of indexation mechanisms, in particular, effectively tempered its effects. Moreover, the engine of economic growth, the state, did not encounter any difficulties in financing itself. At one time, monetary indexation was an important tool used by the military government to assure the financing of the public sector. Prior to that time, the government issued bonds without indexation, which the financial market was forced to accept.

With the evolution of this process, as well as with the successive measures designed to combat it, and an interruption in financing flows, inflation became dysfunctional. First, growing inflation discredited indexation. Different adjustment indexes emerged, and economic agents began to search for better indexation mechanisms. Second, price indexes always lagged behind inflation, especially when the inflation rate accelerated more rapidly. As a result, indexation based on *ex post facto* indexes was insufficient to assure that nominal values would be appropriately adjusted despite a shortening of intervals between adjustments.

Third, and perhaps most important, the successive measures adopted by the government to combat inflation and to solve its financing problems generated mistrust among economic agents, who, in turn, responded by not saving and decreasing available financing for the government sector. This mistrust emerged because on various other occasions under different economic plans, indexation mechanisms were interrupted. Following the procedures in existence since the 1970s, the government interfered with indexes by purging price increases, redefining their weighting system, and carrying out other measures that resulted in serious losses to economic agents who held financial assets at the time.

Fourth, intervention became more audacious at each turn, culminating with the confiscation of financial assets tied to specific taxation policies carried out during the Collor administration. Economic agents, therefore, became reluctant to finance the government sector because of uncertainties; this became the main reason for rising interest rates. The consequences were twofold: the state deprived itself of the financial resources needed for its investments, and private creditors suffered losses, causing savings to contract and reducing money available for investment in the private sector.

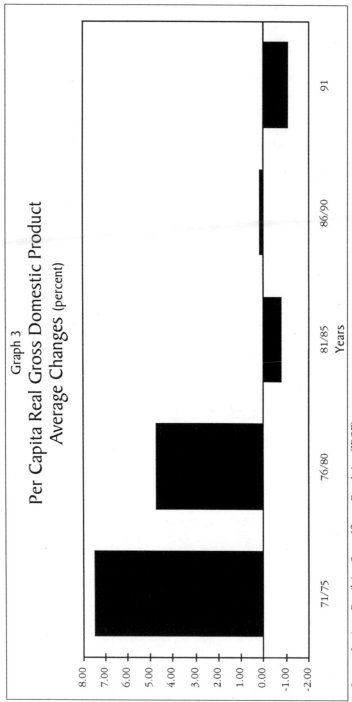

Graph 3
Per Capita Real Gross Domestic Product
Average Changes (percent)

Source: Instituto Brasileiro Geográfico e Estatístico (IBGE).

The inflationary problem in Brazil and its repercussions on the rate of investment and economic growth may be best understood if the public sector is viewed as a private enterprise that had filed for Chapter 11. By extending this analogy further and likening it to a poorly resolved Chapter 11 case in the private sector, the government, in experiencing chronic deficits and debts, had no other alternative than to proceed as enterprises in this situation typically do: "clean house," by balancing revenues and expenditures — fiscal reform — and negotiating debt payments with creditors, eventually sacrificing assets, particularly state-owned enterprises, via programs of privatization. Contrary to expectations, the government did not "clean house." By failing to refinance the debt and by forcibly liquidating its liabilities by intervening in indexation mechanisms until it finally resorted to the confiscation of society's financial assets, the administration lost credibility and caused its lenders significant monetary losses.

In order to resolve its problems effectively, the government's first task should be to balance its revenues and expenditures. The tax structure is less than perfect, and tax evasion is a pervasive problem. At the same time, the government must promote cost containment and restructuring measures by limiting its expenditures to necessities, such as road maintenance, and by stopping the enormous waste of resources taking place in the form of political concessions, ill-defined investments, and current expenditures on unsustainable privileges such as full-salary retirement pensions.

The debt should be restructured by reducing interest payments and by lengthening the maturity period, provisions that were only recently adopted with foreign creditors. Internally, fiscal reform and the sale of government assets clearly might be sufficient to cover debt service, which would result in an increase in credibility that could open the way for negotiations to reduce interest rates and extend repayment schedules. It is particularly important that the privatization process be resumed. The government would be following those enterprises that have filed for Chapter 11: disposing of assets as a way to reduce liabilities.

It is worth noting that intervention in indexation mechanisms resulted in vast gains for those who had financed their housing purchases and for those who had financed industrial, agricultural, and regional development through the banking system. These gains, however, seriously impaired new investments. The funds were not renewed for additional lending, and their growth was threatened by stagnation and a retraction in savings.

One important question related to the root of the Brazilian inflation and stagnation problems remains to be answered. No rational solution has been found for this poorly resolved Chapter 11. The frustrating experiences with plans and teams of economic advisers have demonstrated that the problem is conditioned by institutional and political elements. In its five hundred-year

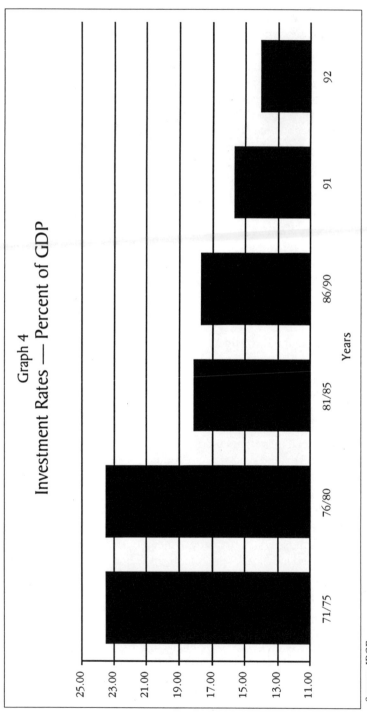

Graph 4
Investment Rates — Percent of GDP

history, Brazil has evolved through consecutive economic cycles that began with timber extraction, were followed by sugarcane, cotton, gold, and coffee extractions, and, since the middle of the twentieth century, have been based on import substitution industrialization. These cycles took place in different regions and resulted in demographic and productive bases that are widely dispersed throughout the country. Heterogeneous interests committed to the maintenance of these bases were also formed, as is the case of sugarcane in the Northeast and coffee in the Southeast.

Paralleling these economic cycles, the country received successive waves of immigrants of different ethnic origins who mixed with the local population and formed a new population of racially mixed groups. Add to these factors the vastness of the country's territory. Taken altogether, these factors prevented the creation of an hegemonic force within Brazilian society, be it political, ideological, ethnic, or even religious, that could clearly define a stabilization program and gain support for it. In general, previous experiences show that ancillary measures of heterodox plans, such as price freezes, find strong support among politicians. However, when the policy aims at the root of the problem, such as fiscal control, several interest groups switch sides, thereby leaving the stabilization plan without any chance of success.

After a series of military administrations, civilian leaders came to power. However, even if a government is in favor of structural reform, as was the case of the Collor administration, any structural reform program that involves fiscal adjustment is bound to face opposition. As reform measures are presented to Congress, it reacts as an advocate of vested interests, be they personal, familial, regional, local, or corporate.

Once elected, Collor had a political hedge. He exhausted it, however, by seeking congressional approval for measures such as price freezes, the withholding of assets, and the adoption of specific taxation policies.

When the fiscal reforms proposed by Marcílio Marques Moreira were presented to Congress, they were immediately rejected. Eventually, the government was able to negotiate the approval of some higher taxes, although these measures were of dubious efficacy. The tax reform as a package was never approved, and the proposal to cut government expenditures was completely ignored. The approval of a few new taxes was conditioned on using proceeds partially to cover programs in education and housing.

The frustrating aspect of the whole situation is that the country is losing time in its race toward development and has already lagged behind many other countries. These frustrations explain why so many observers, Brazilian and foreign, have adopted a cautious "wait and see" attitude. They are concerned that the Brazilian case is too complicated to be fixed readily, but also that Brazil is too large to be ignored.

# Notes

1.  This section draws heavily on Barbosa and Mussi 1991, from which the data were obtained.

2.  In reality, the gradual increase of external commitments was functional in the short term. The public sector, at the time running a deficit and hungry for resources, was able to count on an additional source of financing when it received payments from the private sector corresponding to that sector's external debt in cruzeiros.

3.  See Mussi, Ohana, and Guedes 1992. It is worth mentioning that the fiscal reform project proposed by Minister Marcílio Marques Moreira contemplated an "own-effort" fiscal system that rewarded the best fiscal performance of each sphere of government in order to boost total fiscal revenues.

4.  Barbosa and Mussi 1991, 70; author's translation.

5.  For a description of the experiences of Israel, Argentina, Brazil, Bolivia, and Mexico, please refer to a discussion on orthodoxy versus heterodoxy in Bruno, Di Tella, Dornbusch, and Fischer 1988.

# References

Barbosa, Fábio, and Carlos Mussi. 1991. *O Déficit do Setor Público e Política Fiscal no Brasil, 1980-1988.* Fiscal Policy Series, No. 15. Brasília: ONU-ECLA.

Bruno, M., G. Di Tella, R. Dornbusch, and S. Fischer, eds. 1988. *Inflación y Estabilización: La Experiencia de Israel, Argentina, Brasil, Bolivia, and México.* Mexico, D.F.: Fondo de Cultura.

Mussi, Carlos, Eduardo Felipe Ohana, and José Rildo de Medeiros Guedes. 1992. *Análise da Estrutura Funcional do Gasto Público no Brasil: 1985-1990.* Discussion Paper No. 154. Brasília, D.F.: IPEA.

# The State and the Liberalization of the Brazilian Economy

## Carlos Alberto Longo

## Historical Background

The last successful stabilization plan in Brazil was the Government Program for Economic Action (Plano de Ação Econômica do Governo — PAEG), implemented during Humberto Castelo Branco's presidency (1964-1967). With an inflation rate threatening to reach 140 percent by March 1964, the program was able to hold it at 70 percent that year, at approximately 35 percent in 1965, and reduce it in 1972 to 14 percent. Like all comprehensive anti-inflationary plans, the PAEG was based on a three-pronged strategy combining fiscal, monetary, and income policy goals (Simonsen 1970). By reprogramming its budget to reduce the fiscal deficit to Cr$753 million in 1964 (it was expected to reach Cr$2 billion that year), the federal government was able to lower the deficit to Cr$748 million. Measures were taken to maintain monetary expansion at Cr$2 billion for 1964, representing a 70 percent increase over the previous year. The actual rate of growth in money supply was 85 percent.

The PAEG was not a radical stabilization program designed to balance the budget at any cost. There was no doubt, however, about the direction of the government's fiscal and monetary policies. Because of this, the recession that resulted was not extensive. Per capita income and industrial output, both stagnant since 1963, began to rise sharply in 1967 — the crisis reached a peak in 1965 as industrial output dropped approximately 5 percent that year (Peláez and Suzigan 1976, 336-367).

Under the PAEG the need for a gradual income policy was acknowledged. There had been extreme variations in real wages due to high inflation and long intervals (two years) between wage adjustments. Instead of calculating wage adjustments to restore purchasing power to its previous peak, the new policy instituted a formula whereby the average real wage for the 12-month period in which the newly adjusted nominal rate was to remain in force would be equal to the average real wage for the preceding 24 months.

In conjunction with the price stabilization program, the government paved the way for far-reaching structural changes in the tax and financial systems. Among the many innovations, the following are worth highlighting: replacement of the Sales and Consignments Tax (Imposto sobre Vendas e Consignações — IVC) with the Merchandise Circulation Tax (Imposto sobre a Circulação de Mercadorias — ICM); reform of the banking system (Law 4595 of December 1964); creation of the Housing Finance System (Sistema Financeiro de Habitação — SFH) and of the indexation system known as monetary correction (Law 4380 of August 1964); and regulation of the capital market (Law 4728 of July 1965). It is often argued that these reforms were relatively easy to implement, given that there were no political constraints under military rule. The truth is, however, that Congress and influential state governors (São Paulo, Minas Gerais, and Guanabara) were highly critical of the federal executive. Moreover, plans for institutional reform had been made public, and draft legislation covering these questions had been sent to Congress well in advance.

After the Castelo Branco administration, no subsequent administration addressed the problem of inflation directly. Hence, over the ensuing 20-year period, inflation rates rose steadily as a result of surges in demand and supply shortages. Limited attempts to implement contractionist policies failed due to the virtually all-inclusive indexation of prices and incomes, creating highly inelastic inflationary expectations. In addition, despite a limited impact on inflation, a fiscal or monetary contraction was expected to lead the economy into a recession — a politically injudicious option.

The administration taking office in 1967 decided it was inadvisable to continue policies based upon a reduction in demand. Although the inflation rate was still at 25 percent per year, the government set as its goal the promotion of economic growth and full employment. The "developmentalist" position of President Arthur da Costa e Silva (1967-1969) and President Garrastazú Médici (1969-1974) was motivated in part by the probability of an upswing in the economy resulting from austerity measures and institutional reforms implemented by the previous administration.

The First National Development Plan (Primeiro Plano Nacional de Desenvolvimento — PND I) consolidated and extended the import substitution model introduced by President Juscelino Kubitschek (1955-1960). PND I emphasized exports and, contrary to PAEG's liberalizing framework, put its trust in central planning and state intervention in the economy. Indexation through the monetary correction mechanism was extended to all markets; prices were placed under government control (through the Council on National Prices, Conselho Nacional de Preços — CONEP, and later by the Interministerial Council on Prices, Conselho Interministerial de Preços — CIP); wage adjustment regulations were maintained; credit controls were introduced; and interest rates were capped. The program achieved its goals: high levels of production and employment, a foreign trade surplus, and stabilized inflation (at approximately 20 percent per year).

The cost of such positive results, called the "Brazilian miracle," was the freezing of relative prices through monetary correction and excessive state intervention in the economy. Other results of the First National Development Plan were wide-ranging — generous tax and credit subsidies favoring agriculture, exports, and industry; concentration of ownership in the banking industry; loss of independence by the Central Bank; the direct subordination of all official banks to the Finance Ministry; and an increase in state-owned enterprises occupying gaps not filled by private enterprise.

During the Ernesto Geisel administration (1974-1979), economic policy often changed track under the pressure of new circumstances, especially the inertial inflation inherited from the previous administration that was aggravated by the first oil shock. In view of the ineffectiveness of conventional economic policy instruments, the government chose to accommodate the external shock by permitting inflation to rise. The vicious circle created by the indexation of prices, wages, and exchange rates, together with structural balance-of-payments deficits, was alleviated by an abundance of cheap external credit and by the compression of prices and rates charged by state-owned enterprises (SOEs).

The main goal of the Second National Development Plan (Segundo Plano Nacional de Desenvolvimento — II PND) was to proceed with the import substitution development model (primarily, in heavy industry, fine chemicals, and pulp and paper) as well as to launch an ambitious program of investment in energy and infrastructure commanded by the state and funded by foreign resources. The plan was backed by the same instruments employed by the previous administration: prices, wages, and exchange rate and credit controls. These policies, however, created major distortions in relative prices. Domestic demand was buoyed by subsidies given to the consumption and production of public services. The re-lending of foreign loans underwritten by the Treasury was crucial to the financing of the balance-of-payments deficit.

The second oil shock (1979) and the refusal by the governments of developed countries to accommodate their rising inflation presented Brazil with a serious dilemma in the early 1980s. The challenge was to restrict aggregate demand, realign relative prices, and temporarily accept low rates of economic growth with high unemployment. The fatal mistake made by the João Baptista Figueiredo administration (1979-1985) was to press on with the then-outdated 1970s development program. Its argument was that Brazil was unique and that through public investment, subsidies to import-substituting industries (Proálcool, coal, and petroleum prospecting), and preferential treatment for natural resources exports (agricultural products, such as soybeans and orange juice, and primary goods such as ores), continuous growth could be achieved despite new external constraints and internal distortions inherited from previous administrations.

In fact, Brazil began the 1980s without any planning framework whatsoever. Without explicit performance targets and with increasingly weak instruments of government action, the executive branch made even more extensive and intensive use of administrative controls. It centralized control of public expenditures and merged all operations relating to the financing of state-owned enterprises and official banks into a single consolidated agency — Special Secretary of State Enterprises Control (Secretaria Especial de Controle das Empresas Estatais — SEST). It created additional systems for monitoring and controlling prices and wages: Conselho Interministerial de Preços, CIP; Secretaria Especial de Abastecimento e Preços, SEAP; and Superintendência Nacional do Abastecimento, SUNAB. It stepped up the frequency of unexpected and sudden changes in the rules of the game by implementing measures such as setting the monetary correction and exchange rates in advance (in other words, not indexing them to actual inflation), announcing massive exchange rate devaluations, and changing the mechanism for wage adjustments. The results of these opportunistic, ill-managed policies were a steadily rising inflation and prolonged recession (1980-1983).

Although another historic opportunity to redirect economic policy arose in the mid-1980s, the government preferred facile measures with popular appeal. This strategy is summed up in the motto of the José Sarney administration, "Tudo pelo Social" (Everything for Social Development). Under President Sarney (1985-1990), the government recognized that combatting inflation must be an end in itself. Yet, stabilization plans continued to be plagued by major flaws in conceptual terms as with the Cruzado Plan, and in their implementation, as with the Bresser and Summer Plans. The nation had not yet become accustomed to the tug of war between contending forces that is typical of democratic processes. The federal administration's shortsightedness and incompetence were compounded by the inexperience of Congress and even of the courts of law, both of which failed to present constructive solutions to the crises linked to attempts at economic stabilization.

With the economy teetering on the brink of hyperinflation, Fernando Collor was inaugurated as president in March 1990 and within a short time announced bold measures to contain the price spiral, implement institutional reform, and improve social welfare. Such objectives, on the other hand, cannot be attained overnight. They are the result of a long process with a painful and intrinsically necessary chronology that consists of wiping the slate clean of past errors, permitting the rate of growth to step up, and distributing the benefits of higher growth. Thus, while economic policymakers during the "economic miracle" capitalized on the effects of austerity measures and reforms implemented under Castelo Branco, the administrations of the 1980s lacked the wherewithal for fulfilling their promises, though manifestly populist.

## The State as "Entrepreneur"[1]

A pragmatic analysis of the functions of the state consists of weighing the costs and benefits of its presence in the economy. The quality of the public sector depends on the effectiveness of its components: federal, state, and municipal governments; state-run banks; and state-owned enterprises. However, obscure fiscal and financial relationships not only distort the application of funds by the state but actually make it impossible to identify how such funds are used.[2]

SOEs are often used as instruments of stabilization, with the Treasury acting as controlling shareholder and the official banks providing the main source of financing. Interbudgetary transfers may take the form of loans, capital increases, or subsidies. The way in which transfers are classified for accounting purposes does not necessarily correspond to the economic nature of the operation. Capital transfers (loans and investments) are frequently transformed into current transfers (subsidies) during the fiscal year. Thus, when SOEs are turned into an instrument of macroeconomic policy, the budgetary process fails to provide clear-cut information in terms of the nature and effective availability of funds. As a result, the elaboration and evaluation of the Treasury budget become a process of aggregation, combining central guidelines on the scarcity of funds with requirements for financing SOEs (Premchand 1988).

A major criticism of Brazil's development model is that the state's participation in the economy is excessive. Clientelism, corporatism, and the absence of stimuli for private investment are among the basic causes of the state's insolvency; there are not enough funds to cover the simplest everyday items of public spending. Wages have been depressed incessantly by the decline in investment. The mismatch between public revenue and public expenditure is largely determined by long-standing commitments inherited from previous administrations. The consolidated budget procedure recently adopted by the federal executive branch failed to eliminate several sources of long-term disequilibrium. The draft budget currently being debated in Congress is no more than a desperate attempt at containing the fiscal deficit by imposing arbitrary tax hikes and increasing tariffs. The exhaustion of traditional sources for financing the public deficit explains the failure of so many stabilization plans.

Structural disequilibrium derives from the excessive indebtedness of the public sector, including federal, state, and municipal governments, SOEs, and financial institutions. Because no clear definition exists as to who is legally accountable for these liabilities, it is virtually impossible to formulate a set of alternative solutions. Systematic transfers of funds (in current and capital budgets) from one part of the public sector to cover default or government guarantees of a debt in another are incompatible with proper budgetary and administrative practices.

Functions within the public sector need to be defined clearly in order to prevent the present situation of interlocking arrears and cross-defaults between agencies from jeopardizing operational efficiency and increasing the fiscal deficit. The concern here is microeconomic as well as aggregate. It is difficult to envisage any possibility of administrative rationality in the production and sale of goods and services when prices are controlled by the Finance Ministry and levels of indebtedness are determined by the Central Bank. The cash flow of SOEs is determined by what may be called the "national interest." As a result, priorities are not set with the objective of protecting the "interests of the consumer" (quality and price) nor those of the shareholder (profit).

If the fiscal debt is to be contained and the process of development reinitiated, the functions of the federal, state, and municipal treasuries should be separated, and SOEs and banks should be made administratively independent of one another. Assets and cash flow accounts of large SOEs and financial institutions should also be examined and evaluated. Surety bonds (or collateral securities) and mutual debts should be examined, and the residual balance of their assets and liabilities should be indicated explicitly. It is imperative that the sources and uses of resources be reorganized if a reduction in subsidies and a reestablishment of administrative and budgetary autonomy for public sector entities are to take place. The reorganization of excessively indebted SOEs is yet another prerequisite for the state's financial recovery. Their assets and liabilities should be scrutinized to determine net assets and to allocate losses to the appropriate debtor. Once rescued, these enterprises could be exclusively administered from operational resources without market share allocations and with minimal government interference.

What this involves is a major overhaul of the financial system, administrative decentralization, and even massive privatization. All remaining debts and debtors, once identified, would go through a consolidation phase. At the same time, interbudgetary transfers to cover entrepreneurial expenses, investments, and financial responsibilities would be reduced. State enterprises then would be administered as if they were private enterprises, resulting in the Central Bank operating independently of the Treasury Department and the Bank of Brazil (Banco do Brasil) and Federal Savings Bank (Caixa Econômica Federal) competing with other financial institutions.

The federal budget would consolidate financial and contractual liabilities unsustainable by state-owned banks and enterprises so that such liabilities can be secured and renegotiated with domestic and foreign creditors. The process would have to include not only federal enterprises and their financial institutions but also the Bank of Brazil. Once the federal budget is freed of its moral obligations to other government enterprises, the federal government finally will have attained control over its resources. All fiscal decisions would be discussed thereafter while in the process of defining and implementing federal budget legislation, since only a credible federal budget would make a reduction in inflation viable in the long run.

## Attempts at Stabilization[3]
### First Collor Plan

The essence of the <u>First Collor Plan</u> centered on three presidential decrees issued in March 1990, known as Provisional Measures under the Federal Constitution of Brazil. These decrees contained a set of fiscal, monetary, and income policies. Other parts of the plan (civil service and administrative reforms, subsidy cutbacks, elimination of tax evasion, government property sales, as well as SOE privatizations) can be considered complementary components. Although eventually they may come to represent the "New Brazil" (Collor's election slogan), alone they hold little significance for the success or failure of the stabilization program.

Price and wage hikes were forbidden for some time. To help balance the budget, public service charges and prices of key SOE goods were raised, as was the Financial Operations Tax (levied on money market transactions, among others). Inflation dropped sharply. The initial effectiveness of Collor Plan I was guaranteed by an immediate reduction of liquidity; only about one-quarter of all financial assets remained at the public's disposal. Inflationary expectations were reversed abruptly.

Collor Plan I's weakest points included excessive centralization of decisionmaking, violation of property rights, and a high degree of risk that the government could have avoided without impairing the effectiveness of the plan if it had opted to modernize the instruments of economic policy and empower other decision-making bodies. The Central Bank, for example, remained dependent; Congress was not informed of the executive's budget projections; and the judiciary was obliged to perform legal acrobatics to benefit a plan with no room for second thoughts or second opinions.

Rather than reprogram the budget inherited from the Sarney administration and seek an agreement with Brazil's creditors, Collor's team chose drastic measures designed to balance revenues and expenditures quickly. New taxes, surcharges, and compulsory loans were created, while liquid assets were seized, measures deemed both inadvisable and of doubtful legality. Moreover, their social cost could soon be appreciated: inflation once again was running high.

It is difficult to appraise the federal sector's real fiscal situation because budgets are out of date or nonexistent. Furthermore, excessive financial interpenetration of public entities confuses priorities and discourages the sound application of funds. The only consistent source of information is the federal treasury's cash-flow statement, but since it makes no clear distinction between the rights and obligations of different jurisdictions, it is considered an indicator of a permanent balance in the budget.

Three months after the Collor Plan was announced, people were beginning to realize that the government was losing control of its stabilization program. With respect to pricing mechanisms, the return of high inflation after three months is attributable to adjustments in public sector and other prices for inflation. On the demand side, pressure was increasing despite a lower level of economic activity because of the exacerbation of inflationary expectations.

By August 1990, gross errors committed in implementing measures led to a 10 percent rise in prices. Difficulties in communicating with workers, the business community, the courts, and Congress, as well as delays in the negotiations of foreign debt rescheduling, illustrated the government's growing inability to conduct the stabilization program effectively. It is not enough to reduce inflation by decree, to ensure that the treasury has a balanced cash flow, to allow interest rates to rise to unprecedented heights, and at the same time to lift import restrictions. Such an approach failed in the well-known cases of Chile under Augusto Pinochet and in Argentina under Finance Minister José Martínez de Hoz.

The risk of opening the economy too quickly and providing investors with excessive incentives, typically accompanied by a currency overvaluation, is that decapitalization and obsolescence will ensue; severe social costs (in job losses and wasted production) will be incurred; and only limited gains in reducing inflation will be made.

## Second Collor Plan

Impatient with economic developments, the executive branch launched Collor Plan II in January 1991, another incomplete and hastily prepared economic package, which unfortunately did nothing to compensate for the succession of errors committed during the First Collor Plan. The Second Collor Plan, like the first, consisted almost entirely of measures entailing a high degree of risk and high social costs — a sharp hike in public sector prices, another wage and price freeze, as well as complicated changes in the rules for financial markets.

A second attempt at stabilizing the currency was claimed to be an "extension" or "deepening" of the first. The irony, however, is that the government's claim was not altogether unfounded: the Second Collor Plan did little more than repeat the initial failure to stamp out inflation. The style, form, and substance of the initiatives associated with the Collor Plan II were similar in every respect to those of the previous package. The executive branch again behaved in a presumptuous and arbitrary manner; it abruptly changed the rules of the game without consulting with organized social groups and representative institutions (the legislative and judiciary branches), let alone gaining their support. The new package consisted of one more batch of provisional measures, presidential decrees, and Central Bank resolutions.

Collor Plan II ignored and, in many cases, actually contradicted accepted principles of administrative decentralization and tax prerogatives and failed to perform a comprehensive review of the management, instruments, and aims of the federal administration. No consideration was given to the institutions of a democratic government, nor was power shared.

## Changes of Style

The Collor administration's disastrous management of the economy in its first year was mirrored by a lack of confidence in the executive branch (verging on deadlock, if not direct confrontation) by the other two branches of government and by both labor and industry. Misgivings derived from a reaction to the prevalence in May 1990 of voluntaristic and incoherent economic policymaking and target setting.

While the executive branch focused its attention on combating inflation with short-term mechanisms, it avoided any attempt at genuine structural reform of the public sector. It did not address, for example, tax reform, consolidation of the budgetary process, or an overhaul of the financial system. Instead, it swiftly and expeditiously seized assets, froze prices, altered indicators, and arrested tax evaders.

The legacy of the two stabilization plans is mediocre. The meaning and usefulness of such pyrotechnical innovations in the financial market as the Overnight Money Fund (Fundão, in which overnight balances may be kept) and the Referential Interest Rate (Taxa Referencial, an official rate applied to previously indexed bonds) need to be reconsidered, and a market solution must be sought for a excessively regulated financial market. Today, a lack of intermediation in corporate and financial investment is becoming as prevalent as it was in the early 1960s.

Reacting to a widespread perception that the country was becoming ungovernable, the federal government suddenly "softened" its style in May 1991 by replacing Finance Minister Zélia Cardoso de Mello with Minister Marcílio Marques Moreira. Congress was reluctant to ratify any more provisional measures; the Supreme Court halted the dubious legal maneuverings of the outgoing economic team by implementing more and more restraining orders to annul the effects of the two plans. A balance of power among the three branches of government apparently was restored.

As price and exchange controls were lifted, the economy slowly turned toward the free market. There was no risk of the hyperinflation experienced after the price freezes imposed by past stabilization plans. For speculative reasons, prices were not raised except as an adjustment to repressed costs. Demand continued to be suppressed temporarily with wages low and liquidity tight. Although inflation was still rising, its pace was slow.

Hereafter, the problem was how to administer the price-wage spiral in the absence of reliable inflation indices. The search would have to begin for a means of avoiding universal informal indexation; thus, the solution for the Collor administration would reside in yet another stabilization plan. As the second half of 1992 wore on, it became likely that the executive branch would change the direction of its economic policy — based this time on a general examination of public finances.

A new stabilization plan requires fiscal reforms focused on long-run performance. It is imperative that anachronistic and ill-conceived institutions be abandoned and that the social security system be revised. It is critical that SOEs and official banks be reorganized, the federal budget revitalized, double taxation and special contributions eliminated, and the foreign and domestic debts rescheduled. As of 1993, the federal government had not implemented a permanent fiscal adjustment. Measures taken during 1990-1991 to achieve a balanced budget were based on an increase in taxes and duties that created a more regressive, inefficient, and complex tax system. The government also placed excessively strict caps on outlays for current expenditures (operating costs) and hindered investment through cuts, restrictions, and levies of doubtful legality and legitimacy.

Although the federal Constitution determines how tax revenues are to be shared, it is incompatible with an effort to modernize the budget's structure. The burden of obligations inherited from previous administrations and the economic and social heterogeneity of regions and classes make it impossible to transfer most federal government expenditures to states and municipalities. Since this stripped the federal government of most traditional sources of revenue (income tax and tax on manufactured products), in order to guarantee a precariously balanced cash flow, the executive branch will have to continue resorting to new cumulative taxes not shared with subnational governments. It becomes advisable to eliminate additional primary fiscal contributions at the federal level (such as Finsocial; Imposto sobre Operações Financeiras, IOF; PIS/PASEP; contributions on enterprise profits; and others) and to reduce intergovernmental transfers.

At the state level, it would be beneficial to increase the scope of sales taxes (ICMS) by taxing a large portion of services currently under the Services

Tax (Imposto sobre Serviços — ISS), which ultimately would be abolished. Local governments could have their share of the ICMS' revenue increased as a compensation for loss of ISS revenues and would also be allowed to tax rural properties, supplementing the Property Tax on Urban Land and Structures (Imposto Predial e Territorial Urbano).

Little effort has been made to pass legislation that minimizes these distortions or that regulates the Constitution in the areas of public finance and the financial system. The current budgetary process gropes in the dark for ways to adapt the new Constitution to the laws and traditions in force before 1988. However, aside from the normative vacuum, resulting contradictions are very great. Provisions such as the 12 percent cap on real interest rates, the abolition of the National Monetary Council, the procedure for enacting budgetary laws, the ban on fiscal advances by the Central Bank, and parliamentary intervention in the administration of public debt are obvious examples of issues that require urgent review and implementation.

## The Issue of Governability

If the government is to regain the nation's confidence, its legal and institutional framework must be modernized. Although ambitious stabilization plans have been implemented, they have flouted numerous legal norms in the name of the "collective interest." The government has been strong as well as weak: strong, when it legislates in a way not determined by law, and weak, when it is forced to resort to an "inflation tax" to defray current expenditures. A resurgence of inflation after so much shock therapy calls into question the efficacy of these measures. Therefore, it is necessary to examine not only the legality but the economic legitimacy of such economic packages.

When inflation is high and chronic, it becomes a controversial (if not illegal) source of funds for the federal government. Its illegality derives from the fact that there are no provisions in Brazilian law for an "inflation tax." Such a tax, moreover, runs counter to the customary principles of taxation: equal rights to persons in equal positions and neutral allocation of resources. On the other hand, stabilization packages based on shock treatment weaken government institutions because they entail vast and frequent changes in the rules. Provisional measures, decrees, and directives are often not only mutually conflicting but seem to be designed to correct administrative errors or serve the interests of the federal executive branch rather than to modernize institutions.

It is important to examine the concept of representation and governability in light of the "social contract." Difficulties exist in applying the principle of majority rule to a socially and economically heterogeneous population that during most of its history has been under oligarchic, populist, military, or monarchical rule. The rule of law and the legitimacy of government are violated frequently under the system of presidential representation because the government can make as many mistakes as it likes for a predetermined period.

Bearing in mind Brazil's presidential system, its history, and the heterogeneity of its population, it appears that effective government can be achieved only through permanent assembly representation, such as the parliamentary system wherein attempts to stabilize the economy and reform institutions would lead to a convergence of ideas and to a stable cabinet. Under parliamentary rule, government instability is neither frightening nor threatening to institutions. On the contrary, the principle that the government is secure for an undetermined period makes for stronger institutions.

# The Liberalization of the Economy
## Privatization[4]

The Brazilian privatization experience began timidly with the National De-bureaucratization Program (July 1979), the main goals of which were to strengthen the role of market forces, stop the indiscriminate creation of state enterprises, and promote conditions for transferring SOE control to private enterprise. In 1981 (Decree 86215) and again in 1985 (Decree 91991), rules were made for issuing SOE stocks to the public, selling control to private sector investors, and even shutting some SOEs down. Although the Interministerial Privatization Council (Conselho Interministerial de Privatização — CIP) was created, legislation was changed in 1986 (Decree 93606) when the council's decision-making powers were enhanced and the National Development Bank (Banco Nacional de Desenvolvimento — BNDES) was placed in charge of executing the program.

In 1988 (Decree 95886), liberalization underwent an intense process of reinforcement, partly because the federal government was on the verge of insolvency. The CIP was abolished, and the Federal Council for Privatization (Conselho Federal de Desestatização — CFD), consisting of representatives of the BNDES, the stock market, workers, and the business community, took its place. Restrictions imposed on participation by foreign capital in privatization were lifted.

Finally, Law 8031 (December 1990), which is still in existence, created the National Privatization Program (Programa Nacional de Privatização). The Privatization Steering Committee (Comissão Diretora de Privatização) was appointed with eleven members, four from the public sector and seven from the private sector. The BNDES remained in charge of implementation. Foreign investors were allowed to acquire up to 40 percent of voting shares and 100 percent of non-voting shares. Between 1979 and March 1990, when Collor took office, the program was restricted to the privatization of public enterprises that were previously privately owned but had since been nationalized because of past financial difficulties. The privatization of 38 companies generated US$824 million into government coffers through direct sales, tender, and auctions.

Hereafter, the plan includes the sale of SOEs that in the past had been federally owned. Monopolies enshrined in the Constitution (oil, gas, and ore extraction, and shipping lines) will be respected. The program has three main objectives: reduction of the public sector debt, reinforcement of market laws, and the further democratization of companies. As of April 1991, privatization projects totalling US$12 billion have been approved for 25 SOEs in the steel, petrochemical, and fertilizer industries. Payment can be made in the form of chirographic credits, public debt bonds, transfer of title to Cruzados Novos (old currency) held by the Central Bank, or similar means.

Given the excessive indebtedness of the public sector, the supply of credit (internal and external) for acquisition of these companies is potentially high. Funds deposited with the Central Bank (MYDFA) — largely overdue external public debt, totaling US$40 billion, in principal and interest — entitle the holder to participate in privatization with a 25 percent discount on face value. It is worth noting that these credits are traded on the secondary market with a discount of 70 percent. The availability of funds for debt-equity swaps was reinforced by the seizure of financial market investments during the First Collor Plan; the Central Bank held a total of about US$27 billion equivalent in Cruzados Novos deposits (by mid-1991). Other public sector debts that can be used for privatization include debentures issued by Siderbrás (Companhia Siderúgica Brasileira, the steel holding company), land reform bonds, and quota holdings in the National Development Fund (Fundo Nacional de Desenvolvimento — FND).

The total of these credits is enough to acquire all federally owned SOEs, estimated to be worth US$60 billion. The government should have little trouble selling the shares of the most efficient companies, at least during this first stage. The Brazilian privatization experience began with the path of least resistance: first, devolution of nationalized companies to private ownership and now the sale of the most profitable SOEs. When appropriate, the situation will change to privatize those utilities and commercial SOEs with chronic deficits.

## Deregulation

The "patrimonial" state in Brazil, in which the interests of the bureaucracy interlock with those of the private sector, has deep historical roots. Portuguese laws played a more positive role in political organization than in trade and the private economy. The codification of existing *Ordenações* (laws) enacted by Manuel I and Felipe II were concerned primarily with allocating public office, including military rank, as well as church property and privileges. Only after the administration's base had been laid did they proceed to specify civil, criminal, and procedural law. Knowledge of the rights inherent in sovereignty was not acquired by studying the ancient customs of the Portuguese kingdom but was borrowed instead from Roman law. The *Ordenações* were essentially a case of state intervention in the economy, business, shipping, domestic commercial transactions, pricing, and export embargoes (Faoro 1957, 64-65).

In strict terms, administrative law existed, but there was no civil or commercial law. Thus, the discipline imposed on individuals was not economically inspired but political in content; it did not serve the interests of individuals, rational in economic terms, but the interests of the patrimonial state. The logic of laws and decisions was very distant from the impersonal and fair nature of values; it was subordinated to the arbitrary rule of the Prince. England, the home of classical capitalism, did not need to consolidate its laws so its economy could expand to plenitude. It dispensed with codes and Roman law, and it was driven by the realities of economics, grounded in private property within a context of flourishing industrialization. Thus, through centuries of ancestral assimilation, Brazil became the heir to a long history dating back to the revolution of John of Aviz and the court of Manuel I (Faoro 1957, 66-69).

To cut costs and enhance the efficiency of federal public administration, Collor announced a radical change in the ministerial structure during his first few days in office. He reduced the number of ministries from 30 to 12, created secretariats, closed public bodies, eliminated posts in top administrative ranks, fired or laid off public employees, and sold government buildings, apartments, and vehicles.

The results were insignificant both financially and in terms of administrative reorganization. While macroeconomic instability continued to prevail, it would be difficult to reform institutions. Many measures that had been announced were never implemented, and as many more would be revised or abandoned.

In addition to the usual economic, political, and legal obstacles, reforms floundered because of insufficient preparation. No solution was found to the problem of whether to increase the productivity of the civil service or to improve low salaries. The Constitution guarantees job security for civil servants; therefore, it is difficult for the government to cut the size of its work force. The haste with which ministries were merged and autonomous authorities closed down meant that the same functions are now performed by super-ministries or super-secretariats reporting directly to the president. No significant savings or gains in effectiveness have been made by such a reorganization.

## Liberalization[5]

In June 1990, the executive branch announced its Industrial and Trade Policy (Política Industrial e de Comércio Exterior — PICE), reproducing with few differences the provisions of Decree-Law 2433 (May 1988) enacted by the Sarney administration. PICE's objective is "to enhance the efficiency of production and trade of goods and services by modernizing and restructuring industry." Its distinguishing feature is full integration between macroeconomic, industrial, and trade policies. Growth in imports will play a key role in fighting inflation, given that investments will be stimulated and competitiveness sharpened. Among PICE strengths is the recognition that the effectiveness of industrial policy depends on the overall macroeconomic environment and its liberalizing drift. Changes in industrial and trade policy carried out since 1988 and expanded in mid-1991 have been designed to alter the development model prevalent in the 1980s — a closed, non-competitive, inefficient model that helped undermine the economic and technological dynamism of the decade.

A number of import restrictions were lifted — significantly the Tax on Financial Operations (IOF), duties for renovating the merchant navy and port improvements, the obligation that companies submit import schedules in advance, controls on import licenses (*Anexo C*), the similarity test, and compulsory financing of imports. Trade policy in 1990 became more open through the implementation of the following measures: 1) replacement of the crawling-peg devaluation system with a market-oriented system of floating exchange rates; 2) elimination of all special import schemes except the drawback, the Manaus Free Zone, and international agreements; and 3) a phased-in reduction of all tariffs by 1994, designed to achieve an average tariff of 14.2 percent (with a small standard deviation of approximately 7.9 percent). Between 1990 and 1991, nominal tariff protection on average dropped from 32.2 percent to 14.2 percent. Zero tariffs were placed on sectors where Brazil has a competitive advantage and on products without a locally produced equivalent. A 20 percent tariff will be applied to sectors that would be afforded temporary protection.

The problems faced by countries that attempt to liberalize their economies in the midst of failed stabilization programs are well-known. When initiated concurrently with a trade liberalization program, a stabilization program tends to place excessive pressure on the all-important substitution sector. Above all, the dynamism of the export sector derives from the behavior of the exchange rate throughout the liberalization process. Liberalization generally should be preceded by a real devaluation so that adjustment by the import-substitution sector and the export sector can attenuate the impact of greater foreign competition. Macroeconomic stabilization also should be achieved before the liberalization process is fully implemented.

The flexible exchange policy introduced during the second half of 1990 was accompanied by a provision of more credit for exporters. The lead time for negotiating foreign exchange contracts in advance of an export operation was increased, bills of exchange for export could now be secured, and (faced with high domestic interest rates) exporters easily obtained external lines of credit to finance their activities.

However, a permanent recovery of exports is far from guaranteed. Although the accumulated trade surplus in 1988 was US$19.1 billion, it dropped to US$16.1 billion in 1989, stabilized at US$11 billion in 1990 and 1991, and has fallen to considerably lower levels in recent years. In fact, exports after having remained flat for three years (1989-1991) at around US$33 billion per annum, have increased since then, although at a much slower pace than imports. Such a weak performance was caused by the suspension of foreign debt service. Hereafter, for the current recovery actually to become a trend, it would be necessary to pay off debt arrears, revive exports, and accelerate exchange rate devaluations.

Brazil's current trade policy is becoming more harmonized with its neighbors' policies through the creation of regional blocs, in the hope that strategic partnerships will spread to other countries on the continent. The latest regional integration agreement is the Southern Cone Common Market (Mercado Comum do Cone Sul — MERCOSUL), signed by Brazil and Argentina in 1986 and later joined by Uruguay and Paraguay (Treaty of Asunción 1990). Concessions are being made at the same time to other trading partners within the General Agreement on Tariffs and Trade (GATT) framework in order to eliminate disputes with developed countries. Examples of this include an effort to introduce stricter laws on intellectual property rights and a commitment not to resort to Article 18b of the GATT allowing for import restriction measures.

## MERCOSUL[6]

Integration can be seen as a move in the direction of a common market; independent member states relinquish sovereignty in exchange for political participation in a multilateral forum. The issue, therefore, has broader implications than the immediate costs and benefits of trade liberalization and a customs union. In addition to consumer advantages in the short run, qualitative gains will be made from the regional harmonization of economic policies now that domestic market protection is being stripped away. The main benefit will be a boost to the dynamics of growth, which will more than compensate for the potential disadvantages of a regional agreement.

This type of broad perspective inspired the Treaty of Rome (1957) as Western Europe pulled itself together after World War II. The process began with a free trade zone, progressed to a customs union, and finally to a common market. By contrast, Latin American integration efforts, such as the 1960 Treaty of Montevideo, which set up the Latin American Free Trade Association (LAFTA) and the Latin American Integration Association (LAIA) (1981), have never been much more than expressions of diplomatic intentions. In the past 30 years, when military governments were in power in many Latin American countries, prevailing views were typical of the ideas espoused by the UN Economic Commission for Latin America (ECLA).

Once the winds of democracy and liberalism swept through the hemisphere, the countries of Latin America decided to forge stronger relations with each other by setting up regional blocs aimed at building strategic partnerships. The ambitious goal of MERCOSUL was to create a common market and regional parliament by the year 1995.

Brazil's complacency toward the MERCOSUL effort was in marked contrast to the excitement shown by its Latin American partners. Uruguay and Paraguay, of course, have much at stake; their intraregional trade is almost 50 percent of their total trade. In Argentina, intraregional trade is closer to 15 percent, while in Brazil it is no more than 5 percent. Moreover, neighboring domestic policies have a more immediate and strong effect on small, open economies such as Uruguay and Paraguay.

Argentina's strong support of MERCOSUL stems from the progress of its liberalization and stabilization programs. The political strength of traditional sectors, especially agriculture and the financial community, has helped the government reduce average import tariffs to less than 10 percent (compared to approximately 40 percent in Brazil) and to carry out stringent fiscal, monetary, and exchange rate adjustments.

Brazil is less committed to MERCOSUL than the other members. Aside from having its own special weight (in terms of a consumer market and industrial base) and being a closed economy (imports accounted for less than 5 percent of GDP) with high levels of protection for industry, the Brazilian government has not succeeded in controlling the chaotic macroeconomic situation. It is a strategic error for Brazil to turn its back on the Southern Cone simply because 80 percent of its trade lies north of the equator. The developed nations have already begun integrating economically and, in some cases, politically. Any concessions from these blocs will come only as a result of pressure from regional blocs. Thus, it is easier for Latin America to stop the decline in its share of international trade (from 8.5 percent to 3.5 percent) of the early 1990s by resorting to the advantages of economic integration. Indeed, the multilateral diplomacy of the GATT negotiations has proved incapable of dealing with key issues such as farm subsidies in industrial countries that affect the MERCOSUL region, especially Brazil.

The main advantage of integration, however, is that it forces countries to harmonize stabilization policies in order to enter the common market. During negotiations toward MERCOSUL formation, Brazil lagged behind and ran the risk of missing yet another opportunity to diminish macroeconomic uncertainty. Unlike the other MERCOSUL countries, Brazil's government fell behind in producing a reliable plan of action. Harmonization of fiscal, monetary, and foreign exchange policies requires uniform, stable rules of the game. Thus, before concentration on setting an agenda for the establishment of free movements of people, services, and merchandise, a common external tariff, standardized capital markets, and homogeneous public services, the Brazilian government first needed to bring inflation down to tolerable levels. Not only was Brazil at the back of the queue at that time, but it offered no short-term prospects of normalcy. Closer relations with its neighboring countries and stronger commitment to MERCOSUL may be the anchor that will help Brazil to realize its plans to reach price stabilization.

# Notes

1.   An expanded version of the arguments in this section can be found in Longo 1990a and 1990b and in Longo 1992. Editor's note: As of 1996, the state has significantly altered its role in the economy and, in many ways, has pursued a course of action similar to the suggestions made by the author of this chapter.

2.   The budgetary obscurity that results from cross-subsidies between the fiscal budget and state enterprises is characteristic of many developing, newly industrialized countries. For a comparative analysis, grounded in statistical information and accompanied by suggestions for reform, see World Bank 1988. This problem, however, is not confined to developing nations; it permeates discussions of deregulation and privatization in Western Europe and the former socialist countries. See, for example, the case of the USSR in V.K. Senchagov et al. 1989.

3.   For a less schematic presentation of the Collor Plan and related issues, see C.A. Longo 1990c, 1991a, and 1991b.

4.   This section draws heavily on Figueira de Mello 1992 and BNDES 1991.

5.   For more detailed information, see Silber 1990 and 1991 and Braga 1990.

6.   MERCOSUL, also known by the Spanish term MERCOSUR, has been advanced significantly since the original writing of this chapter in 1992. Likewise, Brazil's position toward the MERCOSUL is currently far more positive and supportive than it was a few years ago.

# References

Banco Nacional de Desenvolvimento (BNDES). 1991. *The Brazilian Privatization Program*. Rio de Janeiro: BNDES.

Braga, C.A.P. 1990. "U.S. Policies and the Prospects for Latin American Economic Integration." In *U.S. Policies and the Latin American Economics*, eds. W. Baer and D. Coes. New York: Praeger.

Faoro, R. 1957. *Os Donos do Poder*. Vol. 1. Porto Alegre: Globo.

Figueira de Mello, M. 1992. *A Privatização no Brasil: Análise dos seus Fundamentos e Experiências Internacionais*. Ph.D. dissertation presented to the University of São Paulo.

Longo, C.A. 1990a. *Estado Brasileiro: Diagnósticos e Alternativas*. São Paulo: Atlas.

Longo, C.A. 1990b. "Crises e Revisão das Contas Públicas." In *Brasil: Agenda para Sair da Crise — Inflação e Déficit*, ed. J. P. Reis Velloso. Rio de Janeiro: José Olympio.

Longo, C.A. 1990c. "O Plano Collor em Perspectiva." In *Plano Collor, Avaliação e Perspectivas*, ed. C. de Faro. Rio de Janeiro: Livros Técnicos e Científicos.

Longo, C.A. 1991a. "O Plano Collor aos Nove Meses." In *Condições para a Retomada do Desenvolvimento*, ed. J. P. Reis Velloso. Rio de Janeiro: Nobel.

Longo, C.A. 1991b. "A Questão da Governabilidade." In *Análise e Perspectivas pós Plano Collor II*, ed. C. de Faro. Rio de Janeiro: Livros Técnicos e Científicos.

Longo, C.A. 1992. "Brazil: Monetary and Financial System." *The New Palgrave Dictionary of Money and Finance*. London: Macmillan Press, Ltd..

Peláez, C.M., and W. Suzigan. 1976. *História Monetária do Brasil*. Série Monográfica. No. 23. Rio de Janeiro: IPEA.

Premchand, A. 1988. "El estado y las empresas públicas: relaciones presupuestarias." In *Aspectos del presupuesto público*, eds. A. Premchand and A.L. Antonaya. Washington, D.C.: International Monetary Fund.

Senchagov, V.K., et al. 1989. *Restructuring the Financial System and Its Influence on Economic Development*. Proceedings of the 45th Congress of the International Institute of Public Finance. Buenos Aires: G. Krause-Junk.

Simonsen, M.H. 1970. *Inflação: Gradualismo versus Tratamento de Choque*. Rio de Janeiro: ANPEC.

Silber, S.D. 1991. "Uma Avaliação da Política Brasileira de Comércio Exterior." *Informações FIPE* 130 (May). São Paulo: FIPE.

Silber, S.D. 1990. "Liberalização Comercial e Estabilização." *Informações FIPE* 121 (August). São Paulo: FIPE.

World Bank. 1988. *World Development Report 1988*. Chapter 8. Oxford University Press.

# Industry and Technology

## Hélio Nogueira da Cruz
## Marcos Eugênio da Silva

## Macroeconomic Analysis
### General Background

Brazilian industry underwent a vigorous period of import substitution throughout the 1940s and 1950s, especially in the durable goods sector (such as the automobile industry) and basic industry (such as the steel and oil industries). Import substitution not only represented the closing of the Brazilian economy to international markets, but also the opening of new import markets as new domestic industries prospered. During the 1960s and especially the 1970s, heavy import substitution of capital and intermediate goods occurred while massive investments were made in the electric sector and the production of raw materials.

In spite of some concern with exports, until the end of the 1970s, the Brazilian industrial sector focused mainly on the internal market. Emphasis on the domestic market created a concentrated production structure marked by maturity and technological sophistication. Practically all technological advances were absorbed by the local production structure. The performance of both the industrial sector and the gross domestic product (GDP) was satisfactory, while inflation was still under relative control, as shown in Table 1.

Initially, the domestic market was small by international standards. It grew rapidly, however, generating favorable investment opportunities derived particularly from the high profit margins of an industrial structure that was strongly oligopolist. The private sector also was favored with fiscal and financial incentives. Whenever these stimuli were insufficient, however, the state surfaced as a main investor, acting in several economic sectors simultaneously.

Table I
# Evolution of Brazil's GDP,
## Industrial Production, Inflation, and Exports

| Year | GDP Annual Rate Change | Industrial Production Annual Rate Change | Price Index Annual Rate Change | Exports US$ Billions |
|------|------|------|------|------|
| 1950 | 6.5 | 11.3 | 10.8 | 1.36 |
| 1951 | 5.9 | 6.4 | 18.2 | 1.77 |
| 1952 | 8.7 | 5.0 | 13.5 | 1.42 |
| 1953 | 2.5 | 8.7 | 15.3 | 1.54 |
| 1954 | 10.1 | 8.7 | 27.2 | 1.56 |
| 1955 | 6.9 | 10.6 | 15.6 | 1.42 |
| 1956 | 3.2 | 6.9 | 19.0 | 1.48 |
| 1957 | 8.1 | 5.7 | 13.9 | 1.39 |
| 1958 | 7.7 | 16.2 | 11.4 | 1.24 |
| 1959 | 5.6 | 11.9 | 39.7 | 1.28 |
| 1960 | 9.7 | 9.6 | 29.1 | 1.27 |
| 1961 | 10.3 | 10.6 | 37.2 | 1.40 |
| 1962 | 5.2 | 7.8 | 51.1 | 1.21 |
| 1963 | 1.6 | 0.2 | 69.0 | 1.41 |
| 1964 | 2.9 | 5.2 | 96.9 | 1.43 |
| 1965 | 2.7 | -4.7 | 57.2 | 1.60 |
| 1966 | 3.8 | 11.7 | 37.9 | 1.74 |
| 1967 | 4.8 | 3.0 | 26.9 | 1.65 |
| 1968 | 11.2 | 15.5 | 24.8 | 1.88 |
| 1969 | 10.0 | 10.8 | 20.2 | 2.31 |
| 1970 | 8.3 | 10.5 | 20.0 | 2.74 |
| 1971 | 12.0 | 11.8 | 20.4 | 2.90 |
| 1972 | 11.1 | 12.7 | 17.4 | 3.99 |
| 1973 | 14.0 | 16.0 | 14.8 | 6.20 |
| 1974 | 9.5 | 9.1 | 28.5 | 7.95 |
| 1975 | 5.6 | 5.6 | 27.8 | 8.67 |
| 1976 | 9.7 | 12.5 | 41.3 | 10.13 |
| 1977 | 5.4 | 3.9 | 42.7 | 12.12 |
| 1978 | 4.8 | 7.4 | 38.7 | 12.16 |
| 1979 | 6.7 | 6.6 | 53.9 | 15.24 |
| 1980 | 7.9 | 7.9 | 100.2 | 20.13 |
| 1981 | -1.9 | -5.4 | 109.9 | 23.29 |
| 1982 | 1.4 | 0.4 | 95.4 | 20.20 |
| 1983 | -3.3 | -7.0 | 154.5 | 21.90 |
| 1984 | 4.5 | 6.0 | 220.6 | 27.01 |
| 1985 | 8.3 | 8.3 | 225.5 | 25.64 |
| 1986 | 8.0 | 12.4 | 124.3 | 22.38 |
| 1987 | 2.9 | 0.2 | 228.7 | 26.23 |
| 1988 | 0.0 | -3.4 | 1061.5 | 33.78 |
| 1989 | 3.6 | 3.9 | 847.7 | 34.39 |
| 1990 | | | | 31.39 |

Source: CACEX; IBGE; FGV - *Conjuntura Econômica*, several issues.

Technological advances were imported from developed countries and were slowly absorbed by local producers. Innovations were adapted to local conditions and were sufficiently numerous to cause significant transformations in the industrial structure.

After 1980, the maturation of investments that were made during the previous decade led to a vigorous increase in exports and increasingly larger trade surpluses, as shown in Table 1. At the same time, however, the burden of foreign debt caused the balance of payments to deteriorate. Structural changes that took place in Brazilian industry, mainly in the 1970s, made possible a reversal of priorities with focus on the external market.

In contrast, the 1980s did not enjoy a dynamic industrial sector comparable to the previous decade. The new wave of technological innovations, such as microelectronics and biotechnology, were not absorbed sufficiently into the production structure. The controversial Market Reserve Law (Lei de Reserva de Mercado) prohibited the entry of foreign firms into the microcomputer sector or into other microelectronic sectors, even in the form of joint ventures. The disappointing results have yet to be fully evaluated.

Despite moments of occasional euphoria, such as with the Cruzado Plan (Plano Cruzado), the foreign debt crisis and large zigzags in Brazil's economic policy were largely responsible for industrial stagnation during the 1980s. Investment fell considerably and, by the end of the decade, it constituted only 17 percent of the gross domestic product (GDP), well below the 25 percent average established during the 1970s.

## The Sectoral Structure of the Economy

In 1989 the Brazilian economy had the ninth-highest GDP in the world, equivalent to approximately US$380 billion. In terms of industrial production, Brazil occupied eighth place. The Brazilian economy, however, fell short in many areas, especially during the 1980s, when the growth rate of GDP per capita was practically zero. In 1989, Brazil occupied fortieth place in terms of per capita GDP and fifteenth in terms of the growth rate of the GDP per capita between 1965 and 1988.

Furthermore, a closer look at GDP shows economic growth was unbalanced. The most significant economic development occurred in the service sector where services represented 47 percent of GDP in 1970, expanding to 55 percent by 1989. Within the service sector, for example, the financial sector's share of the GDP grew from a little over 5 percent in 1970 to almost 13 percent in 1987. The industrial sector also increased its contribution to the GDP from 32 percent in 1970 to 40 percent in 1987. Manufacturing maintained its share at approximately 25 percent, while the construction industry increased its share from 5 percent in 1970 to 7.5 percent in 1987.

The data confirm the generally low levels of economic activity, especially during the 1980s, when per capita income was practically stagnant. Usually a dynamic part of the economy, the industrial sector maintained its share of the GDP, while the service sector — financial services, in particular — grew disproportionately larger. Unfortunately, the growth of the financial sector does not represent the maturation of capitalist institutions in Brazil; it means that this segment of the economy has been appropriating progressively larger shares of GDP without a proportionate contribution to the country's development.

## Indicators of Technological Evolution

The indicators traditionally used to measure the technological evolution of a country are its expenditures on science and technology (S&T), expenditures on research and development (R&D), and the labor productivity index. Unfortunately, in Brazil's particular case, these indicators are scarce and unreliable. The country's expenditures on S&T, much of which was allocated to scientific and technological infrastructure at universities and research centers, correspond to approximately 0.5 percent of GDP, a low figure when compared to international standards, usually above 2 percent. The state, as in most countries, is the largest source of financing for such activities.

One of the most recent studies of the technological effort of Brazilian industrial enterprises was conducted by Braga (1986) based on income tax data for 1978, 1980, and 1982. His analysis shows that expenditures on technology reached US$157 million in 1978 and increased to US$233 million in 1982. From this total, R&D expenditures reached US$145 million in 1982, while expenditures on royalties and technical assistance internally and internationally reached US$35 million that same year.

One importance of these indicators is that they show a high concentration of expenditures of R&D in a few large enterprises. Although industry classification differs, this pattern of R&D expenditure concentration is similar with only slight variations to the international pattern. In the countries of the Organization for Economic Cooperation and Development (OECD), for instance, the largest expenditures in the production sector in 1981 were concentrated in electronics, chemicals, and aerospace. In Brazil, those expenditures for 1982 were concentrated in transportation materials (24 percent), electrical and communications materials (18 percent), the steel industry (14 percent), and the mechanical sector (12 percent).

When compared with the country's needs and the experience of other countries that had reached high levels of industrialization in short periods of time, such as the "Asian Tigers" (Korea, Taiwan, and Singapore, for example), these indicators show Brazil's limited technological effort, especially in leading-edge sectors.

In another study, Santana (1986) has analyzed productivity indicators for Brazilian industry, showing that indicators for labor productivity, though of poor quality and in need of improvement, are among the most reliable. All available data for the period 1978 to 1981 indicate that labor productivity grew at an average annual rate of 3.5 percent.

## Industrial and Technological Policy

It was not until the Target Plan (Plano de Metas, 1956-1961) that industrialization became a clear objective of Brazil's economic policy. Ambitious projects in the energy, transport, steel, and oil refining sectors were proposed. Government participation was decisive, both as a producer and as an inducer of industrialization through incentives. Investments were carried out by large conglomerates of private and state enterprises, as well as by multinational corporations. Despite the importance of technology, the Target Plan did not have an explicit policy for dealing with technological issues.

The Triennial Plan (Plano Trienal, 1963-1965), though never implemented, proposed that the same line followed by the Target Plan be maintained. The Government Program for Economic Action (Plano de Ação Estratégica do Governo — PAEG, 1964-1967) held the battle against inflation as the top economic priority. As industrial and technological policy was not addressed, there resulted a considerable fall in the growth rate of industrial products, which in turn was hastened by a recession that affected the entire economy. Until that time, technology policies were passive in nature; it was as if the country's technological development could be fueled by aggregate demand, through either local innovation or imported technology.

In its Strategic Program for Development (Programa Estratégico de Desenvolvimento — PED, 1968-1970), the government not only set industrial growth as a priority, but also presented a set of detailed objectives for each sector. For the first time, scientific and technological policy was made explicit and emphasized a need for the domestic development of this area with a high degree of autonomy. The National Council of Scientific and Technological Development (Conselho Nacional de Desenvolvimento Científico e Tecnológico — CNPq), which had begun to coordinate all policies for scientific development, and the National Fund for Scientific and Technological Development (Fundo Nacional de Desenvolvimento Científico e Tecnológico — FNDCT), created at that time, both permitted conditions that greatly favored Brazil's industrial and technological development. The government clearly had established stimulation of S&T development as one of its priorities, granting certain privileges to the domestic supply of technology, thereby enhancing its condition as a by-product of aggregate demand growth.

Another important step in the evolution of explicit technological policies was taken with the First National Development Plan (I Plano Nacional de

Desenvolvimento — PND, 1972-1974), which occurred at the time of Brazil's "economic miracle." Priority already was being given to the development of leading-edge technology (such as electronics) as well as to the development of capital goods and basic inputs. The Second National Development Plan (Segundo Plano Nacional de Desenvolvimento — II PND, 1975-1979) followed the same general guidelines as the first and anticipated an acceleration in the import-substitution process, especially in the raw materials, energy, and capital goods sectors. Despite the oil crisis that unfolded in 1973, major industrial expansion with massive investments took place that consolidated Brazil's industrial structure and provided the country with a competitive edge in the international market during the 1980s.

The Third National Development Plan (Terceiro Plano Nacional de Desenvolvimento — III PND, 1980-1985) and the Government Action Program (Programa de Ação Governamental — PAG, 1987-1991) were quite different from previous government plans. Although both programs presented general intentions and government guidelines, they failed to detail projects to be executed and how they were to be financed. Only the information sector had an explicit technological policy — market reserve — but it also went through difficult times caused by internal and external friction.

In 1990, President Fernando Collor de Mello inaugurated a new era for domestic industry. New policies would increase the competitiveness and quality of Brazilian products, open the economy to foreign competition, and reduce the state's presence in the economy. Much of this would be accomplished through the privatization of state-owned enterprises. The Brazilian Program of Quality and Productivity (Programa Brasileiro de Qualidade e Produtividade — PBQP) was created to combat waste and technological backwardness in Brazilian enterprises, including state-owned businesses.

The Industrial and International Trade Policy (Política Industrial de Comércio Exterior — PICE) was initiated progressively to reduce protectionist taxation, eliminate indiscriminate incentives and subsidies, strengthen competition and potentially competitive segments of the economy, introduce local industry to international competition, and increase industry's technological capacity.

The Industrial Competitiveness Program (Programa de Competitividade Industrial — PCI) formed to consolidate guidelines for competitive restructuring and deregulation of the Brazilian economy and for improvements in legislation that stimulates competition.

## Sectoral Analysis
### The Metal-Mechanical Sector

The metal-mechanical sector includes a vast set of interrelationships, from the extraction of minerals to the manufacturing of parts and accessories used in the production of final goods. This sector may be subdivided into eight microsystems: steel, nonferrous metallurgy, metallurgy, machinery and equipment, automotive and other transport materials, chemical, and electric-electronic. The electric-electronic subsector will be dealt with separately.

The metal-mechanical sector originated at the end of the last century. However, it was only after the 1950s that the current production structure began to form, due to the increasing import substitution of durable and capital goods. During the Target Plan era, the "Brazilian miracle" phase, and the II PND, the implementation process prospered the most. Brazil had a metal-mechanical system during the late 1970s that was relatively large and sophisticated and included the marked presence of both foreign and state capital enterprises. New technological challenges emerged because of the depletion of import-substitution possibilities in sectors with stable technological frontiers. Therefore, it became necessary to define a model capable of incorporating technological transformations associated with the electronic, mechanical, and fine chemical sectors. In the information sector in particular, the country adopted strong measures aimed at internalizing production. In past years, exports in this sector have been an important source of foreign exchange for Brazil.

## The Steel Industry

Brazil has a long tradition of steel production, but only recently has it become internationally prominent. In 1988, Brazil became the sixth-largest producer of raw steel in the world at a level of 24.3 million tons — 10.3 percent higher than that achieved the previous year. Government presence in the steel sector was initially strong, including Companhia Siderúrgica Nacional (CSN), Companhia Siderúrgica Tubarão (CST), Companhia Siderúrgica de São Paulo (COSIPA), and Companhia Siderúrgica de Minas Gerais (USIMINAS), among others. This sector was given priority for privatization, and all of these companies have been privatized.

Brazilian exports, reaching nine million tons of raw steel in 1988 and generating US$2.5 billion to US$2.6 billion, are in the form of laminates, ingots, and semifinished products. They are sold all over the globe, primarily in the United States, Canada, Italy, Japan, Korea, and Argentina.

## The Non-ferrous Metallurgic Microcomplex

The non-ferrous metallurgic microcomplex includes the extraction of minerals, production of alloys, laminates, cast iron, wiredraws, and relaminates, production of solders and anodes, as well as the metallurgy of precious metals and powders. Given the variety of items (26 different types) that compose this microcomplex and the lack of available information on it, the following discussion will only examine aluminum — the most important component of this microcomplex to the Brazilian economy.

The consumption of aluminum has increased because of its ease of transformation, good electric and heat conduction, hardness, durability, and ease of combination with other elements. As a result, aluminum is being used in many different sectors, and it competes with steel, iron, and wood in the construction industry and with copper in the electrical industry. In addition, aluminum has various applications in the electronic and aerospace industries.

Aluminum production at the world level is dominated by Alcoa, Alcan, Reynolds, Kaiser, Alusuisse, and Péchiney. These companies control approximately 55 percent of the world's production and are leading producers in the United States, Russia, and Canada.

The Brazilian aluminum industry dates to the early 1900s, but only after 1955 did it begin to gain momentum when Companhia Brasileira de Alumínio (C.A.), a private Brazilian company owned by the Votorantim Group, explored mines in Poços de Caldas, in the state of Minas Gerais. Later, Alcan and Alcoa would establish themselves in Brazil. Aluminum production, once evenly distributed among the three companies, saw substantial growth during the 1970s, increasing from 80,600 tons in 1971 to 260,600 tons in 1980. During this period, Valesul and Bellinton entered the market, bringing production to 454,900 tons in 1984.

The Second National Development Plan directed ambitious efforts toward the expansion of the aluminum industry, particularly for export. The government's aim was to take advantage of the abundance of bauxite and electrical energy in the Amazon region with projects such as Alunorte/ Albrás, a joint venture of foreign and state capital, and the first project of its kind. During the 1970s, the state also participated in the Valesul project (Rio de Janeiro), a joint venture with Shell and Reynolds dedicated to supplying the domestic market. Another such project was Alumar (Alcoa), begun in 1984.

According to the Brazilian Mineral Balance, produced by the National Department of Mineral Products (Departamento Nacional de Produtos Minerais — DNPM), the main consumers of aluminum are civil engineering (22.9 percent of the total in 1983), durable goods (18.8 percent), transportation (18.2 percent), the electric sector (16.31 percent), and packaging (9.3 percent). Demand is heterogenous, varying greatly from product to product.

In the 1980s, Brazil generated increasingly larger surpluses of bauxite (more than 50 percent of total production due to the Trombetas project implemented in 1983) and aluminum. In the 1970s, Brazil imported more than 50 percent of its aluminum. Production expanded so rapidly, however, that aluminum exports from Brazil in 1988 generated the exceptional sum of US$1.5 billion, due in part to high aluminum prices on the international market.

## The Metallurgical Microcomplex

Metallurgical products represented 11 percent of the total value of production in the metals and machinery complex in 1970, 11.5 percent in 1975, and 12.3 percent in 1980. Despite its important role in the sector, specific, detailed information is lacking. As a result, only a few segments of the sector can be studied including metallic packaging, tools and knives, and electric conductors, which together represented 34 percent of the value of production in 1980.

Basic industries of the metallurgical microcomplex are suppliers of raw materials, providing Flanders sheets for packaging, sheets of stainless steel for cutlery, and special types of steel for tool manufacturing, as well as copper, aluminum, and lead for electric conductors. These sectors interact with the rubber industry while CSN and Acesita have substantially increased production of Flanders sheets and stainless steel. CSN, Cosipa, and Usiminas have increased their production of steel sheets (cold and hot).

The metal packaging subsector is comprised of the following types of enterprises: those that manufacture cans for their own consumption (such as Nestlé), those that produce cans for a third party (such as Metalma of the Matarazzo Group), those that manufacture other types of containers (such as Mangels for gas cylinders), and those that produce barrels and cans (manufactured by Metalúrgica Prado and Kheem). The sector shows a presence of both national and foreign capital.

## Machinery and Equipment

The machinery and equipment sector (or capital goods industry) plays an important role in the industrial sector. It is responsible for the production of capital goods and, therefore, incorporates a large part of Brazil's technological advances. It is located almost entirely in the states of São Paulo, Rio de Janeiro, Minas Gerais, and, to a lesser degree, Rio Grande do Sul and Paraná.

The sector has a long history in Brazil, dating to the end of the last century. Initially, its production was limited to basic products but has evolved over time to include truly complex products. During the 1960s, there was a surge in capital goods production, with industrial development fueled by the Target Plan (1956-1961) through the establishment of the Brazilian automobile industry in particular. Production of machine tools such as lathes, drills, and milling and shaping machines grew substantially. Other capital goods related to the textile, printing, and farm equipment sectors also displayed considerable improvements in quality. Domestic production of parts, auto parts, and components, such as motors and ball bearings, made viable "deverticalization of industrial production," in other words, made the change from vertical integration of industrial production to a more horizontal mode viable.

Propelled by orders placed primarily by the steel and oil industries, the production of made-to-order capital goods increased, as did the production of electrical energy, with state enterprises constituting the bulk of demand.

The capital goods sector benefited from several government incentives. The import-substitution policy offered domestic producers a sizeable expanding market, thereby making growth at corresponding rates possible. Moreover, there was financial support provided mainly by the Investment Fund for Machinery and Equipment (Fundo de Investimentos em Máquinas e Equipamentos — Finame), fiscal subsidies of varying size and nature, and a procurement policy adopted by state enterprises, which altogether contributed to sector increases in production and advances in technological capabilities.

During the 1970s, the capital goods sector experienced significant growth and extraordinary expansion in domestic demand. Demand for capital goods tends to stress the oscillations of economic cycles; it grows when the economy is prosperous and is reduced sharply when the economic setting is unfavorable.

After the 1970s, domestic demand declined, causing the sector to seek out international markets. After 1981, the production of capital goods showed a downward trend that reversed itself somewhat during the Cruzado Plan.

## Table 2
## Performance of the Mechanical Sector in Brazil

| Year | Production US$ billions 1989 | Exports US$ billions current | Employment Thousands (annual average) |
|---|---|---|---|
| 1980 | 17.75 | 1.05 | 306.1 |
| 1981 | 16.22 | 1.19 | 296.1 |
| 1982 | 13.69 | 0.91 | 258.8 |
| 1983 | 11.54 | 0.89 | 209.0 |
| 1984 | 12.42 | 1.16 | 204.7 |
| 1985 | 15.02 | 1.34 | 234.9 |
| 1986 | 17.17 | 1.21 | 274.5 |
| 1987 | 17.62 | 1.43 | 289.2 |
| 1988 | 17.11 | 2.00 | 282.7 |
| 1989 | 16.40 | 2.20 | 275.8 |
| 1990 | 15.00 | 2.00 | 265.0 |

Source: ABIMAQ.

In order to present a more complete analysis of the 1980s, it is necessary to look at aspects of the Brazilian mechanics sector using data collected by the Brazilian Association of Producers of Machinery/Syndicate of Machinery Producers (ABIMAQ/SINDIMAQ), which include the production of serial goods, such as tools, machine tools, farm equipment and implements, textile machines, heavy mechanics, printing machines, and machines for the production of plastic products (see Table 2).

Nineteen eighty was a peak year for volume of production and employment levels; despite a period of recovery stimulated by the Cruzado Plan, this kind of domestic economic peak would never repeat itself. Growth in exports could not compensate for the decline in domestic demand. Imports also fell during the period.

Most of the main products for export in 1987 — which included internal combustion engines, with 42.7 percent of the total, and water pumps and other types of pumps, with 9 percent of the total — were destined for the United States and Europe. The expansion in exports did not suffice to maintain operating capacity. Made-to-order capital goods, for example, operated at 50 percent below capacity levels.

As of 1992, Brazil exhibited a mature and significant capital goods sector. Several national and foreign companies possessed the reasonable technological capability as well as production levels that allowed for significant economies of scale. Although the objective of the sector was not necessarily to obtain total self-sufficiency, it gave Brazil a reasonable degree of technological autonomy.

The interrelationship between the machinery and equipment sector and other industrial and agricultural activities, as well as the whole metal-metallic cluster, is very strong. The machinery sector plays an important role in the diffusion of leading technologies and in the industrialization process. It stands to reason that the capital goods sector in Brazil, as in other countries, requires special industrial policy treatment.

Finally, the capital goods sector is facing several dilemmas. Regardless of idle capacity, there is a need to invest in plant modernization. The lack of technical advances (associated with electronics, precision mechanics, and new materials) may render the industrial park cluster obsolete. Specific products, parts, components, and accessories will probably have to be imported, despite the existence of conjunctural excess productive capacity in these segments of the industry. To perform its fundamental role of assuring the efficiency of Brazil's production sector, it also will be necessary for the sector to interact with all other sectors of the economy and the country's scientific-technological base. In light of financial difficulties resulting from prolonged demand crises and macroeconomic instability, this final regard is no longer viable.

## The Brazilian Automobile Industry and the Auto Parts Sector
The automobile sector represents the main segment of the metal-mechanical cluster. Automobile production requires relatively high technical standards for its numerous activities that include steel, mechanical, metallurgical,

chemical, rubber, glass, forging, and alloys. The pace of production is set by the assembling companies, which also define standards for quality control, technical specifications, types of raw materials, and component specifications.

The auto parts sector has demonstrated significant advances in the technological capability of domestic producers. In the 1950s sophisticated production was almost exclusively the mark of international companies. As time has gone by, domestic groups have developed and matured to take their place, and, more recently, auto parts exports have increased, attesting to the quality of Brazilian products.

**Automobile Production at an International Level.** The automobile sector presents important technological advances that have generated waves of investment of a Schumpeterian nature. Since the beginning of the century, the auto industry has been led by North American products under the guidance of Taylor-Ford labor methods and mass production. Toward the end of the 1950s and in the early 1960s, U.S. hegemony in this market was threatened by European production. The hardships of the 1970s, triggered by the oil crises of 1973 and 1979, drew a picture of low growth in demand and an increasing share of the market taken up by Japanese production.

Although the automobile industry is dominated by large enterprises, it is possible to observe the presence of a Schumpeterian-type pattern of competition in which efforts toward quality improvement and aggressive sales techniques are an underlying characteristic. Japanese automobiles — known for low fuel consumption, low maintenance, and competitive prices for comparable quality — are produced with technical and managerial advances (Kanban, Just-in-Time, CCQ) that challenge automobile production methods worldwide.

The Japanese automotive industry accomplished extraordinary growth after the mid-1970s, when it invaded the market, giving American and European products stiff competition. In recent years, the United States and Europe have placed numerous barriers on Japanese imports, causing the Japanese automobile industry to move its operations and promote joint ventures in several other countries, including Organization for Economic Cooperation and Development (OECD) countries and Korea.

**The Brazilian Automobile Industry.** The Brazilian automobile industry is uniquely important to the nation's technical base, due to its economic relations as well as its role as an inducer of technological advancement.

**Evolution of Production.** The development of the Brazilian automobile industry has been manipulated largely by tariffs and other commercial policies implemented in accordance with models of import substitution. Government policies included such requirements as a 95 percent level of nationalization, capital goods import facilitation through nontaxation, financial and fiscal advantages, and restrictions on imports. Response to these policies was immediate and strong, particularly in terms of rapid growth in production and the installation of numerous enterprises. An implementation phase between 1957 and 1962 saw strong pressure exerted to guarantee increases in technical standards in several activities of the productive cluster, particularly capital goods. Between 1963 and 1967, when Brazil endured economic crises ridden with inflation, a rising foreign debt, and falling exports, growth in the industry was limited, as was growth in the GDP. Between 1968 and 1974, a new period of expressive growth took place in which overall automobile production tripled.

The expansion of the automobile industry is related directly to the macroeconomic performance of the Brazilian economy and specific policies aimed at providing the sector with incentives. Expansionist monetary and fiscal policies were aimed at promoting exports. The result was an acceleration in the rate of growth of GDP ultimately affecting the automobile industry because of the high income elasticity of industry demand. On the other hand, an expansion of consumer credit (for the acquisition of durable consumer goods) also encouraged growth in the domestic demand for automobiles.

During the period between the oil shocks of 1973 and 1979, production dropped. The government had adopted macroeconomic policy measures that prevented a more accentuated fall in GDP. A new wave of import substitution resulted, which included an extensive reconversion program of the energy matrix through external financing, leading to a substantial growth in foreign debt. Since exports failed to compensate for the decline in domestic demand, automobile production during most of the 1980s was lower than in 1981.

**The Market Structure.** The automobile industry evolved in the midst of important changes in the production structure. Two periods characterize the evolution of the automobile industry: the first extends to 1968, and the second spans from 1968 to the present.

During the first period, Volkswagen's (VW) participation was overwhelming. In 1959, it accounted for 58.3 percent of the market; in 1968, its share reached 77.5 percent of sales. VW's growing importance was associated with economies of scale and was derived from the mass production of small cars. During this same period, other enterprises, such as SIMCA, VEMAG, WILLYS, and FNM, experienced a loss in market shares.

At the beginning of the second period, the production structure underwent an important reorganization when General Motors (GM), Ford, and Chrysler entered the market. In 1976, Fiat also began its operations. The local firms, FNM and VEMAG, were absorbed by multinational corporations. Prior to the oil crisis, most investment went to the production of mid-sized and large cars. Thereafter, a renewed emphasis on the production of small cars attracted other firms to compete with VW, whose market share dropped in 1985 to 38.5 percent. During the recession years of the 1980s, the so-called "world cars" — the Monza by GM (1982), the Escort by Ford (1983), the Santana by VW (1984), and the Uno by Fiat (1984), for example — were introduced. Changes in the production structure ranged from modifications in a car's external appearance to modifications in the engine, as well as other quality improvements. New production processes, such as *Kanban* and "Just-in-Time," as well as large-scale automation, were introduced but have not yet been implemented throughout the entire sector. Implemented during the Collor administration, a liberalization program that eased automobile imports represents an important challenge to the industry during the 1990s.

**The Auto Parts Sector.** The parts industry comprises 4,000 firms that produce about 5,000 different products. The industry is marked by wide differences in production conditions and in technological and physical capacity, as well as a lack of detailed sectoral data. National and foreign businesses of the most diverse sizes and technological standards coexist within this sector.

Important transformations have been observed in the sector. Strategies, distinguished by a search for better products, reduction of inventories, and the formation of associations for R&D, as mainly pursued by Japanese industries, have been disseminated internationally. Introduced in Brazil, albeit in a discrete manner, these strategies have transformed relationships between international enterprises and the assembling businesses, mainly in areas related to rigid quality control in which large companies (such as Metal Leve, Cofap, Varga, and Brosol) participate. Regardless of the origin of a firm's capital (domestic or foreign), production standards are the stiffest standards found in the international sphere.

Brazilian exports of auto parts increased dramatically from US$700 million in 1974 to US$2 billion in 1988. They are mainly destined for sale in the United States (50.9 percent), Germany (16 percent), and Argentina (6.1 percent).

The tire industry (which includes inner tubes and other rubber products) encompasses 15 enterprises, among which Pirelli, Firestone, and Michelin are leaders with more than 90 percent of the market.

**Exports.** Exports from the Brazilian automobile industry showed rapid growth between 1972 and 1981, followed by a period of relative stabilization between 1982 and 1987. Exports, as a share of total production, increased significantly during the same period. Export growth during the first period was mainly a result of new incentives provided by the BEFIEX Program (Comissão para a Concessão de Benefícios Fiscais e Programas Especiais de Exportação). Initiated in 1972 between the government and multinational corporations, the program aimed at stimulating exports in products manufactured by multinational corporations. It established export targets in exchange for special authorization to import capital goods, parts and components, with tariff exemptions capped at one-third of export value. Such subsidies, as well as other privileges related to the Industrial Products Tax (Imposto sobre Produto Industrializado — IPI), were given to exports in automobiles, small trucks, jeeps, buses, and larger trucks that had a nationalization index of at least 85, 82, 95, 82, and 78 percent, respectively. The volume of investments related to exports between 1973 and 1977 was quite heavy.

In the second period, the growth of exports was prompted by a strong fall in domestic demand, the modernization of plants and car models, and changes in government policy. The external market was pivotal for six corporations: Fiat, GM, Ford, Mercedes Benz, VW, and Volvo. In 1987, for example, the percent of total production sold to foreign markets by Fiat, VW, Volvo, and Mercedes was 64.5, 42.5, 37.4, and 26.6 percent, respectively. In the cases of Mercedes Benz and Fiat (producers of large trucks), a large portion of their exports was destined for industrialized countries, whereas exports from the other firms were mainly bound for less developed countries.

Parallel to the growth in car sales, there was an increase in auto parts sales, particularly engines and components. The change is representative of the growing internationalization of the whole sector in which the effects of new technologies and products, such as the "world car," offer new challenges to international producers. In 1988, automobile and auto parts exports soared to more than US$3 billion.

Since the 1970s, the paradigm for the automobile industry has been the Japanese case. The Japanese industry has implemented cost reductions and quality improvements, thereby threatening both American and European companies in their own markets for small cars. Japan's technology has migrated to European countries, the United States, and Korea. The Brazilian automobile industry will have to operate within this competitive environment if it intends to export large portions of its production. The risk of running into technical obsolescence and unfavorable exchange rate schedules will have to be faced in order to avoid the depreciation of such an inestimable asset.

## Chemical Industry

The chemical industry is extremely important because of its strong interrelationship with the rest of the economy. According to Haguenauer (1985), although some foreign producers of consumer goods had started production approximately 40 years earlier, this production cluster has its roots in the 1954 creation of Petrobrás (Petróleo do Brasil).

Until the end of the 1960s, advances in the petrochemical area were minimal. At the time, there was no foreign capital, and domestic capital was insufficient to finance needed levels of investment. Once Petroquisa, a subsidiary of Petrobrás, was created after 1967, a performance model was defined involving the state as well as private capital from national and foreign sources. The state not only eased the supply of basic inputs but also created favorable conditions under which private capital could function by defining priorities and large investments.

The government created three petrochemical poles in Brazil: the Northeast (1971), São Paulo (1972), and the South (Rio Grande do Sul). Initial plans for the South, however, underwent changes as the oil crisis unfolded; subsequently, the plans have not been fully implemented. A strategy to stimulate the petrochemical industry was part of the II PND and was designed to consolidate the vertical integration of the Brazilian industrial structure through the production of basic inputs. In 1987, another petrochemical pole was launched in Rio de Janeiro.

Despite the difficulties faced by Brazilian enterprises in managing a sector that uses such sophisticated technology, the results were positive. The industry shows a solid financial and technical performance, as indicated by its recent superior export record. The petrochemical complex is now consolidated and fully integrated with the rest of the economy and operates with highly modern technology. It exhibits a significant participation on the part of domestic firms, especially in the production of basic and intermediate inputs.

In the area of finished goods — pharmaceuticals, perfumes, dyes and pigments, fertilizers, herbicides and pesticides, preservatives and flavoring for foods, and all kinds of additives — the picture is quite different. Multinational corporations practically control this part of the market, import most of its inputs, and are slightly integrated with the rest of the industrial cluster. Therefore, the finished goods segment of the chemical industry exhibits a high degree of dependence on foreign technology and input.

In contrast, the finished goods segment of the non-petroleum-based chemical industry (organic and inorganic) is highly heterogeneous in terms of production, production scale, technological complexity, and capital ownership. This segment of the industry is poorly developed in Brazil and has reported a structural deficit in its balance of payments.

The Brazilian chemical industry overall is marked by a major disequilibrium in terms of technological development. According to Haguenauer (1985), basic chemistry is well developed and shows the strong presence of solid domestic firms (many of them highly regarded by private groups during the privatization process). They typically operate on the edge of the technological frontier and generate a significant level of exports.

In the segment of final goods, the picture is not as bright. With the exception of some areas, such as plastics and fertilizer, the final goods sector is dominated by multinational corporations and is highly dependent on the external sector to fill domestic demand. Another area of poor performance is fine chemistry, in which Brazil has not developed technological sophistication. The recent approval of the patent law, however, should foster development in this area.

## Electric-electronics and Information

**Electronics Microcomplex.** Comprising a true Schumpeterian cluster, the electronics sector is representative of the great technological advancement experienced by capitalist economies. The sector's technological sophistication positively affects other economic spheres, such as the production of capital goods, and the automation of the industrial sector. It even brings about changes in current consumption patterns.

During the 1980s, the Brazilian electronics industry received close attention from the federal government, whose concern was translated into many measures aimed at internalizing production and technological capacity within Brazil. Among these were direct intervention to create companies, the creation of technical and human resources advancement centers, financial support, restrictions on imports (such as the Informatics Law — Lei da Informática), and rigorous control over the electronics industry. The direction of the electronics and information sector is affected by political as well as other controversial issues impacting on economic policy. Sometimes, the sector responds to measures that have potentially negative effects on the existing technical base, as apparently was the case of the Free Trade Zone.

The electronics sector deserves special consideration in the study of the technological progress of the productive sector in economies such as Brazil's. Despite the fact that most of this industry is located in the state of São Paulo, with important technological hubs in Campinas, São Carlos, São José dos Campos, and in the capital itself, it will not be discussed in great detail. Export figures from this sector are significantly lower than those of other sectors such as automotive.

The Brazilian electronics microcomplex is comprised of about 380 firms, dispersed throughout the subsectors of telecommunications, radio communications, electronic consumer goods, data processing, and electronic components.

The major challenge confronting the industry in the 1990s is to be competitive in international markets. Relationships between multinational corporations and national businesses are advancing rapidly, with several joint ventures already established; among them, the most noteworthy is a consortium between SID and IBM. During the current process of market liberalization and in the face of intense technological change, the joint venture approach appears to be the most rational survival strategy for Brazilian enterprises in this industry.

*Manufacturing of Electronic Materials and Equipment.* The electronic materials and equipment industry includes electronic components such as semiconductors, capacitors, and resistors, as well as computers and equipment used for controls and instrumentation, the defense industry, and the practice of medicine.

The components sector has more than 2,000 manufacturing units, mainly small and medium sized. Twenty-six percent of these enterprises are multinational corporations; the remainder are Brazilian companies. This sector is still under consolidation due to swift technical changes and the fast growth of the domestic market.

The main market niche of the electronics equipment industry is computer equipment. The data processing industry may be classified in two subsectors: 1) large and medium-sized computers and 2) small-sized computers, microcomputers, and peripheral components. Large multinational corporations (IBM, Digital, and UNISYS) dominate the production of large and medium-sized computers in Brazil. The manufacturing of small computers and microcomputers was begun in Brazil in 1978, primarily by the Brazilian companies Cobra, Edisa, Lobo, SID, and SISCO. As liberalization proceeds, this subsector of the electronics industry that is largely affected by the Informatics Law is expected to undergo a radical reorganization.

*Radio, TV, and Sound Industry.* Known as "electronics for final consumption," this sector accounts for approximately 80 percent of all sales in the electronics sector. In 1983, the radio subsector was responsible for 79 percent of the radio, television, and sound industry. The subsector of electronic appliances for domestic use has shown a very high rate of growth, although it suffered a strong reduction only during the 1980 and 1981 economic crises.

Until the mid-1970s, the radio receiver industry was located in the Central-South region of the country and was characterized by a strong presence of national enterprises and low levels of technology. With the implementation of the Free Zone and the adoption of the PAL-M system for color TVs, a significant restructuring took place. Small businesses could not compete with the large firms; a majority of those that survived moved to Manaus. In the audio equipment sector, the strategy was to incorporate modern technology by importing kits and making technological assistance agreements with international firms, a process that altered the sector's production structure. Firms such as Gradiente, Sharp, and CCD lead the market, followed closely by Phillips, Evadin, and Semp. Only a few small companies remain in the market.

*Communications Equipment Industry.* At the beginning of the 1970s, the telecommunications industry was comprised of a few small national companies that used low levels of technology and four large foreign enterprises (Ericsson, SESA, Siemens, and NEC) that produced equipment and systems for public communication. Until 1977, almost all large-scale equipment was imported.

The Interministry Group of Components and Materials (Grupo Interministerial de Componentes e Materiais — Geicon) and the Center for Research and Development of Brazilian Communication (Centro de Pesquisa e Desenvolvimento da Telebrás — CPqD) initiated an aggressive procurement policy under the administration of the Ministry of Communication that would benefit Brazilian companies. The ensuing market structure remained concentrated, with 73 percent of the country's 1983 production supplied by the 15 largest companies. The largest four companies alone were responsible for more than 45 percent of total production. Among the 15 largest companies, 11 were at least partially foreign owned.

Using modern technology and local resources, about 40 Brazilian enterprises supply the domestic market with radio production, filling the demand especially for broadcast and rebroadcast.

**Information and Data Processing.** Notwithstanding its recent establishment in Brazil, the information sector has been extraordinarily dynamic not only in its rate of growth but also in terms of technological change. In spite of criticism of how information technology was introduced into Brazil, with respect to the Market Reserve Law in particular, this industry has imposed important transformations on the entire industrial sector.

Between 1980 and 1983, Brazil's market was between US$3.3 billion and US$3.7 billion, about 10 percent the size of the U.S. market. Brazilian companies filled 33 percent of the demand. In 1985 the sector exported the equivalent of US$578 million (3.4 percent of all Brazilian exports that year) and imported US$1.045 billion. In 1988, total sales for the sector amounted to US$5.9 billion, 67 percent of which was produced by domestic enterprises.

In 1986, about 50 percent of imports were components, 10.9 percent were entertainment products, and 39.1 percent were products for professional use. Exports of components represented 25 percent of total exports, entertainment goods amounted to 42.7 percent, and products for professional use totaled 31.7 percent. From the beginning of the 1980s, the sector's trade balance showed a deficit (US$491 million) for 1986, due to the impossibility of import substitution caused by the phenomenally fast technological advances of more developed countries.

According to information provided by the Special Secretary of Informatics (Secretaria Especial de Informática — SEI), the number of installed computers in Brazil increased by approximately 400 percent between 1984 and 1987. As of the early 1990s, about one million units had been installed (including data processing for general use, automatic banking, and business). In terms of value, national enterprises were responsible for almost 40 percent of the total (estimated at US$5.4 billion). The production of 16-bit microcomputers, for instance, jumped from 2,300 units in 1984 to about 100,000 units in 1987.

In the early 1970s, the Commission of Electronic Processing Activities (Comissão de Atividades de Processamento Eletrônico — CAPRE), associated with the Planning Ministry, was established. Its creation marked the beginning of a government policy that would stimulate scientific and technological development and protect the interests of national capital.

In the II PND (1974-1979), the government's attempt to stimulate the foundation of a domestic information industry was explicit, granting special treatment to companies of national origin. CAPRE began to define those market areas to benefit from market reserve and, after 1976, imposed several restrictions on imports by the sector.

A market reserve policy was implemented in 1977, guaranteeing the exclusive production and distribution of new products manufactured in the industry to national companies (especially small-sized computers).

The policy was expanded in 1979 with the establishment of the SEI in association with the National Security Council (Conselho de Segurança Nacional — CSN), and in 1982, with the creation of the Informatics Technological Center (Centro Tecnológico de Informática — CTI). In 1984, the National Congress approved the Informatics Law, which introduced more democratic principles and created the National Council of Informatics and Automation (Conselho Nacional de Informática e Automação — CONIN), an agency consisting of representatives from the public and private sectors charged with the task of debating and proposing new strategies. The law ratified temporarily (until 1992) the principles of technological advancement and market reserve for the sector.

The Informatics Law was implemented by the National Plan for Informatics and Automation (Plano Nacional de Informática e Automação — PLANIN) and was approved by the Congress in 1985. PLANIN reinforces the position of national enterprises by defining fiscal incentives aimed at technological development. The Market Reserve Law has been criticized heavily in national and international arenas. It is alleged that it not only inhibits Brazil's technological progress and makes information products more costly, but that it has also imposed difficulties on external debt renegotiation.

The truth is that the law is cumbersome, especially in attempting to preserve all the markets that use computers. Since microelectronics is a technology that extends well beyond its own market frontier, this law would ultimately affect other sectors, including mechanics, metallurgy, and automotive. The price Brazil paid to establish its own microelectronics industry was extremely high, in that it inhibited the growth of other important sectors.

Expenditures of national enterprises on R&D represent another problem. R&D support is below the level needed to keep the industry up to date and positioned to compete in international markets. The government is responsible for assisting the productive sector by making technology available and by creating demand for information products. Firms benefiting from the Market Reserve Law, however, must realize that they cannot survive under a long-term strategy of manufacturing clones of foreign products. Without innovation all efforts taken by the country to establish this industry may be in vain.

## Biotechnology

Biotechnology is not an economic sector as such. It represents a set of techniques, many of which (such as those for beverage fermentation and food processing) have been known for a long time. More recent practices of modern biotechnology consist of the manipulation of cellular and subcellular processes that use recombinant DNA technology as a core for the identification, isolation, and cloning of genes through biochemical methods. Cloning is a technique that reproduces and augments an isolated gene usually found in the genetic material of a virus or bacteria.

Besides recombinant DNA, other processes of applied cellular biology are being used that combine recent advances in microbiology, biochemistry, and chemical engineering. In leading-edge areas of modern biotechnology, new products and processes quite often are developed in small and medium-sized companies, many of which, however, are subsequently forced to associate with large conglomerates to begin production on an industrial scale. These associations, undertaken to secure new technology and efficiency, usually lead to the absorption of small-sized companies by large groups.

In Brazil, several important productive sectors are typical users of classical biotechnology, and it is expected that they will adopt this technique. The following are the economic sectors that are the most vulnerable to intense biotechnological transformation: agriculture (mainly livestock), paper and cellulose, sugar-alcohol production, pharmaceuticals, and production of vaccines. Although utilizing biotechnological products and processes of relatively low monetary value that are consistently restricted to classical biotechnology, these sectors play a strategic role in industrial production because of their interactions with the rest of the economy.

The establishment of a market reserve policy for biotechnology is extremely controversial. Contrary to what happens in microelectronics, in biotechnology it is difficult to utilize the copying technique, also known as "reverse engineering," and it is often impossible to acquire the generating sources of products and biotechnological processes (such as cells and cloned genes) on the international market. A monoclonal antibody, for instance, can be commercialized on a world scale even when the sale of its originating cells does not take place.

With the exception of the pharmaceutical sector, Brazilian capital dominates the biotechnology industry. The pharmaceutical sector is basically controlled by multinational corporations that import a considerable portion of their technology from their headquarters. Despite important achievements in the area of input production (such as insulin), it would be quite difficult for Brazilian enterprises to obtain the indispensable technological capacity to become competitive in the international market.

Sugar-alcohol, paper and cellulose, and livestock sectors are controlled by domestic capital, and it is within these segments of the industry that modern biotechnology is expected to modify traditional biotechnology substantially, bringing considerable economic and social benefits to the country. Modifications occurring in these sectors on a global scale may make current techniques obsolete and imply a loss of domestic and foreign markets, especially in industries dominated by national capital.

In Brazil, paper pulp and cellulose is the sector that will be impacted first by new production techniques. Climatic conditions, the integration of business and university in research areas (forest engineering and vegetable physiology), and the predominance of national conglomerates clearly indicate a thriving future for the sector.

In livestock, extensive production with low productivity can be observed together with "technological pockets" where experiments with artificial insemination and embryo transfers have been successful. In the next few years, embryo transfers will be employed more extensively, bringing about an increase in productivity of up to 5,000 percent in embryo generation. In the future, techniques that allow choosing the sex of embryos (sex determination), as well as physical characteristics (size and weight), will be available on an industrial scale. Although such techniques are currently used in laboratories, the transfer of their knowledge to the industrial scale for livestock is difficult. One might expect Brazil to be a large meat exporter in the near future.

The sugar-alcohol sector has undergone very little biotechnological innovation and exhibits a lower productivity than the highest international averages. A University of São Paulo achievement in this area was significant. It was able to clone amylase genes, thereby making the use of cassava a viable alternative input for alcohol production. The adoption of such a technique, however, depends on more favorable conditions. Since only 3 percent of the alcohol produced in Brazil is obtained from cassava, technological achievements and economic incentives are still needed to stimulate extensive cultivation of this crop.

For the National Program of Alcohol Production (Programa Nacional do Álcool — Proálcool) — a government program aimed at generating alternative energy sources — developing existing projects for improvements in sugarcane genetics that will increase productivity is of paramount importance. New research on yeast must be performed to ameliorate the efficiency of the fermentation process.

In agriculture, especially in the production of staples such as corn, rice, beans, and potatoes, modern biotechnology can help produce "engineered" seeds (inserting genes with higher economic value through recombinant DNA technology) and plants more resistant to pests and herbicides.

The production of serum and vaccines for human use is exclusively a government responsibility and should be evaluated from a social perspective, not from a market viewpoint. Research to combat diseases such as the barber bug fever (*Doença de Chagas*), *esquistossomose* (a tropical disease), and malaria has been of much interest to the scientific community and is an agenda to which the government has become sensitive. Since the health sector is moving toward the leading edge of technological innovation, it is possible that such efforts may generate a biotechnology with broader uses.

## Conclusion

The long-term performance of the Brazilian industrial sector looks very satisfactory. As production has grown quite rapidly, a high level of technological capability has been attained. Since the end of the 1970s, great effort has been made to increase exports with favorable results. By the early 1980s, Brazil's industrial production structure was already diversified and sophisticated.

During the 1980s, the economy faced difficulties that resulted in a less commendable performance. The domestic macroeconomic environment was marked by a painful adjustment to an external debt crisis that had manifested itself in low GDP growth, an acceleration of inflation, and low investment. The production sector was forced to explore expansion into the international market. During the 1980s, investment levels in the Brazilian industrial sector were quite low. Projects involving large steel production and paper pulp and cellulose were completed, and the production of basic inputs was increased. Significant efforts were made to develop the electronics sector, which underwent a technological revolution in the 1980s.

Strategic (industrial) activities used to maintain dynamism in Brazilian industry are linked to the external sectors that use high technology, especially in the production of capital goods, automobiles, and electronics.

The capital goods sector maintains a strategic position within the current production structure because of the high level of value added this sector is able to generate. It also has played an important role in the diffusion of technologies for machines and other equipment. Although a mature sector, it requires continuous modernization to be efficient; its newest challenge is the incorporation of technology, such as precision mechanics and industrial automation.

Another highly strategic activity is the automotive sector. Its impact on other productive activities such as steel, glass, rubber, capital goods, and several other activities linked to the mechanical and metallurgical sectors is considerable. Its introduction in Brazil was one of the most decisive contributions to the technological improvement of Brazilian industry. Its current success will certainly affect the future configuration of a significant portion of the industrial sector.

Finally, it should be emphasized that the electronics and biotechnology industries display the most revolutionary technological advancements of the international productive sphere, and they are having a major impact on numerous productive systems. Innovations are altering the productive processes through the use of robots, flexible production systems, industrial automation, and significant increases in agricultural productivity. Innovations also affect durable and nondurable goods. The development of the electronics sector in particular has needed strong legislation (the Informatics Law) and financial support. The success of these industries also requires the articulation of scientific, technological, and industrial policies.

The challenge of the 1990s will be to confront international competition and improve the quality and competitiveness of domestic products. Significant changes in Brazil's productive structure will take place and will yield noticeable gains in efficiency. The new production configuration will occur within the context of a greater international involvement and with a less interventionist state. However, it is necessary that the continuing economic instability be resolved (or at least kept under control) to ease the occurrence of structural changes. If economic instability is not controlled, the country is at risk of experiencing another decade of economic stagnation.

# References

ABIMAQ/SINDIMAQ. *Bens de Produção Mecânicos*. Several years.

Baptista, M.A.C. 1987. *A Indústria Eletrônica de Consumo a Nível Internacional e no Brasil: Padrões de Concorrência, Inovação Tecnológica e Caráter da Intervenção do Estado*. Campinas: M.A. thesis, University of São Paulo at Campinas.

Braga, H. 1986. *Progresso Técnico na Indústria Brasileira: Indicadores e Análise de seus Fatores Determinantes*. Rio de Janeiro: FTI.

CACEX/DEPEC. *Comércio Exterior: Exportações*. Several issues.

CACEX/DEPEC. *Comércio Exterior: Estatísticas*. Several issues.

Cruz, H.N. 1985. *Mudança Tecnológica no Setor Metal Mecânico do Brasil*. São Paulo: FIPE-USP.

Cruz, H.N., and S.B. de Holanda Filho. 1988. *Exportações de Manufaturados Paulistas*. São Paulo: FIPE-USP.

Fajnzylber, F. 1971. *Sistema Industrial e Exportações de Manufaturados*. Rio de Janeiro: IPEA/INPES.

FIPE/DECON. 1975-80. *Levantamento de Conjunture, Indices FIESP*. São Paulo.

Gadelha, M.F., and J.A. Reis. 1986. *O Complexo Industrial Metal Mecânico*. Brasília: PADCT/STI.

Haguenauer, L. 1985. *Organização e Dinâmica Interna dos Complexos: Agroindústria, Química, Construção Civil e Têxtil*. Rio de Janeiro: IEI/Federal University of Rio de Janeiro.

Haguenauer, L., J.T. Araujo, V. Prochinik, and E.A. Guimarães. 1984. *Os Complexos Industriais na Economia Brasileira*. Rio de Janeiro: IEI/Federal University of Rio de Janeiro.

IBGE. *Censos Industriais* from 1960, 1970, 1975, and 1980.

Lipkin, S., and L. Naidin. 1986. *O Complexo Industrial Têxtil e Calçados*. Brasília: PADCT, STI.

Malcher, J. 1986. *A Indústria de Mecânica Pesada e os Programas Estatais de Investimento*. Brasília: PADCT/STI.

Moreira, C.A., and M.E. da Silva. 1987. *Biotecnologia: Oportunidades e Desafios*. Texto para Discussão No. 20.

Naidin, L. 1986. *O Complexo Industrial Papel e Gráfica*. Brasília: PADCT/ STI.

Sant'Ana, M.A.A. 1986. *A Construção dos Índices de Produtividade de Fatores de Produção como Indicadores de Profresso Técnico na Indústria Brasileira*. Rio de Janeiro: FTI.

SEADE. 1988. *São Paulo e Conjuntura*. February.

Tadini, V. 1986. *O Setor de Bens de Capital sob Encomenda: Análise do Desenvolvimento Recente*. São Paulo: FIPE/USP.

Tavares, M.C. 1978. *Ciclo e Crises: O Movimento Recente da Industrialização Brasileira.* Rio de Janeiro: Federal University of Rio de Janeiro (mimeo).

Tigre, P.B. 1986. *Desenvolvimento da Indústria Brasileira de Computadores: Análise e Perspectivas à Luz das Tendências Internacionais.* Rio de Janeiro: IEI/UFRJ.

# FOUR

# Brazilian Agriculture: A New Horizon of Growth

## Fernando Homem de Melo

B razilian agriculture and agroindustry offer significant comparative advantages and considerable potential for growth. During the last four decades, however, economic policies have inhibited Brazil from achieving its potential in these sectors. During the early 1990s, the agricultural sector experienced a serious financial crisis at a time when the country needed this sector to grow. The changes taking place through Brazil's development strategies will favor growth as long as a new concept of agricultural policy is adopted.

This chapter examines some specific questions related to Brazilian agriculture. The first section diagnoses the situation of the early 1990s and its problems. The second analyzes various scenarios of economic growth and their impacts on food demand and on the supply of agricultural products. In the third section, the new growth horizon of the agricultural sector is discussed, and emphasis is placed on the need to reform agricultural policy with priority given to medium-term policy instruments, such as infrastructure and tariffs.

## Agriculture at a Time of Macroeconomic Transition

I n analyzing the relationship between Brazil's macroeconomic condition and its agricultural sector during the last 40 years, two basic facts stand out:

1.  The agricultural sector always has functioned below its growth potential as a result of the type of economic development strategy — industrialization via import substitution — adopted by Brazil after the 1950s (Homem de Melo 1979, 43-116), involving strong (sometimes extreme) protectionism of certain sectors.

2.  The recent crisis (post-1986) in the agricultural sector — characterized by loss of income, decapitalization, and indebtedness — was largely

a result of the macroeconomic disequilibrium that persisted until March 1990 (Rezende 1990) in the form of an acceleration of inflation.

Regarding Brazil's development strategy, the mechanism of discriminating against the agricultural sector included the overvaluation of Brazilian currency, an increase in input prices (through tariff protection), and the insufficiency of public investment. After initiating import substitution of consumer durable goods in the 1950s, Brazil proceeded with the import substitution of agricultural equipment in the 1960s and import substitution of basic inputs, capital goods, and energy in the 1970s. The highest degree of protection was granted the informatics sector in the 1980s. Agricultural policy was passive, and, because of its low priority within the government's development strategy, it was given secondary consideration. The creation and expansion of the Brazilian Enterprise for Research in Agriculture (Empresa Brasileira de Pesquisa Agropecuária — EMBRAPA) during the 1970s was one of the few long-term meritorious initiatives that permitted the sector to maintain a reasonable rate of growth and productivity (Alves and Contini 1988, 49-96). Lack of investment in agricultural research in previous years was one cause for the segmentation of products into export and domestic products (Homem de Melo 1981). Table 1 summarizes agricultural performance during the 1950-1989 period, which includes a crisis in domestic crop production occurring in the 1970s.

Products, producers, and regions did not suffer at the same rate; however, gains were obtained in some cases. Good performances resulted in cases such as agricultural credits, special programs (Polocentro, Proálcool, Profir, and Provárzea), periods of high international prices (the first half of the 1970s, for instance), and protection of domestic wheat production. In this context, the credit policy can be interpreted as a mechanism to counteract the industrial bias of the development strategy through strong protectionism. Such a compensation mechanism would remain in place until the early 1980s, when it was removed by anti-inflationary policies.

## Table I
## Growth Rates of Brazilian Agricultural Production
### 1950-1989 (percent per year)

| Period | Total | Domestic | Exports |
|--------|-------|----------|---------|
| 1950/89 | 4.18 | 2.99 | 5.48 |
| 1950/59 | 4.67 | 3.45 | 6.38 |
| 1960/69 | 1.87 | 4.68 | zero |
| 1970/79 | 3.89 | zero | 7.64 |
| 1980/89 | 3.20 | 2.20 | 3.34 |

Sources: Production data from IBGE. Aggregation and estimates by the author. Domestic Products: rice, potatoes, onions, beans, cassava, corn, and tomatoes. Export Products: cotton, peanuts, cacao, coffee, sugarcane, tobacco, oranges, castor beans, and soybeans.

It is important to mention the relevance of subsidized credit policies and special programs in Brazil's agricultural economy, as they characterize a sector that is strongly controlled by the government and, therefore, highly dependent on its protection. During the period, the market played a minor role in the economy. Wheat, milk, and cane-alcohol are good examples of markets administered by the government. Naturally, after the 1980s, credit policies and special programs lost importance, and the agricultural sector became "unprotected."

In the context of the macroeconomic disequilibrium experienced after 1986, four factors were prejudiced particularly against the agricultural sector: 1) agricultural prices that were unable to keep pace with prices in the manufacturing sector during the high inflationary period of 1986-1990, 2) appreciation of the cruzeiro through the imposition of two moratoriums during the period, 3) periodic attempts to implement austere monetary and fiscal policies (Bacha 1982), and 4) the economic stagnation during which domestic demand fell significantly.

There undoubtedly were attempts made to implement an agricultural policy, or at least to replace and compensate the loss of the previous scheme of support, especially during the José Sarney administration. Examples of such attempts were the implementation of pluri-annual minimum prices, price controls, buffer stocks, commercial policy, and many other instruments. These attempts gradually became unfeasible, nonetheless, due to an inflation that rose from 1 percent per month at the apex of the Cruzado Plan's "success" in 1986 to 84 percent per month in March 1990, the last month of the Sarney administration. High inflation combined with a continuous fiscal crisis substantially decreased the already precarious resource base that supported rural credit in the form of demand deposits (Vellutini 1991).

Graph 1 illustrates the severity of this recent agricultural crisis. Between 1986 and 1990, the index of real prices received by producers (deflator IGP-DI) for 15 vegetable and animal products dropped 50.9 percent. On the other hand, terms of trade fell during this same period by 37.9 percent. Added to these difficulties was the problem of price indexes to correct agriculture's financing contracts during the economic plans adopted at the time. It is no surprise that the sector's current picture is marked by losses in income, decapitalization, indebtedness, and, ultimately, a lack of motivation among farmers.

This crisis becomes more apparent in Table 2. With the exception of 1989, the index of physical production per capita was below the 1985 level, due especially to climatic problems experienced in 1986, 1990, and 1991.

Low levels of physical production were combined with lower real prices (Graph 1), resulting in a sharp decrease in the value of production of a composite product that is based on 20 vegetable products and on the average exchange rate from January to August 1991. Between 1985 and 1990, the value of agricultural production dropped 51.4 percent, corresponding to a loss of US$18.904 billion. The disequilibrium of the Brazilian economy put a heavy burden on the agricultural sector, manifested by high indebtedness, decapitalization, a drop in revenues, and lack of investments in the agricultural sector.

Graph I

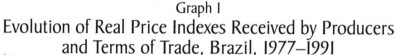

## Evolution of Real Price Indexes Received by Producers and Terms of Trade, Brazil, 1977–1991

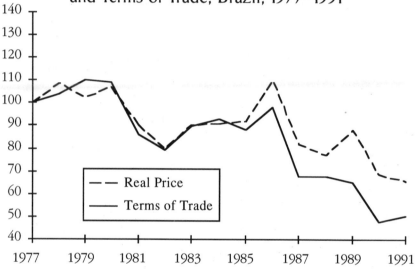

The appreciation of the cruzeiro played a crucial part in agriculture's deterioration as well. Between 1985 and March 1990, the cruzeiro appreciated 56.3 percent in relation to the U.S. dollar and 45.1 percent in relation to the currencies of Brazil's other main trade partners. The two moratoriums imposed on the external debt were very important in allowing the strong appreciation to progress without causing an exchange rate crisis.

What is happening in the current situation? Are there any signs that the picture will be reversed? Regarding macroeconomic disequilibrium, the crisis remains despite the implementation of Collor Plans I and II; it will continue to be a potential inhibitor of sustainable growth in the agricultural sector.

On the other hand, the first basic problem — bias against agriculture embedded in the import substitution development strategy — seems to have been resolved gradually. The new strategy of "competitive restructuring" of the Brazilian economy already under way will bring important incentives to the growth of agriculture. As described in the National Reconstruction

## Table 2
# Brazilian Agriculture: Some Basic Data for the Period 1985-1991, Twenty Vegetable Products

| Years | Physical Quantity Index | Index of Per Capita Output (Quantity) | Value of Production (US$ million) | Value of Production Index |
|-------|-------|-------|-------|-------|
| 1985 | 100.0 | 100.0 | 36.800 | 100.0 |
| 1986 | 88.8 | 87.2 | 34.500 | 93.9 |
| 1987 | 102.7 | 99.1 | 26.210 | 71.2 |
| 1988 | 103.1 | 97.7 | 26.509 | 72.0 |
| 1989 | 110.8 | 103.2 | 19.822 | 53.9 |
| 1990 | 97.9 | 89.6 | 17.896 | 48.6 |
| 1991 | 97.2 | 87.3 | 19.147 | 52.0 |

Sources: Basic data from IBGE and FGV. Elaborated by the author.

Program (Programa de Reconstrução Nacional), the strategy has two main components: 1) reform of the state and 2) productive transformation. The first component includes deregulation of economic activities, privatization, administrative reform, and the redefinition of public sector functions. The second includes foreign trade liberalization (mainly through tariff reductions), economic integration through MERCOSUL, and industrial and agricultural competitiveness. All of these were initiated under the Collor administration, though Southern Cone integration through MERCOSUL effectively had commenced when the Sarney administration signed a trade agreement with Argentina. This growth strategy is more dependent on market forces than on state control and will be enforced even in the case of agriculture.

Incentives for agricultural growth are expected to stem from the following: 1) an adjusted exchange rate, 2) lower import tariffs for inputs and capital goods, 3) export financing, 4) a reduction in port operation costs, 5) a reduction in transportation costs, and 6) a reduction in export taxes.

Clearly, many aspects of these incentives are mere intentions; other aspects, such as a privatization program and administrative reform, face serious difficulties before approval. However, a real opportunity exists to push agriculture toward its full potential through a process marked by market influence, which can create a new growth horizon. The exchange rate (illustrated in Graph 2), for instance, already showed signs of a real devaluation after March 1990, due to the opening of the economy to imports and to a partial renegotiation of the external debt. This was a radical new direction for the agricultural sector that previously had been completely dependent on state control; as a result, it experienced a general feeling of "abandonment."

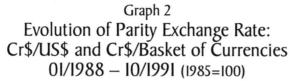

Graph 2
## Evolution of Parity Exchange Rate: Cr$/US$ and Cr$/Basket of Currencies 01/1988 − 10/1991 (1985=100)

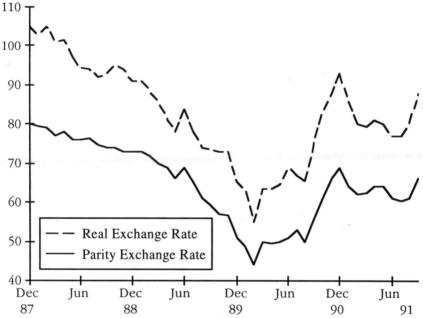

## A New Horizon for Agricultural Growth

Depending on the rate and the type of economic growth Brazil experiences during the 1990s, demand for agricultural products will vary. As a consequence, agricultural supply also will undergo different degrees of adjustment depending on variables related to economic growth and income distribution.

Four different macroeconomic scenarios for the growth and level of food consumption in the next ten years are shown in Tables 3 and 4. Three of the four scenarios have already been examined by Homem de Melo (1990) in connection with the work of Fritsch and Modiano (1988). A fourth scenario of *low growth* is added.

The main characteristics of the four scenarios in terms of their use for projections on food consumption are the following: 1) *low growth*: a growth rate in the range of 2.5 to 3.0 percent of gross domestic product (GDP) and a population growth of 1.6 percent on average for the next ten years; 2) *medium growth*: at 4.5 percent of GDP, with the same increase in population; 3) *high growth*: at 7.5 percent of GDP, with the same increase in population;

Table 3
# Annual Average Growth Rates of Food Consumption under the Four Scenarios

(percent per year)

| | Scenarios | | | |
| Products | Low Growth | Medium Growth | High Growth | Social Growth |
| --- | --- | --- | --- | --- |
| Rice | 1,60 | 1,60 | 1,60 | 1,26 |
| Beans | 1,50 | 1,26 | 1,04 | 0,40 |
| Corn | 2,34 | 4,01 | 5,27 | 5,93 |
| Soybeans | 2,34 | 4,01 | 5,27 | 6,35 |
| Wheat | 2,08 | 3,08 | 3,91 | 3,86 |
| Grains-Total | 2,18 | 3,50 | 4,53 | 4,99 |
| Potatoes | 2,31 | 3,71 | 4,83 | 3,99 |
| Cassava | 1,23 | 0,30 | - 0,60 | - 1,16 |
| Sugar | 1,90 | 2,54 | 3,09 | 2,63 |
| Beef | 2,62 | 4,51 | 5,98 | 6,78 |
| Chicken | 2,34 | 3,79 | 4,95 | 5,57 |
| Pork | 1,90 | 2,54 | 3,09 | 3,33 |
| Eggs | 2,13 | 3,20 | 4,08 | 4,61 |
| Milk | 2,73 | 4,78 | 6,37 | 7,26 |
| Coffee | 1,89 | 2,54 | 3,09 | 3,05 |
| Fruits | 2,48 | 5,27 | 7,41 | 8,44 |
| Vegetables | 2,19 | 3,52 | 4,69 | 5,35 |

and 4) *social growth*: at 6.5 percent of GDP, with the same increase in population and better income distribution. As for the external demand for food, the assumption is that it will be higher in the scenarios of *high growth* and *social growth*.

A comment must be made specifically about *social growth*. When there was relatively high growth paralleled by better income distribution, the "graduation effect" became more pronounced (Yotopoulos 1985). It occurred as a result of an increase in middle-income households and their ensuing adoption of middle-income eating habits. It is considered an important driving force in food economics at both the international and the domestic levels. As a result of this "graduation," there was a considerable increase in the consumption of animal proteins, vegetables, and fruits, and a consequent substantial increase in demand for cereals and oleaginous seeds used in the production of animal food, such as peanuts and sunflower seeds, as the demand for their final consumption increased (Homem de Melo et al. 1988, 18-19).

Table 3 shows the expected average annual growth rate for the most important foodstuffs in the next ten years under the four macroeconomic scenarios. Table 4 shows the absolute figures for consumption of these edibles,

Table 4

# Projection of Food Consumption from 1991–2001, within the Four Economic Scenarios

(1,000 t)[a]

| | Scenarios | | | |
|---|---|---|---|---|
| Products | Low Growth | Medium Growth | High Growth | Social Growth |
| Rice | 12,006 | 12,006 | 12,006 | 11,565 |
| Beans | 3,436 | 3,349 | 3,269 | 3,072 |
| Corn | 35,709 | 42,657 | 48,697 | 52,164 |
| Soybeans | 28,222 | 33,714 | 38,486 | 41,227 |
| Wheat | 7,521 | 8,376 | 9,145 | 9,098 |
| Grains-Total | 86,894 | 100,102 | 111,603 | 117,126 |
| Potatoes | 2,980 | 3,461 | 3,897 | 3,565 |
| Cassava | 29,800 | 26,933 | 24,378 | 22,908 |
| Sugar | 11,020 | 11,809 | 12,517 | 11,915 |
| Beef | 3,658 | 4,469 | 5,212 | 5,663 |
| Chicken | 2,443 | 2,852 | 3,224 | 3,438 |
| Pork | 1,399 | 1,449 | 1,589 | 1,630 |
| Eggs[a] | 2,407 | 2,700 | 2,965 | 3,134 |
| Milk[b] | 20,655 | 25,674 | 30,279 | 33,190 |

Note: a = eggs, millions of dozens; b = milk, millions of liters.

with the exception of coffee, fruits, and vegetables. The *social growth* scenario, which is characterized by a resurgence of economic growth, implying a solution to the macroeconomic disequilibrium but with emphasis on a better distribution of income, clearly reveals the population's hopes of significantly changing consumption patterns. Change involves a shift from basic products, such as rice, beans, and cassava that are high in calories, to vegetables, fruits, and foodstuffs rich in animal protein. Products such as wheat and its derivatives, potatoes, pork, coffee, and sugar would be found in an intermediary position. This evolving dynamic in food demand, stemming from economic growth and better income distribution, contrasts with the pattern observed since the 1970s when rice, beans, and cassava predominated. To date, these products have been responsible for 40 percent of the total calories and 30 percent of the total proteins consumed by Brazilians. Henceforth, the importance of these foodstuffs will diminish, especially if social growth takes place.

The discussion below analyzes the various scenarios of growth in agricultural demand and corresponding increases in aggregate agricultural supply. It examines what supply growth rates are necessary under each of the four scenarios to meet the expected demand increases over the next ten years and to avoid a change in relative prices, a decrease in exports, or an increase in imports.

Table 5 presents information on agricultural growth. Annual growth rates are 2.1 percent in the *low growth* scenario, 3.8 percent for *medium growth*, 4.9 percent for *high growth*, and 5.3 percent for *social growth*. With the exception of *low growth*, all other rates are higher than those of the 1980s. The reason for the overall increase is that the annual growth rate for the economy as a whole in the three scenarios is large enough to compensate for a relatively low population growth. Examination of the other aggregates presented in Table 5 indicates that agriculture's positive performance is based on the relatively higher growth rates of animal products, which could reach annual rates of 5.1, 6.4, or 6.9 percent in the three most optimistic scenarios, respectively. These rates are significantly higher than those of the 1980s. Under the *social growth* scenario, the growth rate in the supply of animal products would be almost twice as high as 1980 rates, partially due to the "graduation effect" and the presumed growth in external demand.

## Table 5
# Average Annual Rates of Agricultural Growth Required in the Four Economic Scenarios Considered for 1991–2000

### (in percent per year)

|  | | Scenarios | | |
| --- | --- | --- | --- | --- |
| Products | 1980 Decade | Low Growth | Medium Growth | High Growth | Social Growth |
| Agriculture/grains | 3.6 | 2.1 | 3.5 | 4.5 | 5.0 |
| Vegetable Agriculture/ Total | 3.1 | 2.0 | 3.0 | 3.9 | 4.2 |
| Livestock | 3.4 | 2.5 | 5.1 | 6.4 | 6.9 |
| Total Agriculture | 3.2 | 2.2 | 3.8 | 4.9 | 5.3 |

Sources: Table 4 for data in physical quantity; Laspeyres indices with estimates for 1988.

Additionally, this picture shows how Brazilian agriculture would have to alter its production pattern by increasing the production of grains and animal products. Increases in these areas would be factored into the annual growth rate under the *social growth* scenario of 8.4 percent in the supply of fruits and 5.3 percent in the production of vegetables (Table 3).

Expected growth rates for vegetables in the 1990s fall into a lower range. The annual growth rates for overall vegetable production are 2.0, 3.0, 3.9, and 4.2 percent in respective scenarios. The last two rates, 3.9 under *high growth* and 4.2 for *social growth*, are significantly higher than 1980s' rates, while the rate in the *medium growth* scenario is roughly the same as those for the 1980s period.

In the case of grains such as rice, beans, corn, soybeans, and wheat, the anticipated growth rates for *high growth* and *social growth* scenarios are also

Table 6

## Pivotal Variables for the Possible Growth of Agricultural Supply During the 1990s

| Variables | Scenarios | | | |
|---|---|---|---|---|
| | Low Growth (2.2%) | Medium Growth (3.8%) | High Growth (4.9%) | Social Growth (5.3%) |
| 1. Technological Change and Human Resources | Low pace | Moderate pace | High pace | High pace |
| 2. Exchange Rate and Tariffs | No change Stable Tariffs | Small Devaluation Stable Tariffs | High Devaluation Lower Tariffs | High Devaluation Lower Tariffs |
| 3. External Economic Growth | Moderate Growth | Moderate Growth | High Growth | High Growth |
| 4. Domestic Economic Growth | Low Growth | Moderate Growth | High Growth | High Growth |
| 5. Income Distribution | No Change | No Change | No Change | More Equal |
| 6. Indirect Taxes | No Change | No Change | No Change | Reduced/Eliminated |
| 7. Terms of Trade | No Change | Small Improvement | Large Improvement | Large Improvement |
| 8. Commercial Costs | No Change | Little Lower | Much Lower | Much Lower |
| 9. International Prices | Little Higher | Little Higher | Higher | Higher |
| 10. Agricultural Policy | Undefined | Undefined | Defined/Implemented | Defined/Implemented |
| 11. Special Programs Proálcool | No Emphasis | No Emphasis | Emphasis | No Emphasis |
| 12. External Protectionism | No Change | No Change | Lower | Lower |

higher than those of the 1980s — 4.5 percent and 5.0 percent per year, compared to 3.6 percent per year. In the *low* and *medium growth* scenarios, however, predicted rates for grains are lower than those prevailing during the 1980s.

In summary, higher growth rates than those found in the 1980s can be expected in the agricultural sector under the three most optimistic macroeconomic scenarios. Meanwhile, a shift in the composition of this growth, occurring mainly in the *social growth* scenario, must be emphasized. In the latter, the leading agricultural subsectors would be animal products and grains such as soybeans and corn needed for animal production, as well as fruits and vegetables.

## Preconditions for the New Agricultural Policy

Twelve variables are considered pivotal in defining each scenario. Table 6 discusses the importance of each variable and notes its expected behavior.

The first variable is technological change, characterized by higher productivity with reduced production costs. While technological change requires moderate productivity growth, the other two more optimistic scenarios *(high growth* and *social growth)* command a much higher level. In this context, moderate productivity growth in the 1990s is defined as a rate comparable to the annual average growth rate of 1.8 percent for the basket of products in the 1980s (see Table 1). High productivity is characterized by an annual growth rate close to 3.0 percent. Such a scenario, however, requires higher investment in research and development in the public and private sectors, a higher adoption rate by farmers, and stronger emphasis on improving human resources.

Higher real devaluations of the exchange rate and lower import tariffs for agricultural inputs and raw materials as well as components would make the two scenarios that are characterized by a higher supply of agricultural products more feasible. This occurred to a certain degree in the Collor administration, where an expressive real devaluation took place (at least until October 1991) (Graph 2). The combination of this devaluation with less external protectionism, higher international prices for Brazilian export products (ninth variable), and lower tariffs for inputs would result in an improvement in the terms of trade (seventh variable).

A substantial decrease in commercialization costs (eighth variable), together with a reduction or elimination of indirect taxes (sixth variable), such as sales taxes and social contributions on food products and domestic inputs, also would contribute to an improvement in terms of trade and consequently to increases in productivity through greater use of fertilizers, herbicides, and pesticides. A reduction in commercial costs would encourage the expansion of cultivated areas, especially in Brazil's Central region. The magnitude of these costs is demonstrated in Table 7 specifically for Rondonópolis in the state of Mato Grosso in Central Brazil. Table 8, on the other hand, shows high indirect taxes charged on food. It is important to mention that the elimination or reduction of these taxes can increase agricultural production for both domestic and external markets.

The expansion of cultivated areas will be necessary in the three most optimistic scenarios since anticipated improvements in productivity (per area) will not be sufficient to reach the expected growth level in overall agricultural production. The amount of land used for agriculture is expected to increase 2 percent per year for each of these scenarios, corresponding to an increase of 1 million hectares in the production of vegetable products and conceivably 2 million hectares for all agriculture including pastures.

The tenth variable — agricultural policy for short-term instruments — will be pivotal in the two most optimistic scenarios (*high growth* and *social growth*). In general, this policy will provide financial resources for investment in productivity and expansion into new areas. It will implement measures leading to a price stabilization by setting minimum prices and administering prices for inventory sales and will adopt an international trade policy with import conditions defined. Some of these measures already have been implemented under the conditions of the agricultural packages prepared by the Collor administration.

Table 7

# Decomposition of Soybean Price - FOB - Santos to Orlândia, SP and Rondonópolis, MT $US/ton ([a])

| Items | Orlândia-SP | Rondonópolis-MT |
|---|---|---|
| Price Santos | 220.56 | 220.56 |
| Port Charges | 7.63 | 7.63 |
| Domestic Freight | 11.73 | 29.34 |
| ICMS | 28.67 | 28.67 |
| PIS | 1.65 | 1.65 |
| Weight Loss | 0.55 | 0.55 |
| Exchange Rate Contract | 0.41 | 0.41 |
| FUNRURAL | 3.90 | 3.16 |
| Producer Price | 166.02 | 149.15 |

Note: [a]The decomposition is based on price quoted at the closing of Chicago's commodities market, March 9, 1990.
Rondonópolis distance from Santos is 1,400 km. (875 miles), and Orlândia distance from Santos is 450 km (281 miles). Freight expenses refer to a private terminal. The exchange rate refers to December 1988.

## Tabel 8
# Estimates of Indirect Taxes Levied on Food Products
### (Percent of Value Added)

| Products | ICMS | Social Contributions | Total |
|---|---|---|---|
| Meats | 13.64 | 8.80 | 22.14 |
| Rice | 13.64 | 8.80 | 22.14 |
| Beans | 13.64 | 8.80 | 22.14 |
| Milk | zero | 8.80 | 8.80 |
| Bread | 13.64 | 7.50 | 21.14 |
| Sugar | 21.75 | 7.50 | 29.25 |
| Ground Coffee | 21.75 | 7.50 | 29.25 |
| Edible Oils | 21.75 | 7.50 | 29.25 |
| Pasta | 21.75 | 7.50 | 29.25 |
| Salt | 13.64 | 7.50 | 21.14 |
| Gardenstuffs | zero | 8.80 | 8.80 |

Source: Rezende 1991.

Finally, the following variables differentiate the scenarios of *high growth* and *social growth*: technological change and human resources (first variable), income distribution (fifth variable), indirect taxes (sixth variable), and special programs, such as Proálcool (eleventh variable). The *social growth* scenario would require better income distribution (the graduation effect in food demand), a reduction or elimination of indirect taxes levied on food products in the domestic market, and less emphasis on programs such as Proálcool (or at least an understanding that these programs not be expanded).

## Final Considerations

This study shows that the growth possibilities for Brazilian agriculture in the 1990s within the three most optimistic economic scenarios are greater than the growth rates experienced in the 1980s. The three most promising scenarios suggest that growth rates will range between 3.8 and 5.3 percent annually — much higher than the 3.2 percent rate of the 1980s. In the pessimistic scenario, agricultural growth will remain low at 2.2 percent per year.

It is common knowledge that the 1980s were economically difficult years. It is important to highlight, however, that the potential growth of the agricultural sector may be as high as 5.3 percent per year, an impressive rate even when compared to other sectors of the economy.

The highest growth rate, 5.3 percent, would occur under the *social growth* scenario, which is characterized by growth with equity. As mentioned earlier, the graduation effect under this scenario would bring about changes in consumption patterns — more animal proteins and fruits and vegetables — as well as higher export levels.

The *high growth* and *social growth* scenarios would require large increases in agricultural productivity in the range of 3.0 percent annually, compared to 1.8 percent in the 1980s. Besides demanding higher investments in agricultural research, more farmers will be required to implement technological innovations, such as new products, fertilizers, pesticides, herbicides, and machinery, and to improve their labor resources.

Finally, in the three best scenarios analyzed, the amount of cultivated land must increase at a rate of 2 percent per year. Considering that there is no room for agricultural expansion in the South and Southeast regions of Brazil, this expansion should develop in the Central-West region. For this to happen, however, the country will have to solve the problem it currently has with high transportation costs. Otherwise, the promising Central-West region's full potential cannot be realized. Expansion also should take into consideration ecological concerns that have created conflicts for Brazil in the international community.

# References

Alves, E.R.A., and E. Contini. 1988. "A Modernização da Agricultura Brasileira." In *Os Principais Problemas da Agricultura Brasileira: Análise e Sugestões*, ed. A.S.P. Brandão. Rio de Janeiro: PNPE-IPEA, Série PNPE no. 18.

Bacha, E.L. 1982. *Introdução à Macroeconomia: Uma Perspectiva Brasileira*. Rio de Janeiro: Campus.

Fritsch, W., and E.M. Modiano. 1988. "A Restrição Externa ao Crecimento Econômico Brasileiro: Uma Perspectiva de Longo Prazo." *Pesquisa e Planejamento Econômico* 18(2): 271-296.

Homem de Melo, F. 1990. "O Crescimento Agrícola Brasileiro dos Anos 80 e as Perspectivas para os Anos 90." *Revista de Economia Política* 10(3): 22-30, July/September.

Homem de Melo, F. 1981. "Política Comercial, Tecnologia e Preços de Alimentos no Brasil." *Estudos Econômicos* 11(2): 123-142, May/August.

Homem de Melo, F. 1979. "Políticas de Desenvolvimento Agrícola no Brasil." In *Resenhas de Economia Brasileira*, ed. J. Sayad. São Paulo: Saraiva.

Homem de Melo, F. et al. 1988. *A Questão da Produção e do Abastecimento no Brasil.* Brasília: SEPLAN/PNUD/ABC.

Neupert, R.F. 1987. *Novas Projeções da População Brasileira: Hipóteses Baseadas na PNAD de 1984*. Brasília: IPLAN.

Rezende, F. 1991. *O Peso dos Impostos no Custo da Alimentação: Análise do Problema e Propostas de Redução*. São Paulo.

Rezende, G.C. 1990. *Do Cruzado ao Collor: Os Planos de Establização e a Agricultura* (versão preliminar).

Sayad, J. 1980. *Crédito Rural no Brasil*. São Paulo: IPE-USP, Relatório de Pesquisa no. 1.

Vellutini, R. 1991. "Financiamento do Desenvolvimento Agrícola." *Revista de Economia Política* 11(2): 106-114.

Yotopoulos, P. A. 1985. "Middle-Income Classes and Food Crises: The New Food-Feed Competition." *Economic Development and Cultural Change* 33(3): 463-483.

# FIVE

# The Brazilian Energy Sector: Challenges for Development, Environment, and Commercial Policy

## Eli Roberto Pelin

The main objective of this chapter is to offer basic guidelines for an eventual plan for Brazil's energy sector. To reach this objective, three background conditions are considered: an economy in transformation, in relation to its need to overcome the current crisis; the gradual establishment of liberalized trade policies in the industrial sector; and growing concerns about the environment. The industrial sector accordingly would have to adapt itself by increasing its competitiveness in internal and external markets, fostering growth, and taking environmental restrictions into consideration. The implication of such changes for the energy sector is the need to supply sufficient quantities of energy to industry in the cleanest and most efficient manner possible.

In order to create an energy plan along these guidelines, the following questions must be answered:

1. What is the structure of the Brazilian energy sector, and, particularly, what is the energy consumption structure of the industrial sector?

2. How did the energy sector perform during the 1980s as measured by production, investment, and cost?

3. What challenges are anticipated in the future?

4. What guidelines could be adopted in the energy sector, given existing conditions?

The answers to each of these questions can be found in the four sections of this chapter: market structure of the energy sector, performance of the energy sector during the 1980s, challenges for the future, and guidelines for an energy policy.

## Market Structure of the Energy Sector

The energy sector of any country is not an engine of growth in the sense that it should be provided incentives from an economic development program. This privilege is normally reserved for sectors that produce final goods because of their capacity to leverage economies. However, energy is a fundamental input in any productive process and, in a majority of cases — due to strategic issues or resource availability — it is treated distinctly as a domestic product. With rare exceptions, such as in Japan, the vast majority of energy products consumed by countries are produced internally and frequently are produced by enterprises under direct government control, as in Brazil. In situations where governments do not manage the energy sector directly, there is at least one government agency or ministry responsible for maintaining some control over the sector. Moreover, energy production, which is likely to be capital intensive, requires enormous, long-maturity investments.

All of these elements imply that investment decisions must anticipate demand for periods as long as ten years in the case of electric power, or five years in the case of oil, in order to prevent the formation of future bottlenecks in the market.

The demand for energy is typically a derivative in that it expands and shrinks according to the level of activity in the country. It is closely related to gross domestic product (GDP), and, in the long run, energy/GDP elasticity tends to be equal to one. For example, a 10 percent increase in GDP would result in approximately a 10 percent increase in the demand for energy. Because investments in the sector are of long maturity, the energy sector begins to attract special attention, which is especially important when implementing new industrial and commercial policies that promote economic growth and greater foreign competition. In such a situation, energy pricing and availability are crucial, especially for sectors producing or utilizing tradable inputs.

In the Brazilian case, the state controls the production and prices of the most important energy products, including oil and its derivatives, natural gas, electric power, and coal. The Brazilian government produces and establishes prices for all of these energy sources except for coal, which is produced by private firms while still subject to government prices. For oil and its derivatives and for natural gas, the state acts through Petrobrás, a monopoly involved in exploration, production, refining, and distribution.

In the production and, to a lesser degree, the distribution of electric power, the state acts through federal concessionaires and state subsidiaries.

The electric sector as defined is controlled by the holding company ELETROBRÁS, which began operations in 1963-1964. In addition to playing the controlling role in the subsector, the holding company also acts as a central agency for financing and obtaining loans for the sector. More important, it is responsible for implementing electrical energy policy, which includes defining the main projects necessary for the generation and transmission of electrical energy. Another important agency is the National Department of Water and Energy (Departamento Nacional de Águas e Energia — DNAE), whose role is to establish industry regulations and monitor compliance. For all of these energy sectors, the federal government, through its secretaries, defines energy price policies as a last resort in making adjustments in macroeconomic policies. At least, this is the type of intervention that has taken place in recent years.

## Structure of Production According to Energy Type

Unlike most countries, Brazil's energy sources are highly diverse, which allows the country to produce different sources of energy for different uses. With few exceptions, such as charcoal and firewood, the supply of energy is concentrated among a few producers, particularly in the cases of hydroelectric power, petroleum, natural gas, and coal.

Table 1 illustrates production levels of primary energy in Brazil between 1979 and 1988. More than two-thirds of the country's energy production is from renewable sources, primarily in the form of hydroelectric power and charcoal (from wood). It is worth mentioning that charcoal's contribution declined during the 1980s, while products from sugarcane became increasingly important within the energy production matrix. The largest part of this increase in sugarcane use has been in the form of ethanol production, which, as a result of the Proácool program, increased from 3 billion liters in 1980 to about 12 billion liters in 1988. Sugarcane bagasse (plant residue), a byproduct of ethanol production, is the other major component of sugarcane's increasing importance in the energy matrix. Depending on humidity levels and geographical distances, sugarcane bagasse can replace oil in powering industrial boilers, or it may even generate a surplus of electrical energy in its own distillery.

Less than one-third of the energy production in Brazil is derived from nonrenewable sources. Among them, petroleum is the most important, accounting for approximately 20 percent of all primary energy produced in the second half of the 1980s, compared to less than 10 percent at the end of the 1970s. This increase over the last decades is largely due to massive investments in exploration and production along the continental shelf of the Campos Basin in the state of Rio de Janeiro. It is worth mentioning that the national production of petroleum was approximately 170,000 barrels per day in 1973, the year of the first oil shock.

Table I

Production Structure of Primary Energy, 1979-1988

(percent)

| | | | | | Years | | | | | |
|---|---|---|---|---|---|---|---|---|---|---|
| | 1979 | 1980 | 1981 | 1982 | 1983 | 1984 | 1985 | 1986 | 1987 | 1988 |
| Non-renewables | 14.5 | 14.8 | 16.5 | 20.5 | 22.1 | 24.8 | 26.2 | 26.7 | 26.0 | 25.0 |
| Petroleum | 9.7 | 9.9 | 11.3 | 12.4 | 14.4 | 17.7 | 19.5 | 20.4 | 19.5 | 19.0 |
| Natural Gas | 2.0 | 2.2 | 2.4 | 2.6 | 3.2 | 3.4 | 3.5 | 3.7 | 3.7 | 3.6 |
| Coal Steam | 1.6 | 1.6 | 2.0 | 2.1 | 2.0 | 2.0 | 1.8 | 1.7 | 1.6 | 1.7 |
| Coal (Metallurgic) | 1.2 | 1.1 | 0.8 | 0.7 | 0.6 | 0.6 | 0.6 | 0.6 | 0.4 | 0.5 |
| Uranium | | | | 2.7 | 1.9 | 1.1 | 0.8 | 0.3 | 0.8 | 0.2 |
| Renewables | 85.5 | 85.2 | 83.5 | 79.5 | 77.9 | 75.2 | 73.8 | 73.3 | 74.0 | 75.0 |
| Hydroelectricity | 39.9 | 40.8 | 40.2 | 39.2 | 38.1 | 36.8 | 36.7 | 37.6 | 36.9 | 39.4 |
| Charcoal | 35.2 | 33.4 | 31.6 | 27.9 | 25.7 | 24.9 | 22.8 | 22.6 | 22.0 | 21.7 |
| Sugarcane | 9.5 | 9.9 | 10.6 | 11.3 | 13.0 | 12.5 | 13.2 | 11.9 | 13.9 | 12.6 |
| Others | 0.9 | 1.1 | 1.1 | 1.1 | 1.1 | 1.0 | 1.1 | 1.2 | 1.2 | 1.3 |
| | 100.0 | 100.0 | 100.0 | 100.0 | 100.0 | 100.0 | 100.0 | 100.0 | 100.0 | 100.0 |

Source: IBGE. *Anuário Estatístico.* 1989.

New discoveries along the Campos Basin in 1974 immediately increased Brazilian reserves, permitting greater production after 1978-1979 through a system of anticipated exploration, which reduced the time necessary for commercial exploration from approximately eight to three years. Due to these new discoveries, the share of petroleum in the energy production matrix more than doubled in the 1980s; production reached 600,000 barrels per day. Once replaced by petroleum and electricity, coal production, after increasing in the mid-1980s, decreased to its former level at the beginning of the decade.

The Campos Basin discoveries also resulted in increased production since natural gas usually can be found in petroleum wells. Additional natural gas sources were found during the petroleum exploration phase. The share of natural gas in the matrix almost doubled between 1979 and 1988, and there is potential for further increases.

## Structure of Consumption According to Energy Type

The energy sector looks somewhat different from a consumer perspective than from a producer perspective. Table 2 shows the structure of primary energy consumption in Brazil. More than 40 percent of the country's consumption of primary energy is in the form of non-renewable sources, with petroleum consumption accounting for nearly all of this category. The relative importance of oil in the consumer market is due to the fact that, despite a dramatic increase in domestic production, Brazil produces only slightly more than one-half of the petroleum it consumes. Consequently, the country is highly dependent on external sources of supply. Regardless of this external dependence, however, the overall importance of petroleum within the consumption matrix has declined almost 10 percent since 1979, due to advances in renewable sources of energy, particularly hydroelectric power in the mid-1980s when it began to replace petroleum, coal, and alternative sources of energy, such as ethanol and sugarcane bagasse. While the consumption of electric power increased by 5 percent, the consumption of energy from sugarcane derivatives almost doubled.

Given the increase in the availability of natural gas, resulting from the discoveries along the continental shelf and elsewhere, the use of this energy product increased over the last decade. Among other uses, natural gas is used for household cooking, especially in the states of São Paulo and Rio de Janeiro, and as a substitute for diesel fuel in urban transportation fleets, particularly in the state of Rio de Janeiro. Another increasingly important use of natural gas has been to power steam boilers for industrial use.

The utility of natural gas has been made possible by agreements between Petrobrás and gas companies in the states of Rio de Janeiro and São Paulo, which made existing gas pipelines more accessible and began constructing new ones. The use of natural gas can be expected to increase in the coming years as it becomes more readily available, especially for

Table 2
## Consumption Structure of Primary Energy, 1979-1988
(percent)

| | Years | | | | | | | | | |
|---|---|---|---|---|---|---|---|---|---|---|
| | 1979 | 1980 | 1981 | 1982 | 1983 | 1984 | 1985 | 1986 | 1987 | 1988 |
| Non-renewables | 45.9 | 43.7 | 42.8 | 42.1 | 39.9 | 39.6 | 39.2 | 40.9 | 40.6 | 39.9 |
| Petroleum | 41.5 | 39.2 | 38.1 | 36.1 | 34.1 | 33.1 | 31.9 | 33.2 | 32.7 | 32.6 |
| Natural Gas | 0.7 | 0.8 | 0.8 | 1.0 | 1.3 | 1.5 | 1.8 | 2.0 | 1.9 | 1.8 |
| Coal Steam | 0.8 | 0.9 | 1.3 | 1.5 | 1.4 | 1.3 | 1.4 | 1.7 | 1.5 | 1.3 |
| Coal (Metallurgic) | 2.9 | 2.9 | 2.6 | 2.6 | 3.0 | 3.7 | 4.1 | 4.0 | 4.0 | 4.2 |
| Uranium | | | | | | | 0.5 | | | |
| Renewables | 54.1 | 56.3 | 57.2 | 57.9 | 60.1 | 60.4 | 60.8 | 59.1 | 59.4 | 60.1 |
| Hydroelectricity | 25.2 | 26.9 | 27.5 | 28.5 | 29.4 | 29.5 | 30.3 | 30.3 | 29.6 | 31.6 |
| Charcoal | 22.2 | 22.1 | 21.6 | 20.3 | 19.9 | 20.0 | 18.8 | 18.2 | 17.7 | 17.4 |
| Sugarcane | 6.0 | 6.5 | 7.2 | 8.3 | 10.0 | 10.0 | 10.9 | 9.6 | 11.1 | 10.1 |
| Others | 0.7 | 0.8 | 0.9 | 0.8 | 0.8 | 0.9 | 0.8 | 1.0 | 1.0 | 1.0 |
| | 100.0 | 100.0 | 100.0 | 100.0 | 100.0 | 100.0 | 100.0 | 100.0 | 100.0 | 100.0 |

Source: IBGE. *Anuário Estatístico.* 1989.

industrial consumption — a more impressive use than for cooking and automotive fuel.

## Structure of Consumption According to Consumer Groups

In Table 3, the consumption patterns of primary energy and secondary energy (such as oil derivatives) of the various consumer types are shown for the 1979-1988 period.

The industrial sector is by far the largest consumer of primary and secondary energy in Brazil, although there had been no clear increase in the sector's share of energy consumption, at least not during the 1980s. Despite fluctuations, its share of consumption remained close to 40 percent, with electricity and oil accounting for most of this amount. However, there was a perceptible substitution of energy products as a result of the second oil crisis in 1979 and the resulting price policy implemented by the government.

The second largest consumer of energy in the country is the transportation sector, accounting for approximately one-fifth of total consumption. Despite a slight decline in share of consumption during the 1980s, no clear tendency exists for the sector. Similar to trends in the industrial sector, energy consumption in the transportation sector is associated with fluctuations in the country's level of economic activity. During periods of economic expansion, the share of this sector's energy consumption tends to increase; in recessionary periods, its share tends to decline. The main type of energy consumed by this sector is diesel fuel, which is used for ground, rail, and maritime transport of cargo and passengers.

Residential consumption is the third largest sector in Brazil's energy consumption patterns. Its share reached levels comparable to those of the transportation sector at the end of the 1970s and has remained within approximately 2 percent of the transportation sector in 1988. The principal types of residential energy consumption are electric power and natural gas. Increases in real prices, mainly of electric power, during the 1980s are accountable for a decrease in shares of the residential sector in total energy consumption.

When considered separately, other sectors listed in Table 3 account for only a small share of total consumption, while, altogether, they account for one-fifth of the total. The agricultural sector's share is slightly below 5 percent. Diesel fuel, used to power tractors and agricultural equipment, accounts for the bulk of this consumption, while oil consumption is also important in the process of drying grains.

It is interesting to examine the energy sector's share in energy consumption, which increased from slightly less than 5 percent in 1979 to 8 percent by 1988. There is, therefore, a proportionately smaller quantity of energy available for consumption by other sectors.

Table 3

## Structure of Final Consumption of Primary and Secondary Energy by Type of Consumer, 1979-1988

(percent)

| | Years | | | | | | | | | |
|---|---|---|---|---|---|---|---|---|---|---|
| | 1979 | 1980 | 1981 | 1982 | 1983 | 1984 | 1985 | 1986 | 1987 | 1988 |
| Industry | 37.9 | 39.5 | 37.6 | 37.4 | 37.7 | 39.4 | 39.6 | 40.1 | 40.0 | 40.4 |
| Transportation | 21.1 | 19.8 | 20.2 | 20.2 | 18.9 | 18.0 | 18.2 | 19.3 | 18.2 | 18.1 |
| Residential | 20.1 | 19.9 | 20.5 | 19.2 | 18.7 | 17.9 | 16.6 | 15.8 | 16.0 | 15.8 |
| Energy | 5.4 | 5.2 | 5.4 | 6.1 | 7.2 | 7.7 | 8.3 | 7.6 | 8.3 | 7.7 |
| Agriculture | 4.7 | 4.7 | 4.9 | 4.8 | 4.8 | 4.4 | 4.2 | 4.4 | 4.6 | 4.6 |
| Commercial | 3.4 | 3.6 | 3.9 | 4.0 | 4.1 | 4.0 | 3.9 | 4.0 | 4.0 | 4.0 |
| Public Sector | 2.4 | 2.6 | 2.7 | 2.8 | 3.0 | 2.9 | 2.9 | 2.8 | 2.9 | 3.1 |
| Non-energy Consumption | 5.0 | 4.7 | 4.8 | 5.5 | 5.6 | 5.7 | 6.3 | 6.0 | 6.0 | 6.3 |
| | 100.0 | 100.0 | 100.0 | 100.0 | 100.0 | 100.0 | 100.0 | 100.0 | 100.0 | 100.0 |

Source: IBGE. *Anuário Estatístico*. 1989.

## Structure of Consumption within the Industrial Sector

As seen in Table 3, the industrial sector is the largest consumer of primary and secondary energy, accounting for approximately 40 percent of the total. The forms of energy comprising the bulk of the industrial sector's consumption are particularly significant. The consumption of these forms of energy by the industrial sector is detailed in Table 4, while the types of industries and their shares of total energy consumption are detailed in Table 5.

Electricity is the main form of energy consumed by the Brazilian industrial sector, accounting for almost one-half of its total energy consumption. However, this has not always been the case. In 1979, electricity accounted for less than 40 percent of the industrial sector's total consumption of energy. Additionally, oil consumption by the industrial sector fell drastically from almost 30 percent of the total in 1979 to less than 10 percent in 1988. The industrial sector concurrently began to increase its relative consumption of other forms of energy without compensating for declines, however. The only noteworthy exception was the consumption of charcoal, which increased by nearly 50 percent, from 6.6 percent in 1979 to 8.4 percent in 1988.

The data clearly illustrate the industrial sector's substitution of traditional forms of energy by new forms during the 1980s. Two main factors will help explain this trend. First came the oil shock of 1979, when the price of petroleum increased from US$13.33 per barrel in January of that year to US$32 in November 1980. These increases at the international level resulted in significant increases in the domestic price of petroleum derivatives, especially oil. One must keep in mind that Brazil's domestic production of oil at that time was much lower than it is today. At the time of the oil shock, domestic production was only 180,000 barrels per day and was highly dependent on external supplies at elevated prices. The second major factor contributing to the shift away from oil consumption was the introduction of a government program that supplied electric power at highly subsidized rates, resulting in rates as low as one-third of real rates. The objective of this program, made possible by surplus energy production at the new Itaipu hydroelectric power plant (HPP), was to replace oil in industrial steam boilers.

Paralleling the success of the government program of substituting oil with hydroelectric power, the energy market developed additional substitutes for oil products. Since substitute products produced internally were not subject to price increases, as petroleum products were, they often became competitive vis-à-vis petroleum. Sugarcane bagasse, firewood, and charcoal all played important roles in the substitution process.

Table 4

Structure of Energy Consumption by the Industrial Sector by Type of Energy Source,
1979-1988

(percent)

|  | Years | | | | | | | | | |
|---|---|---|---|---|---|---|---|---|---|---|
|  | 1979 | 1980 | 1981 | 1982 | 1983 | 1984 | 1985 | 1986 | 1987 | 1988 |
| Electricity | 38.1 | 39.4 | 42.0 | 42.7 | 44.0 | 45.4 | 47.1 | 47.8 | 46.1 | 47.7 |
| Oil | 27.6 | 25.3 | 20.2 | 16.9 | 12.1 | 9.6 | 9.0 | 9.2 | 10.0 | 9.6 |
| Sugarcane Bagasse | 8.7 | 9.1 | 10.5 | 10.5 | 10.9 | 9.5 | 8.3 | 7.7 | 8.2 | 7.1 |
| Wood | 7.0 | 6.9 | 8.1 | 9.1 | 10.2 | 10.5 | 10.1 | 9.6 | 9.1 | 8.4 |
| Coke | 6.4 | 6.2 | 5.5 | 5.8 | 6.6 | 7.8 | 8.2 | 7.6 | 8.2 | 9.0 |
| Charcoal | 6.6 | 6.4 | 6.3 | 6.8 | 7.4 | 8.7 | 8.6 | 8.6 | 8.1 | 8.4 |
| Others | 6.6 | 6.7 | 7.4 | 8.2 | 8.8 | 8.5 | 8.7 | 9.5 | 10.3 | 9.8 |
|  | 100.0 | 100.0 | 100.0 | 100.0 | 100.0 | 100.0 | 100.0 | 100.0 | 100.0 | 100.0 |

Source: IBGE. *Anuário Estatístico.* 1989.

According to the data in Table 5, the industrial sector was less vulnerable to future oil shocks in the late 1980s than it was at the beginning of the 1980s. The international competitiveness of Brazilian products, from an energy point of view, depends more on energy products produced internally than on those supplied by the international market.

Table 5 lists the main types of industries in Brazil, which constitute almost 90 percent of the industrial sector's energy consumption. The main consumers of energy in this sector are industries that produce primary and intermediary goods, accounting as a whole for 65 percent of the industrial sector's energy consumption. Within this sector, industries producing pig iron and steel consume the largest share of energy, more than 24 percent of the total. The nonferrous and other metals sector, accounting for 12 percent of the total, consume the second largest share of energy, followed by the chemical sector, which accounts for approximately 10 percent of the total. All of these sectors generally maintained their respective shares of consumption during the 1980s. Cement producers showed the greatest change, declining from 7 percent of total consumption in 1979 to 4.2 percent in 1988, primarily a result of the completion of numerous large-scale infrastructure projects begun in the 1970s. The paper and cellulose sector reported a slight increase in share of overall consumption of energy, and it remains an important consumer. Mineral extraction and pig iron production occupy the last position in this industrial category, accounting for a little more than 7 percent of total energy consumption.

With respect to the final goods segment of the industrial sector, the production of food and beverages stands out, consuming two-thirds the amount of energy used by the pig iron and steel segment. The energy consumption of food and beverage producers has varied between 15 and 20 percent of the sector's total throughout the decade, responding to fluctuations in the economy. The ceramics and textile industries are two other important components within the final goods segment, each consuming approximately 3 to 5 percent of the industrial sector's total.

*Evolution of Real Prices of Main Energy Products Consumed by Industry.* This section has examined the actual substitution of energy products consumed by Brazilian industries and the importance of oil and electric power in the national energy matrix. Table 6 shows the evolution of price indices for oil and forms of electric energy between 1979 and 1988 and the obvious deterioration in the terms of exchange of electric power vis-à-vis oil during the 1980s. After the second oil shock, real oil prices increased almost systemically, while electric power prices declined, especially after 1981. Between 1980 and 1985, the process of substituting electric power for oil reached its maximum level as the price of electric power fell in relation to the price of oil.

Table 5

## Structure of Primary and Secondary Energy Consumption by Type of Industry, 1979-1988
(percent)

| | Years | | | | | | | | | |
|---|---|---|---|---|---|---|---|---|---|---|
| | 1979 | 1980 | 1981 | 1982 | 1983 | 1984 | 1985 | 1986 | 1987 | 1988 |
| Pig Iron and Steel | 21.0 | 20.7 | 19.2 | 18.9 | 20.0 | 22.8 | 23.0 | 23.0 | 23.6 | 24.6 |
| Food and Beverages | 18.1 | 18.4 | 20.3 | 20.2 | 21.2 | 19.4 | 17.9 | 16.8 | 17.0 | 15.6 |
| Chemical Products | 10.6 | 10.6 | 10.3 | 10.0 | 10.4 | 10.5 | 11.1 | 10.5 | 10.0 | 10.3 |
| Non-ferrous and Other Metallics | 8.1 | 7.7 | 7.1 | 7.4 | 8.4 | 8.9 | 9.8 | 10.7 | 11.1 | 11.6 |
| Cement | 7.0 | 6.7 | 7.1 | 7.0 | 5.2 | 4.1 | 4.3 | 4.7 | 4.4 | 4.2 |
| Paper Pulp and Cellulose | 6.7 | 7.3 | 7.7 | 7.7 | 7.8 | 7.3 | 7.4 | 7.1 | 7.3 | 7.3 |
| Ceramics | 4.8 | 5.0 | 5.5 | 5.4 | 5.2 | 4.7 | 4.5 | 4.6 | 4.7 | 4.5 |
| Textile | 4.1 | 4.1 | 4.1 | 4.2 | 3.8 | 3.6 | 3.6 | 3.7 | 3.5 | 3.5 |
| Mining | 3.3 | 3.5 | 4.0 | 3.8 | 3.8 | 4.0 | 4.0 | 3.9 | 3.8 | 3.7 |
| Cast Iron | 1.6 | 2.1 | 2.4 | 2.7 | 2.6 | 2.7 | 2.8 | 3.0 | 3.0 | 3.4 |
| Others | 14.7 | 13.9 | 12.3 | 12.7 | 11.6 | 12.0 | 11.6 | 12.0 | 11.6 | 11.3 |
| | 100.0 | 100.0 | 100.0 | 100.0 | 100.0 | 100.0 | 100.0 | 100.0 | 100.0 | 100.0 |

Source: IBGE. *Anuário Estatístico.* 1989.

The decrease in the average real prices of electric power resulted from macroeconomic policy changes implemented to combat inflation and the introduction of a subsidized electric power program for industrial steam boilers. With the drop in oil prices after 1986, the trend began to reverse, as steam boilers were reconverted to use conventional oil. With new conditions in the international oil market and changes in the price of electric power, there may be a return to the use of electric power as a means of generating steam for industrial production. Any potential changes, however, will depend on oil prices remaining high for extended periods of time.

## Table 6
# Indices of Real Prices of Electrical Energy and Oil Utilized by Industry
### (1987=100)

| Year | Electricity[1] | Oil[2] |
|------|------------|--------|
| 1979 | 90.9 | 62.2 |
| 1980 | 90.3 | 108.8 |
| 1981 | 107.7 | 155.5 |
| 1982 | 100.0 | 136.3 |
| 1983 | 86.4 | 148.8 |
| 1984 | 86.4 | 153.2 |
| 1985 | 90.5 | 139.7 |
| 1986 | 77.6 | 103.0 |
| 1987 | 100.0 | 100.0 |
| 1988 | 96.4 | 78.1 |

[1] DEME/ELETROBRAS.
[2] CNP. *Anuários Estatísticos*. 1988/1989.

*Consumption Elasticity of Energy/GDP.* It has already been mentioned that the energy/GDP elasticity will tend to be equal to 1. This type of elasticity is obviously applicable to the energy sector taken as a whole and in the long term. Individually, however, the elasticity of one particular energy product (such as electric power) may be greater or less than 1, depending on the time period and relative price. Even when the energy sector is examined as an aggregate of its various forms, there may be short-term fluctuations in its elasticity, as occurred in the periods following the two oil crises when prices rose and recessions developed. In order to test the elasticity hypothesis of the energy sector, Table 7 was used, which shows the relationship between the industrial consumption of primary and secondary energy and real industrial GDP for the 1970-1987 time period. To represent energy/GDP elasticity, the following expression was used:

$$C = bY + u \qquad\qquad (1)$$

where:

C is industrial energy consumption,

Y is the industrial sector's gross domestic product (GDP),

b is energy/GDP elasticity, and

u is the residual.

Estimation of the parameters according to the least square method, after linearization of equation (1), had the following result:

$$C = 0.13552\ Y + 0.93028 \qquad\qquad (2)$$

## Table 7
# Industrial Consumption of Primary and Secondary Energy and Real Gross Domestic Product (GDP) of the Industrial Sector, 1970-1987

| Years | Industrial Consumption of Energy *(in billions of TEP)*[1] | Real Industrial Product *(in millions Cr$ of 1980)*[2] |
|---|---|---|
| 1970 | 21.2 | 2.08 |
| 1971 | 23.2 | 2.34 |
| 1972 | 25.3 | 2.67 |
| 1973 | 28.4 | 3.23 |
| 1974 | 31.0 | 3.60 |
| 1975 | 33.0 | 3.79 |
| 1976 | 36.8 | 4.15 |
| 1977 | 40.8 | 4.23 |
| 1978 | 43.7 | 4.58 |
| 1979 | 47.1 | 4.94 |
| 1980 | 50.6 | 5.43 |
| 1981 | 47.0 | 5.13 |
| 1982 | 48.1 | 5.33 |
| 1983 | 49.8 | 4.93 |
| 1984 | 55.6 | 5.35 |
| 1985 | 59.3 | 5.72 |
| 1986 | 63.4 | 6.06 |
| 1987 | 66.2 | 6.47 |

[1] IBGE. *Anuário Estatístico.* 1989.
[2] IBGE. *Sistema de Contas Nacionais Consolidadas*-Brasil Série Relatórios Metodológicos. 1990.
v. 8. Consumo Industrial de Produto Industrial Real.

The test of hypothesis $H_0 = 1$, using the t-statistics, revealed that the null hypothesis cannot be rejected. Therefore, it is possible to assume that the energy/GDP elasticity for the Brazilian industrial sector is equal to 1 in the long term, implying that increases in production will be matched by equivalent increases in the consumption of energy.

## Performance of the Energy Sector in the 1980s

Given its size and abundant variety of energy sources, Brazil is capable of producing different forms of energy. However, the country still depends on external sources of oil; increases in oil prices in the 1970s were partially responsible for the country's accumulation of a massive foreign debt. Of the total energy supply, approximately 60 percent is from renewable resources and 40 percent from non-renewable resources. Electric power and oil are the two main forms of energy consumed in the country, accounting for 33 percent and 30 percent of the total, respectively.

### Table 8
### Petroleum, Alcohol, and Natural Gas Sector Performances According to Reserves and Production
(1974 and 1990)

| | Data on Production | |
|---|---|---|
| | 1974 | 1990 |
| **1. PETROLEUM** | | |
| Reserves | 780 million barrels | 5 billion barrels |
| Production | 177,000 barrels/day | 630,000 barrels/day |
| Extraction Rate | 8% | 4.6% |
| Lifetime of Reserves | 12 years | 22 years |
| **2. ALCOHOL** | | |
| Installed capacity | 0 | 200,000 barrels/day |
| Production | 0 | 160,000 barrels/day |
| Lifetime of Reserves | 0 | 20 years |
| **3. NATURAL GAS** | | |
| Reserves | 20 billion cubic meters | 200 billion cubic meters* |
| Production | 1 billion cubic meters | 6 billion cubic meters* |
| Lifetime of Reserves | 20 years | 33 years |

Note: * = Data for 1988
Source: Balanço Energético Nacional. 1990.

During the 1980s, the country's energy sector faced important challenges, which were surmounted with relative efficacy. The only exception was the ethanol program, which was a success in terms of production and consumption, but prices for ethanol could not compete with those of petroleum derivatives. Table 8 shows the performance of the petroleum, gas, and ethanol sectors according to reserve and production levels.

Due to the important discoveries of new oil reserves in the Campos continental shelf, the result of vigorous exploration efforts following the first oil shock during the latter half of the 1970s, petroleum production practically quadrupled. By the early 1990s, the country produced approximately one-half of what it consumed. Thirty-two percent of domestic production is extracted from inland wells, while 68 percent is from offshore wells. In 1990, domestic production reached 630,000 barrels per day, most of which came from inland regions in the state of Bahia (approximately 13 percent of the total production) and from the Campos Basin on the continental shelf next to the state of Rio de Janeiro, approximately 58 percent of the total (Pelin 1990, 19). One measure of the efficacy of domestic exploration may be assessed from the following data: In 1974, immediately following the first oil shock, Brazil's reserves amounted to approximately 780 million barrels, while domestic production amounted to approximately 177,000 barrels per day, at an 8 percent extraction rate, which implied that reserves would be exhausted in 12 years. In 1990, explorable reserves reached 5 billion barrels, and production reached 630,000 barrels per day, at a 4.6 extraction rate that would result in a depletion of reserves within 22 years (at 1990 production levels).

Likewise, the country's reserves of natural gas (an energy product that satisfies every condition, even environmental, to be considered an alternative energy source par excellence) increased substantially. From 1982 to 1988, production doubled (from three to six billion cubic meters per year); there are currently substantial reserves both inland and offshore. Brazilian reserves of natural gas are estimated at 200 billion cubic meters (Pelin 1990, 20). Of the total production of natural gas in 1988, approximately 64 percent was extracted from continental shelves (mostly during oil production) and 36 percent from inland sources. Campos Basin, in Rio de Janeiro, was the largest producer with 40 percent of the total production and 62 percent of offshore production. Inland, the state of Bahia is the primary source of natural gas, accounting for 61 percent of the total, followed by the state of Alagoas with 19 percent (Pelin 1990, 20). Santos Basin may also become an important source of natural gas.

Fuel alcohol production for powering automobiles was nil in 1974, but by 1990 it reached approximately 160,000 barrels per day in gasoline equivalency. Available capacity that year was already above 200,000 barrels per year in gasoline equivalency.

Table 9 shows the performance of the petroleum and fuel alcohol sectors according to investments and costs. Investments in exploration and development of new petroleum fields amounted to approximately US$24 billion[1] for the period, or US$2 billion per year, representing an investment of US$5.43 per barrel of reserves.[2] The Alcohol Program required investments of approximately US$10 billion, which produced 1.2 billion barrels in gasoline equivalency during the 20 years that the alcohol distilleries existed. These figures reveal an average investment of US$8.3 per barrel of alcohol.

In terms of investment per output, the petroleum sector performed much better than the alcohol sector. The same occurred in production costs. While the average cost of petroleum produced in Brazil is approximately US$5 per barrel from inland sources and US$15 per barrel from offshore sources, the cost of a barrel of alcohol, equivalent in gasoline, is US$40. Hence, even with early 1990s petroleum prices in the international market at US$18 per barrel, domestic petroleum was produced and sold at competitive prices. The same cannot be said of alcohol, however.

### Table 9
## Performance of the Petroleum and Alcohol Sectors According to Investments and Costs

|  | Investments and Costs |
| --- | --- |
| **1. PETROLEUM** | |
| Investments in Capacity | US$24 billion (1974-1985) |
| Annual Average | US$2 billion |
| Investment per barrel of reserve | US$5.43 |
| Cost of production: | |
| • inland | US$5.00 per barrel |
| • offshore | US$15.00 per barrel |
| **2. ALCOHOL** | |
| Investments in capacity | US$10 billion (1974-1988) |
| Investment per barrel | |
| *(1.2 billion in 20 years)* | US$8.3 |
| Cost of production | US$40.00 per barrel |

Sources: Ministério das Minas e Energia, SNE, several years; and Petrobrás.

The impressive performance of the petroleum sector eventually cannot be repeated in the 1990s, because heavy investments will be needed to continue with explorations and to develop existing fields, such as those at Santos Basin and Marlin and Albacorra. Development of the Marlin field alone will absorb approximately US$2 billion within five years. This is an enormous field that contains approximately 3 billion barrels that are equivalent to 60 percent of the country's total reserves. The petroleum, however, is located in waters as deep as 1,000 meters. It is estimated that the amount of investment required for exploration, development, and extraction of petroleum to produce a certain level of self-sufficiency by the end of the century is between US$2 billion and US$2.5 billion per year until 1995. If such investments are not made, the goal of becoming self-sufficient will be at risk. The most critical factors affecting future explorations are constitutional clauses that prohibit risk contracts, which eliminate, at least momentarily, any share of foreign capital in the exploration of petroleum in Brazil.

In Brazil's electricity sector, approximately 94 percent of the supply is derived from hydroelectric sources, with the Southeast region accounting for 53 percent of the total. The remaining supply of electric energy is derived from thermal sources, including diesel plants, coal, charcoal and firewood, and nuclear reactors. The estimated potential of hydroelectric power in Brazil is at 200 gigawatts (GW), even though current output is approximately 52 GW (Pelin 1990, 21). Despite the difficulties faced by the electric sector, its performance during the 1980s can be considered satisfactory from the standpoint of production. For example, there were no significant interruptions in production supplies, even though industrial consumption increased more than industrial GDP. While the consumption of electric energy increased 4.85 percent in the period 1980-1988, industrial GDP grew only 2.8 percent. Although this difference has been attributed to the informal sector, in my opinion, this is unfounded because GDP estimates already capture at least a good portion of the informal sector, and the growth rate of consumption above industrial GDP is due to the substitution of oil by electricity (detailed in Table 6).

An examination of the electric sector's experience during the 1980s reveals increasing difficulties in the use of hydroelectric power plants with respect to environmental and socioeconomic issues, such as the impact of power plant construction on local populations and the exhaustion of sector financing.

Restrictions were increasingly imposed on projects undertaken after the 1970s, both directly from the population and indirectly through the construction of hydroelectric power plants. Local populations became more organized and began to demand compensation for losses caused by the construction of HPPs. Meanwhile, civil organizations and multilateral financial agencies exerted pressure on the federal government to internalize the benefits of projects in the regions where they were constructed. As a result, the government was forced to create a whole new set of regulations and laws that would strengthen and expand environmental legislation in the area of exploitation of natural resources, particularly those related to water use.

From the electric sector's standpoint, one of the consequences of such developments was an increase in HPP costs because of the additional costs entailed in construction. Henceforth, the construction of HPPs can only take place if part of the additional costs are incorporated into construction costs.

Aside from the environmental and socioeconomic concerns of populations that were being affected directly or indirectly, serious constraints were imposed on investment resources for the sector. On the one hand, its capacity for self-financing was exhausted. As mentioned, the real prices of electric energy used by the industrial sector fell more than 20 percent between 1981 and 1986, thereby reducing the sector's overall profitability. On the other hand, alternative external sources of financing decreased drastically during the period, especially after the 1982 crisis. Practically the only investment sources that were still available came from multilateral financial agencies, which, ironically, gave particularly high priority to the environmental and socioeconomic concerns of the populations affected by hydroelectric dams.

The electric sector was in a very delicate situation. On the one hand, it was forced to meet the growing pressures of local communities that would result in increased construction costs; on the other hand, it faced a cut in investments in the sector, which was derived from its reduced profitability or decreased levels of use in the economy and from difficulties in obtaining external financing.

The first oil crisis of 1973 resulted in a revision of the national energy matrix. An evaluation performed at the time indicated the need to give priority to the generation of energy produced by large hydroelectric power plants, nuclear plants, and alcohol fuel alternatives, as well the need to increase domestic petroleum production.

The construction of large HPPs, such as Itaipu and Tucuruí, benefited from the eagerness of the international financial market to lend money to such projects since they were experiencing a surplus of resources. At the same time, developmentalist policies emphasized the availability of energy as a crucial factor for economic success. The social costs associated with the construction of projects were ignored completely; evaluation criteria were based purely on economic indicators as determined by the allocative efficiency of resources.

The construction of hydroelectric power plants that ignored any social cost to affected populations was authorized by the authoritarian government in power at the time. Opposition to projects that had been approved by the federal government would be interpreted as defiance of national interests and would be strongly repressed.

Despite military repression, certain opposition movements from the affected populations already were flourishing as a growing awareness developed about the unequal distribution of costs and benefits generated by the projects. The emergence of a more open opposition, with national and international repercussions, created an impasse for the electric sector. On the one hand, the sector was forced to take into consideration the demands of the regional population through broader compensatory mechanisms. On the other hand, the emergence of an economic crisis toward the end of the 1970s and the external debt crisis of 1982 placed an increasingly larger number of restrictions on investment sources for the sector.

The impasse was complicated by growing inflationary pressures following the external crisis when state enterprises, by means of which external financing had been attracted, began to be used as instruments of economic policy to control inflation. Tariff adjustments resulted that were below inflation indices. Over the years, this policy practically destroyed the electric sector's ability to self-finance operations through expansions. It was within this socioeconomic and financial environment that the government decided to abandon large-scale HPPs and pursue undertakings on a smaller scale but of equal importance. In general, the implementation of these new projects was made possible because of the situation created by the second oil shock, a factor leading to a policy of replacing petroleum energy sources with electricity.

The electric sector responded to pressures and demands and recognized the need to insert its projects into the regional economy. An initial version of this new posture can be found in the National Plan for Electric Energy 1987-2010 (Plano Nacional de Energia Elétrica), which outlines long-term planning and in which the electric sector accepts, though timidly, regional insertion as a key element for planning the construction and operation of HPPs. The National Plan supports the assumption that the successful construction and operation of new hydroelectric power plants depends not only on their technical and financial viability but also on their socioeconomic and political impact at both the regional and national levels and the positive and negative externalities ultimately associated with their construction. Besides proposing a mitigation of the negative impact that projects have, the plan also proposes actions that will generate a greater number of possible benefits for local populations.

One of the strongest factors affecting this new position was the set of new requirements by multilateral development banks, especially the World Bank and the Inter-American Development Bank (IDB). Such agencies began to include compulsory clauses related to environmental management[3] and socioeconomic aspects in contracts involving large infrastructure projects. With the disappearance of other sources of financing, both domestic and foreign, the electric sector had to accept the new constraints imposed by multilateral development banks.

Another element influencing the adoption of new energy policies was the redemocratization process at the end of the 1980s, which facilitated the proliferation of social movements demanding greater compensation for losses incurred by local populations as a result of hydroelectric dam construction projects. In large urban areas, several movements — primarily made up of ecologists, members of the scientific community, and indigenous rights groups — appeared and began to question the need to construct more HPPs that had been planned in the 1980s. Opposition was most intense in cases involving the flooding of large areas that were sparsely populated, such as the Amazon, or areas occupied by rural and urban populations, such as the São Francisco and Uruguay River regions.

At the regional level, the movements joined those who had been affected directly by the HPPs with elite groups and local associations that were not necessarily affected.[4] The result was a broad set of demands ranging from the adoption of mitigation measures by the electric sector as compensation for the negative externalities of HPP projects, to the adoption of complementary projects that would return at least part of the benefits generated by such projects to the regions where they were constructed (as opposed to exporting these benefits to the major urban centers and to large industrial areas).

Despite these problems, the electric sector was still able to perform satisfactorily. Difficulties in the future, however, are not going to be any less. Financial resources are still greatly limited, and environmental and socioeconomic concerns can only be expected to receive more attention. If energy is to be available for further economic development, new solutions will have to be devised for the electric sector specifically and for the energy sector as a whole.

## Challenges for the Future

In the previous section of this chapter, it was shown that the elasticity of energy to GDP was not significantly greater or less than 1. Any policy, therefore, that gives priority to greater economic growth will have to face the fact that any increase in production will require a positive and equal increase in energy consumption. It should be noted that an energy/GDP elasticity equal to 1 does not imply that the same types of energy will be available; this would only occur if the relative prices of different energy sources were to remain constant. As this is rarely the case, we may find, during different periods, different elasticities for each type of energy source or energy product. Certainly, the elasticity of electricity/industrial GDP was greater than 1 in the period between 1980 and 1988 since the price of electricity dropped in comparison to the prices of other energy sources. This was the main reason for an above-normal consumption rate of electricity, as compared to the rate of growth of industrial GDP. The opposite occurred in the case of oil, as its elasticity was less than 1 during the same time period. By the same token, a more liberal commercial policy will require Brazilian industries to increase their competitiveness in domestic and international markets. In light of the need to promote competitiveness, the cost of energy should be considered, along with the potential for pollution generated by each energy source.

It also has been mentioned that the most important sources of energy in industry were electricity and oil. Although both energy sources performed well during the 1980s, the majority of problems they faced, mainly after 1982, still persisted into the early 1990s. One of the main obstacles facing domestic petroleum production and electric energy production is the lack of investment capacity. Until the beginning of the 1990s, the state, through its enterprises, had been the sole investor in the petroleum and electric sectors. In the majority of cases, needed investments were financed with external savings. With state investments in the energy sector depleting, due to the country's increasing indebtedness, and investments basically restricted by multilateral financial agencies, new economic agents need to be called to intervene in the process. The new Constitution, as mentioned, initially prohibited foreign capital from holding majority participation in the production and exploration of hydraulic resources and subsoil resources.[5] Until such constitutional clauses were revoked, only partial financing could have come from direct investments.

Besides investment capacity, there is also the question of which alternative energy sources could best supplement electricity and oil in providing an adequate level of energy supply to domestic industry at a cost that is competitive with international market rates. The other basic question in establishing energy policy guidelines — assuming policies are geared toward greater liberalization of commerce, industry, and economic growth — is the definition of an initial set of energy sources that would be privileged by such a policy.

In sum, three major challenges await the energy sector in the near future. The first challenge is to define a set of energy sources to be privileged because of their competitive costs. The second challenge is to minimize the negative environmental impacts of new energy sources. The third challenge is to determine an alternative source of financing needed to expand the sector's capacity.

## Alternative Energy Sources

Table 10 lists the energy sources that, from a technical point of view, could be utilized for domestic industrial production. It shows the cost of production (in terms of barrel equivalents to petroleum) of each source, including alcohol. There are eight possible energy sources (excluding alcohol but including conservation) available for industrial consumption. From a technical standpoint, all of these sources are viable, but from an economic standpoint, only some are.

Among the alternatives listed in Table 10, electricity is not analyzed because it is by definition the most appropriate source, technically and economically, for the generation of thermal energy. If this were not the case, it would not be used so extensively by the industrial sector. Other energy sources (excluding alcohol) compete with each other in the generation of thermal energy. Among these (excluding conservation), the best options according to their respective rankings are domestic petroleum (and oil

Table 10

## Production Costs of Some Energy Products

(US$ as of March 1990)

| Domestic oil[1] | Natural gas[2] | Shale oil[3] | Charcoal[4] | Coal[5] | Coal gas[6] | Coal synthetic diesel[7] | Alcohol | Conservation |
|---|---|---|---|---|---|---|---|---|
| 5.00 (inland) | 5.00 (inland) | 43.58 | 26.40 | 13.61 | 73.65 | 61.35 | 40.00 | - |
| 15.00 (in the ocean) | 15.00 (in the ocean) | 52.86 | 33.35 | 21.12 | 95.87 | 92.01 | 45.00 | - |

[1] *Gazeta Mercantil*, 13.
[2] For gas wells only.
[3] For the lower boundary: Petrobrás, August 1981. For the upper boundary: *Folha de São Paulo*, August 16, 1981, 40.
[4] *Gazeta Mercantil*, January 7, 1981, 1, 7.
[5] Modiano and Tourinho, December 1981.
[6] *Gazeta Mercantil*, January 7, 1988, 1, 7.
[7] The World Bank, 1981, 90.

derivatives), natural gas, coal, and charcoal. The remaining energy sources are too expensive to receive a privileged position in the national energy production plan. Instead, such sources should be incorporated into research plans on future energy sources, the strongest candidate of which is shale oil. Estimated reserves for shale amount to 120 billion tons (approximately 5.2 billion barrels), a level equivalent to petroleum reserves.[6]

Although coal and charcoal sources are available to industry at costs competitive with those of oil, they have certain drawbacks. Costs shown in Table 10 do not consider that these are "dirty" sources, because they generate negative externalities such as pollution and critical problems associated with the transportation of large quantities of coal and charcoal into the already congested urban and industrial centers. The problem is multiplied by the lack of space necessary for storing coal and charcoal. Such externalities are yet to be evaluated properly and would tend to increase the cost of these sources because they require additional investments in sophisticated anti-pollutant equipment and transportation networks. However, the traffic problem caused by large trucks would not be as great for industries located outside large urban centers.

Petroleum and natural gas prospects would be, according to Table 10, the best options if their continued availability could be assured. Brazilian reserves of petroleum and gas that are economically available amount to 5 billion barrels and 200 billion cubic meters, respectively, as previously mentioned. However, oil reserves could be expanded to almost 7 billion barrels, depending on investments in deep-water exploration, mainly in the Campos and Santos basins. Similarly, the availability of natural gas could be greatly increased by giving market access to the massive reserves in Bolivia and Argentina through bilateral agreements. Some attempts already have been made in this direction, but due to political reasons (and not economic ones) they have not been successful.

Natural gas could be the best fuel for the generation of thermal energy in industry. Natural gas is cost-competitive with petroleum and has the advantage of being a "clean" fuel in terms of pollution. Even so, a serious economic obstacle to natural gas use is that Brazil's industrial production areas are so widely dispersed; transportation and delivery costs associated with gas are quite high. The use of natural gas, however, would be highly efficient in areas with a high density of industrial firms (such as in the Vale do Paraíba, Baixada Santista, and Greater São Paulo), where investments in infrastructure (such as pipelines) for distribution would be optimized. It is also in these regions that pollution problems are most critical. A system of distribution through gas lines would eliminate other problems, such as the heavy traffic caused by trucks and lack of storage space associated with coal and charcoal in densely populated areas. The gas deposits located at the Campos Basin, for example, made the use of gas viable for industries located in the Baixada Santista, mainly Cubatão.

In regard to conservation, natural gas is obviously the cheapest. In industrial production, it is possible to reduce energy consumption by approximately 10 to 20 percent through equipment adjustments and by decreasing waste. For consumer goods, it is possible to save equivalent levels of energy by improving the performance of domestic appliances. Although there are already specific government programs for financing energy conservation in the industrial sector, at this moment it does not seem sensible to expand such programs. We believe that competition, which will emerge by liberalizing the external sector, will force national industries to move toward energy conservation. In this case, the best policy to follow is to institutionalize broader research programs in conservation. Moreover, it is important to disseminate the results of completed studies.

With respect to the use of alcohol in automobiles, its high cost of production relative to that of petroleum suggests forgoing its production. However, one must consider that the alcohol program has been implemented and was working well, with a capacity of 16 billion liters per year as of 1992. The issue, then, is not whether the program should be implemented but what should be done with it. There are basically three possibilities for alcohol production: 1) let it become obsolete and disappear, 2) maintain the status quo, or 3) expand production. The first option is not suggested for two reasons, one political and the other economic. Since the number of cars in 1992 fueled by alcohol came to approximately 4.5 million, it will be politically impossible to let the program disappear and impose very high costs on the millions of automobile owners. From an economic perspective, given that the bulk of investments already have been made and will last for at least another 15 years, it would be irrational to let the program vanish. For the production and use of alcohol, the sunk costs would have to be incorporated into relevant criteria. Nor would expanding the program be recommended, since alcohol's marginal social cost is greater than US$40 per barrel equivalent of gasoline. This cost is much higher than the actual price of gasoline in the international market, suggesting that the alcohol program is not competitive. In the case of new production facilities, the relevant concept of analysis is the "marginal cost."

The only option that remains available to the Proálcool program is its preservation, which would allow it to expand up to the limits of actual production capacity. From both political and economic points of view, this would be the most sensible recommendation. Other important factors in favor of preservation are environmental issues. As is well known, the substitution of leaded gasoline by anhydrous alcohol (alcohol mixed with gasoline) improves environmental conditions in large cities. As of 1992, only the city of São Paulo used gasoline with a 22 percent concentration of anhydrous alcohol. In other Brazilian cities, the mix is much lower and, in some cases, even nonexistent. This may suggest that the alcohol program should be reconsidered as a possibility to produce, in the long run (about 20 years), only anhydrous alcohol that would be mixed with gasoline. This would move the country toward the adoption of a single type of fuel within its territory, and the hydrous alcohol, currently produced and used by 4.5 million automobiles, gradually would be eliminated and replaced by greater production of anhydrous alcohol.

## Guidelines for an Energy Policy

B ased on what has been discussed, it is possible to produce guidelines for an energy policy designed to accommodate greater economic growth, more liberal commercial policies, and greater consideration of the environment.

Suggestions for types of energy sources:

1. Give priority to electricity as a source of kinetic energy, avoiding its less efficient use in the generation of thermal energy.

2. Give priority to natural gas as a source of thermal energy in regions with high industrial and population density.

3. Consider the use of oil in the generation of thermal energy only in regions of low industrial and population density; charcoal and coal also should be taken into consideration. Local solutions, such as the use of sugarcane bagasse, could be viable alternatives since they meet economic criteria.

4. Give priority to the expansion in production of anhydrous alcohol to be mixed with gasoline at a level of 22 percent, and phase out the production of hydrous alcohol.

5. Expand the scope of research on energy conservation and look for greater efficiency within industries in the dissemination of research results.

Source-specific suggestions:

1. Electricity

   a. Increase discussions on the possibilities and limits of private sector participation in the generation of electric energy, especially in relation to Article 175 of the Constitution, which discusses public utility concessions.

   b. Consider other sources of energy, such as from thermoelectric plants, which require less investment and can be installed, in principle, practically anywhere. (The fact that these plants produce relatively high levels of pollution means that special care should be taken when choosing their locations.)

   c. Improve the self-financing capacity of the electric sector by means of cost rationalization more than raising taxes.

    d. Extend sector royalties to states and municipalities to cover part of the social and environmental costs involved in the installation of HPPs.

    e. Invest sales tax revenues (from the Imposto sobre Circulação de Mercadorias — ICM) in the electric sector in order to improve the financing capacity of new HPPs or thermoelectric plants. This action will help compensate for the sector's loss of revenues caused by the displacement of the Tax on Electric Energy (Imposto Único sobre Energia Elétrica — IUEE) by ICM taxes.

    f. Utilize debt conversion mechanisms as much as possible to generate new investments in HPPs. Similarly, initiate discussions on the viability of using privatization certificates to finance the sector.

    g. Continue with attempts to finance the sector through multilateral development banks, such as the IDB and the World Bank.

2. Petroleum and natural gas

    a. Concentrate efforts on altering the Constitution to allow risk contracts for private foreign and domestic firms to participate in petroleum exploration (recently, the Constitution was altered with respect to this issue).

    b. Improve the self-financing capacity of Petrobrás through cost rationalization.

    c. Use debt conversions as much as possible to generate investment in Petrobrás.

    d. Maintain relative prices for natural gas and oil at levels that will stimulate the use of natural gas in large cities with highly concentrated industrial areas and the use of oil in areas with low densities of industry and population.

    e. Stimulate the diversification of suppliers of natural gas and design a system to maintain a minimum reserve level to buffer against any interruptions in supply in the short term.

3. Alcohol

    a. Move slowly toward establishing a single type of automotive fuel — a gasoline mixture with 22 percent anhydrous alcohol — for the entire country.

    b. Begin phasing out production of hydrous alcohol and phasing in greater production of anhydrous alcohol after at least 20 years, which will be enough time for existing production facilities to become obsolete.

These are the basic guidelines for a national energy policy under the conditions of a more liberal commercial policy and economic growth. To pursue such actions means to implement an energy policy that gives priority to the cheaper sources of energy currently available in the country. Each point in the guidelines raises several questions for practical and legal consideration. Such inquiries are beyond the scope of this chapter, however. They should be studied and debated closely, and their answers eventually could modify the guidelines as proposed here. In any case, the most important point of these discussions is the principle of the efficient allocation of resources, by which only the most competitive energy sources will be prioritized in the development of a national energy plan. Other sources of energy should be researched further and eventually incorporated into Brazil's economy once production costs are lowered.

# Notes

1. See *Brasil-Estatísticas Básicas*, 1990, first edition, Nova Análise Editora, 112.

2. The value of investment per barrel of oil in reserve was obtained by the division of the total investment in the period 1974 to 1985 ($24 billion), by the reserves in 1985 (2.2 billion barrels), plus the consumption in the period (3.0 billion barrels), minus the reserves in 1974 (0.78 billion barrels).

3. The requirement of environmental management became part of a set of conditions imposed by the Department of Water Resources and Electrical Energy (Departamento de Águas e Energia Elétrica) to approve any studies dealing with utilization of water resources.

4. An example of these organized movements is the Commission of Representatives for the Population Affected by the Construction of Dams (Comissão de Representantes dos Atingidos pelas Barragens — RAB), which was very active during the implementation of Eletrosul projects on the Uruguay River.

5. Evidently, the Constitution does not prohibit the financing of investments in the installed capacity.

6. *Gazeta Mercantil*, August 11, 1981, 9.

# References

*Brasil-Estatísticas Básicas.* 1990. Nova Análise Editora, first edition.

CNP. 1988/1989. *Anuários Estatísticos.* Brasília, D.F.

*Folha de São Paulo.* August 16, 1981, 40.

*Gazeta Mercantil.* January 7, 1981, 1, 7; and August 11, 1981, 9.

IBGE. 1989. *Anuário Estatístico.* Rio de Janeiro: IBGE.

IBGE. 1990. *Sistema de Contas Nacionais Consolidadas -Brasil.* Rio de Janeiro: Série Relatórios Metodológicos, v. 8.

Modiano, E.M., and O.A.F. Tourinho. 1981. *A Economia do Carvão Mineral.* IX Encontro da ANPEC.

Pelin, E.R. 1990. *Indicadores do Perfil da Economia Brasileira.* São Paulo: FIPE.

Petrobrás. 1981. *Usina Industrial de Xisto de São Mateus do Sul: Estudo de Economicidade para Diversas Capacidades na 1a. Etapa — Sumário Executivo.* Rio de Janeiro: EPIN/DIPLAN/SESEC.

World Bank. 1981. *Energy in Developing Countries:* Washington, D.C.: World Bank.

# The External Sector of the Brazilian Economy

## Simão Davi Silber

## Introduction

This chapter discusses the evolution of Brazil's external sector and evaluates the main elements of the foreign trade reform initiated in 1988 and scheduled to be completed in 1995. This study stresses that the international trade policies adopted in recent decades were extremely detrimental to the country's international competitiveness because of fluctuations in the real exchange rate and the recurrent use of specific and discriminatory instruments for protection and promotion of sales in domestic and foreign markets. Consequently, the 1980s witnessed a reduction in Brazil's relative participation in the world market in terms of exports of products with low technological sophistication, as well as sectors that involve a more intensive utilization of skilled labor, capital, and technology. In addition, total supply of imports has decreased, transforming the Brazilian economy into one of the most autarkic economies in the world. The central conclusion that can be drawn is that despite the increase in restrictions on international trade after the 1970s, there is room for greater specialization and international integration and for an increase in Brazil's participation in the world economy. This potential exists not only because of Brazil's current low level of participation in the global economy but also because of the expected growth of incomes worldwide and growth of global trade in the 1990s. The final part of this chapter discusses the foreign debt problem and how its direction is conditioned by the future global scenario and Brazil's particular stabilization and liberalization policies.

## Recent Evolution of Brazilian Exports

In this section, the relationship between the degree of openness of the Brazilian economy and the performance of the export sector is discussed.

The main argument is that increasing the openness of the economy to the world, decreasing the excessive verticalization of the economy, and increasing industrial specialization represent a policy based on a comparative advantage that will allow the country to specialize in goods it can produce with lower relative costs.

First, an analysis of transformations in the structure of Brazil's exports is provided that emphasizes the importance of a change in the composition of Brazil's exports toward sectors involving intensive physical capital, human capital, and technology associated with expansion of the import substitution process. This phenomenon was particularly important in the 1970s, indicating that the country's comparative advantages were moving toward those sectors that utilize such production factors more intensively. During the 1980s, the phenomenon reversed itself: the country's relative position in the world market declined in sectors of greater technological sophistication, signaling that something was profoundly wrong with industrial and commercial policy: the country could not obtain the productivity gains needed to expand its competitive power in a world market determined by the pace of creation and diffusion of technological progress.

Following the discussion on the transformation of the export sector, the elements of a strategic commercial and industrial policy that makes it possible for the country to obtain dynamic comparative advantages are considered. The emphasis here is twofold: invest in human capital formation and in basic and applied research and eliminate the variance of protection and incentives, increase competition, and speed up technological transfers to the country. It is argued that priority for new investments must be given to those sectors with a superior — and stable — technological frontier and that the country must be extremely careful in undertaking ventures involving products and productive processes that are rapidly undergoing changes at the global level.

There are important relationships between Brazil's commercial and industrial policies (explicit or implicit) and the changes in the performance of the external sector. When the country opted for a policy of rapid industrialization, it went through four phases of economic policy that conditioned its industrial profile. The first phase, extending from the end of World War II until the mid-1960s, was characterized by high tariff protection that isolated the domestic market from international competition and made rapid economic growth possible. During this period, import substitution of the consumer durable goods sector was completed, and the next phase of import substitution in the capital goods and intermediate inputs sectors was initiated. This phase is characterized by an autarkic industrial development, based on foreign technology imports, without concern for the performance of the export sector. The main instruments utilized to alter relative prices in favor of domestic industrial production were restrictions on imports, subsidies to foreign investment, and overvalued exchange rates.

The second phase, extending from the mid-1960s until 1974, was characterized by a change in trade policy toward increasing the participation of domestic manufactures in the international market. This policy explicitly defined priority sectors and also expanded the import-substitution process in intermediate and capital goods sectors that employed more highly sophisticated technologies.

During the third phase, beginning with the first oil shock and lasting until 1988, the Import Tax Law of 1957 was changed, and taxes of up to 100 percent were introduced in 1974 and 1975 for a large number of products. The rate of taxation further increased the nominal protection of consumer goods at a time when the intermediate and capital goods sectors were industrial development priorities. To control such a disarticulation between tariff and industrial policies, an extensive system of import tariff reductions was created, making investments in the priority sectors more viable.

Parallel to this action, a set of restrictions on imports was introduced, including 1) a tax on financial operations (IOF) of 25 percent on the purchase of foreign exchange, 2) additional taxes on the renovation of the Merchant Navy and on port improvements, 3) business import programs, 4) an import authorization control, 5) "Annex C" (list of products whose imports were temporarily suspended), 6) similarity inspection, and 7) compulsory import financing (for details, see Moreira and Barboza 1984; and Carvalho 1985).

The consequence of import restrictions was the emergence of highly discretionary, subjective, and unstable criteria for import policy — to the detriment of stable and transparent rules, such as tariffs.

To illustrate the dimension of the tariff distortions of the 1970s and 1980s, note that although the average nominal tariff was around 40 percent, import revenues from taxes did not reach 10 percent of the total value of imports (data for 1989). Thus, the stacking of several instruments to control imports weakened the protection embedded in the tariff structure, whose logic only can be reestablished when tariffs recover their role of signaling investment in domestic economic activities.

To compensate exports for the increase in costs resulting from such an excessive restriction on imports and from exchange rate distortions, several incentives such as credit and fiscal subsidies were introduced, all of which were eliminated in 1985 except for the BEFIEX programs, which were maintained until 1989 (Braga and Martone 1987).

The fourth phase of economic policy was initiated with the tariff reform of 1988 and was expanded in 1990 with the elimination of administrative controls on imports, the definition of gradual import tariff reductions, and the change in the exchange rate regime, which sought to liberalize foreign trade and alter Brazil's "closed" style of development.

The change in the composition of value added in the Brazilian industrial sector that resulted from national industrial policies reflects the greater relative importance of the capital and intermediate goods sectors. Taking the value added per worker as a measure of capital (physical and human)/labor ratio, it is apparent that growth in Brazilian industry was more intensive in sectors where capital/labor ratios were higher than the industry's average. According to the 1980 Industrial Census, sectors such as food, lumber and furniture, textiles, and apparel had lower levels of value added per worker than the industry's average; the chemical products, transportation, metallurgy, machinery and equipment, and electrical material sectors exhibited higher per worker value added than the average for the entire industry (for details, see Silber 1983).

Parallel to this structural transformation of Brazil's industry, important modifications in the country's export profile, which reflect changes in the country's international comparative advantages, can be observed.

Tables 1 and 2 present statistics on changes in the composition of Brazil's foreign trade. The evolution of exports of manufactures, which grew from US$366 million in 1968 to US$16.851 billion in 1985, is presented in Table 1. Export growth during the same period reached 26 percent per year (in nominal terms), while the share of manufactures in exports increased from 13 percent to 57 percent of total exports.

## Table I
## Brazilian Exports of Manufactures
## 1968, 1974, 1979 and 1985
### (US$ millions)

| Sectors | 1968 | 1974 | 1979 | 1985 |
|---|---|---|---|---|
| Food, Beverage and Tobacco | 90 | 402 | 1,122 | 2,152 |
| Textile | 15 | 308 | 608 | 656 |
| Apparel | 7 | 297 | 684 | 1,389 |
| Wood and Paper Pulp | 86 | 285 | 623 | 904 |
| Rubber | 2 | 8 | 70 | 223 |
| Chemical | 79 | 468 | 1,043 | 2,556 |
| Oil | 1 | 44 | 215 | 1,617 |
| Non-metallic Minerals | 7 | 34 | 100 | 151 |
| Metallurgy | 32 | 182 | 858 | 2,693 |
| Transport Material | 4 | 176 | 981 | 1,616 |
| Machinery and Other Manufactures | 43 | 555 | 1,770 | 2,810 |
| *Total* | *366* | *2,759* | *8,074* | *16,851* |

Source: United Nations, *Commodity Trade Statistics*, several issues.

As industrialization proceeded toward more dynamic and technologically sophisticated sectors, identical changes took place in the sectoral composition of Brazilian exports. In 1968, for example, 56.5 percent of Brazil's exports of manufactures were concentrated in food, textiles, apparel, lumber, rubber, and non-metallic minerals. In 1985, this level fell to 32.6 percent, and exports of more technologically sophisticated sectors, such as chemical products, oil, metallurgy, transportation, and machinery, increased from 43.5 percent to 67.1 percent (Table 2).

## Table 2
## Brazilian Exports of Manufactures
## 1968, 1974, 1979, 1985
(percent of total exports)

| Sectors | 1968 | 1974 | 1979 | 1985 |
|---|---|---|---|---|
| Food, Beverage and Tobacco | 24.50 | 14.60 | 13.90 | 12.80 |
| Textile | 4.20 | 11.10 | 7.50 | 3.90 |
| Apparel | 1.90 | 10.80 | 8.50 | 8.20 |
| Wood and Paper Pulp | 23.40 | 10.30 | 7.70 | 5.40 |
| Rubber | 0.50 | 0.30 | 0.90 | 1.40 |
| Chemical | 21.50 | 17.00 | 12.90 | 15.20 |
| Oil | 0.30 | 1.60 | 2.70 | 9.60 |
| Non-metallic Minerals | 2.00 | 1.20 | 1.20 | 0.90 |
| Metallurgy | 8.80 | 6.60 | 10.60 | 16.00 |
| Transport Material | 1.10 | 6.40 | 12.20 | 9.60 |
| Machinery and Other Manufactures | 11.80 | 20.10 | 21.90 | 16.70 |
| *Total* | *100.00* | *100.00* | *100.00* | *100.0* |

Source: United Nations, *Commodity Trade Statistics*, several issues.

This phenomenon is an indication that the country's export profile had changed as Brazilian industrialization moved toward more technologically sophisticated sectors. It is safe to conclude, therefore, that exports are shifting to new sectors as a result of the country's industrialization policy.

Using the index of "Revealed Comparative Advantages," the magnitude of these changes can be estimated (see Table 3). The sectors that maintained the highest indices in the initial period (1970) presented a negative performance in terms of specialization in exports. On the other hand, sectors with low indices at the beginning of the period experienced significant increases in comparative advantages, particularly the metallurgy, transportation, machinery, and oil sectors.[1]

## Table 3
# Indices of "Revealed Comparative Advantages"*

| Sectors | 1970 | 1974 | 1979 | 1985 | Annual Growth Rate 70/79 | 79/85 |
|---|---|---|---|---|---|---|
| Food, Beverage and Tobacco | 4.38 | 3.05 | 3.33 | 3.18 | -3.0 | -0.1 |
| Textile | 0.87 | 2.96 | 1.84 | 1.06 | 8.7 | -8.8 |
| Apparel | 1.03 | 4.10 | 2.10 | 1.81 | 8.2 | -2.4 |
| Wood and Paper Pulp | 2.54 | 1.29 | 1.57 | 0.95 | -5.2 | -8.0 |
| Rubber | 0.70 | 0.41 | 1.04 | 1.53 | 4.9 | 6.6 |
| Chemical | 1.41 | 1.66 | 1.20 | 1.32 | -1.7 | 1.6 |
| Oil | 0.22 | 0.07 | 0.12 | 0.51 | -6.5 | 27.3 |
| Non-metallic Minerals | 0.92 | 1.05 | 0.98 | 0.61 | 0.1 | -7.6 |
| Metallurgy | 1.17 | 0.65 | 1.22 | 2.17 | 0.1 | 10.1 |
| Transport Material | 0.16 | 0.62 | 0.94 | 0.61 | 21.7 | -6.9 |
| Machinery and Other Manufactures | 0.45 | 0.78 | 0.85 | 0.62 | 7.3 | -5.1 |

Note: * Defined as $(X_{i,n}/X_n)/(X_{i,w}/X_w)$ where:
  $X_{i,n}$ = Brazilian exports of industry (i)
  $X_n$   = Brazilian exports of manufactures (total)
  $X_{i,w}$ = world exports of industry (i)
  $X_w$   = world exports (total)
Source: United Nations, *Commodity Trade Statistics*, several issues.

It should be emphasized, however, that most of the transformations occurred in the 1970s when growth rates of comparative advantages were high, not only for traditional sectors, such as textiles and apparel, but also for sectors of greater technological sophistication, such as transportation and machinery. During the 1980s, these results were reversed: with the exception of metallurgy and oil, there was a significant reduction in the revealed comparative advantages. It is important to mention the loss that occurred in the competitiveness of sectors of greater technological sophistication, such as transportation and machinery, and in traditional sectors, such as textiles and apparel, indicating that the economy was incapable of keeping up with changes occurring in world trade during the 1980s. Results suggest the urgent need to change industrial and commercial policies in order to increase the competitiveness of Brazilian products in the world market.

Moreover, it is necessary to emphasize that there was an excessive verticalization in Brazil's economy, not only in response to external shocks but also as a consequence of an industrial policy aimed at achieving autonomy regardless of cost. This period was characterized, in addition, by little emphasis on the formation of human resources and on basic and applied research — all of which are essential elements for the creation and transfer of technology. During the period, emphasis was placed on protecting sectors of high technology and those sectors that use skilled labor intensely in research and development (R&D), a scarce factor in the Brazilian economy and one that generally receives low priority from government investments. The concentration of investment in a small number of large firms (producing for domestic and foreign markets) favored the formation and preservation of an oligopolistic structure, which hindered competition and technological change (Silber et al. 1990).

Due to rapid changes in the technological frontier in industrialized countries, a growing number of products and processes that had reached technological maturity were apt to migrate to newly industrialized countries (NICs), which offered favorable costs and institutional conditions for new productive activities. These segments of industry are highly sophisticated and — once having gained technological stability — are often pressured by high labor costs to relocate to countries with special conditions. In this process, multinational corporations have come to play a very important role in terms of technology transfer and the opening of these countries to exports.

It is in this segment of industry, which was marked by high, stable technology, that Brazil's long-run comparative advantages can be found. Brazil's incursions into leading-edge technology sectors should be small, and it should concentrate on areas of the productive process that are transplanted easily into the country without incurring production costs, as in the excessive verticalization of the productive process.

Furthermore, it is important to recognize the distinct nature of the dynamics of a high technology sector in comparison to sectors where technology is stable. In the latter, it is not necessary to make changes in a product or process in order to introduce it into other countries; relative cost factors may transform such products and processes into competitive sectors at the world level. This is not the case for high technology sectors, where products and processes rapidly become obsolete, transforming the creation and diffusion of technology into the crucial element of obtaining products at prices and quality levels compatible with international standards. If a country lacks the necessary conditions to follow such a process, it will be condemned to supporting technologically obsolete sectors, and the whole economy will be negatively affected by their impacts on other sectors. The lack of basic, applied research, the shortage of skilled labor, and the rapid obsolescence of innovations make investments in high technology very risky in recently industrialized countries such as Brazil. Greater emphasis on leading-edge technology should take place when the country will be apt to invest a larger portion of its resources in the formation of human capital and R&D.

It was through the transfer (or imitation) of stable technologies that the NICs were able to increase their comparative advantages significantly after the

1960s, and it is in this segment that Brazil should concentrate its efforts to increase its competitive power. This does not mean that Brazil is predestined to live with inferior living standards. There are several examples of countries, including Canada, Australia, New Zealand, and Spain, that exhibit very high per capita income levels without competing in the area of technological advances.

In order for transfer of technologies to become a reality, it is necessary for Brazil to liberalize its foreign trade by eliminating the variance of protection and incentives, reducing the economy's excessive verticalization, investing in human capital and R&D, eliminating barriers to competition, and eliminating the system of incentives concentrated in companies with significant market power. Through these actions, it will be possible to obtain the productivity gains necessary to expand the country's competitive power in the world market, which is closely determined by the pace of technological progress.

In the last two decades, the participation of NICs in manufactures trade expanded significantly, indicating an increase in the competitive power of Asian and Latin American countries in the trading of products with standard technology and even in some cases in sectors where additional technological effort is still relatively small. Statistical data indicate that the growth of manufactures exports from these countries exceeds that of OECD (Organization for Economic Cooperation and Development) countries. Moreover, a dramatic change in the terms of trade between the two groups of countries apparently has not occurred. What seems to have happened during the 1980s is that the impact of high real interest rates, which reduced the international prices of commodities exported by NICs, eliminated part of the gains in the terms of trade previously obtained.

Despite an increase in nontariff restrictions (NTRs) during the 1980s, Brazilian exports maintained an annual growth rate of 5.6 percent, which was identical to the average growth rate of developing countries while quite lower than those observed in Asian countries, such as Korea (14.3 percent), Hong Kong (11.4 percent), and Thailand (10.2 percent).

Particularly in Brazil's main export market, the United States, there was a great increase in NTRs during the period. At the beginning of the 1980s, there were practically no NTRs on Brazilian exports, while in 1986, 20 percent of Brazilian exports of primary products and 11 percent of manufactures were subject to some form of nontariff restrictions.

It is estimated that the elimination of NTRs on Brazilian exports could increase revenues obtained through foreign trade by as much as 15 percent (US$5 to US$5.5 billion), particularly from gains derived from the liberalization of trade in agricultural products. This would indicate that the country would profit greatly from a liberalization process in trade with emphasis on reciprocity instead of the discrimination typical of U.S. and European

Community requirements within the General Agreement on Tariffs and Trade (GATT). In other words, a major opening of the Brazilian economy to imports should be followed by greater access of Brazilian agricultural and industrial products to the markets of developed countries.

Prospects for high growth in income and trade at the international level should permit high levels of export growth over the next few years, which will enhance the possibilities of inserting Brazil into the global economy. The greatest concern, however, is the formation of economic blocs, which could increase average levels of protection in these regions against external competition. Even in this scenario, there is no strong argument in favor of isolating the Brazilian economy to the extent that it was before, particularly in terms of imports. Even in a less favorable international scenario — given the small participation of Brazil in world trade up to the early 1990s — Brazil should be able to utilize international specialization as an important instrument to gain productivity associated with technological progress, acceleration of economic growth rates, expansion of the domestic market, and more equitable distribution of income.

## Recent Changes in Commercial Policy

Considering the information presented above, it is apparent that Brazil's competitive position in the world market deteriorated during the 1980s due to several factors. First, technological progress accelerated in industrialized countries and rapidly spread (or was imitated) in more recently industrialized countries. In addition, Brazil's commercial and industrial policy made it possible for slow growth rates in productivity to persist during a period when the world was undergoing major transformations.

Initiated in 1988 and expanded in 1991, changes in industrial and foreign trade policies aimed at altering the "closed" development style, which consisted of little competition and poor economic efficiency. This closed style contributed to the decline of the economic and technological dynamism of the Brazilian economy during the 1980s. Beginning in the mid-1970s, the government began to place greater restrictions on international trade, which had important consequences for relative remuneration of sales to domestic and foreign markets (Silber 1991).

In this process, the exchange rate policy will be the most important instrument in eliminating the anti-export bias, a characteristic of an autarkic economy such as the Brazilian one. The exchange rate policy should be part of a larger set of industrial policy measures aimed at revamping the country's competitive capacity at the international level.

The tariff reform completed in 1995, together with the elimination of non-tariff restrictions and special import regimes, will make it possible for the tariff system to recapture its role as the country's main import policy instrument. The revised tariff system will function as an instrument of general application and as such will decrease the level and dispersion of nominal protection; it also will eliminate the import policy's discretionary, subjective, and unstable character (which has not been guided by the rationality of an industrial policy but by the restrictions imposed by balance of payments problems).

It should be noted, additionally, that the opening of the economy to the international market permits the following to occur: the realization of economies of scale, the increased attraction of foreign investment, and the enjoyment of external economies resulting from the domestic economy's increased competitiveness as it is gradually exposed to international competition.

Table 4
## Exports, Imports, GDP, and Degree of Openness*
## 1975-1990
(US$ billions)

|       | World | | | Brazil | | |
|-------|-------------------|----------|---------|-------------------|-------|----------|
| Year  | Export +Import    | GDP      | Openess | Export +Import    | GDP   | Openness |
| 1975  | 1,638.3           | 5,250.0  | 15.6    | 20.5              | 124.3 | 8.3      |
| 1976  | 1,857.3           | 5,729.0  | 16.2    | 22.3              | 152.3 | 7.3      |
| 1977  | 2,118.9           | 6,588.3  | 16.3    | 23.9              | 175.8 | 6.8      |
| 1978  | 2,455.4           | 7,754.4  | 15.8    | 26.1              | 208.3 | 6.3      |
| 1979  | 3,104.5           | 9,588.3  | 16.2    | 33.2              | 234.2 | 7.1      |
| 1980  | 3,838.4           | 11,939.7 | 16.1    | 45.1              | 239.1 | 9.4      |
| 1981  | 3,786.7           | 11,833.8 | 16.0    | 47.4              | 263.0 | 9.0      |
| 1982  | 3,535.0           | 12,859.7 | 13.7    | 41.2              | 270.4 | 7.6      |
| 1983  | 3,428.6           | 12,882.6 | 13.3    | 38.7              | 205.9 | 9.4      |
| 1984  | 3,651.5           | 13,373.3 | 13.7    | 42.2              | 212.6 | 9.9      |
| 1985  | 3,687.1           | 13,853.8 | 13.3    | 40.0              | 227.9 | 8.8      |
| 1986  | 4,053.4           | 16,624.4 | 12.2    | 37.9              | 280.2 | 6.7      |
| 1987  | 4,774.0           | 18,142.6 | 13.2    | 42.8              | 323.6 | 6.6      |
| 1988  | 5,461.9           | 19,547.2 | 14.0    | 49.9              | 333.0 | 7.5      |
| 1989  | 5,912.2           | 22,976.7 | 12.9    | 54.4              | 336.3 | 8.1      |
| 1990  | 6,760.0           | 24,632.8 | 13.7    | 53.9              | 339.7 | 7.9      |

Note: * Degree of openness is defined as the ratio of the average volume of foreign trade (average of export and import totals) to the GDP, measured in percentage terms.
Source: IMF, *International Financial Statistics*, several issues.

For the Brazilian economy to remain isolated from the rest of the world with a captive domestic market for national producers is to condemn the country to technological backwardness, which would ultimately eliminate the country from the export market for manufactures. To a large extent, the stagnation of the 1980s is the result of this strategy, and the consequences could get worse if the country decides to increase its isolation. The statistical information presented in Tables 4, 5, and 6 provides an indication of the Brazilian economy's growing isolation from global flows of trade from 1975 to 1990.

A recently adopted alternative is to open the economy to the world gradually, a strategy that will permit increased rates of economic growth, greater opportunities and improved prospects for investment, higher real salaries, fewer disparities in income distribution, and an enlarged domestic market. Gains associated with greater international specialization may be obtained in a short period of time, mainly due to the Brazilian economy's relative isolation and limited participation in world trade until the 1990s.

In an economy with high levels of protection, companies tend to be less efficient because they are faced with many restrictions on the allocation of production factors and on choices of components for the final product. Absence of foreign competition and imperfections in the domestic capital market help maintain oligopolist market structures with high entry barriers for new companies.

In this environment, there are few incentives to increase productivity, the scale of production is less than optimal, technology becomes outdated relative to the rest of the world, and domestic prices are relatively higher.

A reform of foreign trade policy is an attempt to induce modernization into the production structure by reducing the average levels of protection of the domestic market. The main results obtained from 1988 to 1991, and proposed changes through 1994 follow. In 1988 and 1989, several changes were introduced to reduce the discretionary character of Brazil's trade policy: the redundance of import tariffs was reduced, taxes on foreign purchases were unified (through the elimination of IOF and the port improvement tax), special import regimes were partially removed, and the number of products subject to previous licensing for exports was reduced.

This first attempt to liberalize the external sector had produced the following results: the average import tariff was reduced from approximately 40 percent to 25 percent, and the partial elimination of special regimes reached 15 percent of the value of favored imports. Few non-tariff restrictions were eliminated, however, and the entire bureaucratic structure responsible for the administration of international trade was maintained.

Furthermore, the structure of the effective protection of several sectors of the Brazilian economy changed significantly, particularly in favor of capital goods and consumer goods sectors.[2]

Table 5
Basic Commercial Relations between the Domestic and External Markets
1980-1989
(percent)

| Countries | Degree of Economic Openness | | | | Import Share in Domestic Market* | | | | Share of Exports in GDP | | | |
|---|---|---|---|---|---|---|---|---|---|---|---|---|
| | 1980 | 1983 | 1987 | 1990 | 1980 | 1983 | 1987 | 1990 | 1980 | 1983 | 1987 | 1990 |
| Argentina | 8.0 | 12.2 | 8.0 | 14.6 | 9.0 | 10.3 | 6.4 | 10.6 | 6.7 | 14.7 | 9.8 | 19.7 |
| Australia | 17.4 | 15.3 | 17.0 | 15.4 | 13.7 | 15.8 | 17.5 | 14.8 | 17.0 | 14.5 | 16.3 | 16.3 |
| Brazil | 10.0 | 10.1 | 7.0 | 6.4 | 10.8 | 9.1 | 5.7 | 5.6 | 8.9 | 11.2 | 8.5 | 7.2 |
| Canada | 27.4 | 23.8 | 25.9 | 25.0 | 26.9 | 22.9 | 25.7 | 24.9 | 28.3 | 25.5 | 26.2 | 25.2 |
| Chile | 21.0 | 22.7 | 28.6 | 33.8 | 22.0 | 21.9 | 27.8 | 32.5 | 19.3 | 24.0 | 30.5 | 37.4 |
| Colombia | 13.6 | 11.9 | 14.9 | 16.8 | 14.9 | 12.9 | 13.4 | 14.6 | 15.4 | 10.5 | 17.0 | 20.0 |
| France | 22.1 | 22.6 | 20.8 | 22.7 | 22.5 | 22.6 | 20.7 | 22.7 | 21.5 | 22.5 | 20.9 | 22.6 |
| India | 8.3 | 7.4 | 7.1 | 8.4 | 9.7 | 8.3 | 8.1 | 9.1 | 6.6 | 6.4 | 5.8 | 7.5 |
| Indonesia | 26.1 | 25.4 | 23.2 | 25.5 | 24.2 | 28.8 | 23.2 | 25.2 | 29.7 | 27.7 | 26.0 | 25.9 |
| Italy | 21.9 | 20.5 | 18.2 | 19.5 | 23.0 | 20.8 | 18.2 | 19.6 | 19.8 | 20.0 | 18.0 | 19.2 |
| Japan | 15.3 | 14.6 | 10.9 | 10.0 | 15.6 | 13.9 | 9.3 | 9.4 | 14.9 | 15.5 | 12.8 | 10.7 |
| Mexico | 13.0 | 14.5 | 10.9 | 16.1 | 13.4 | 10.5 | 9.2 | 13.5 | 12.6 | 19.5 | 13.0 | 19.7 |
| Nigeria | 26.3 | 28.3 | 24.6 | 25.0 | 27.9 | 13.4 | 17.3 | 21.7 | 28.8 | 12.8 | 27.6 | 30.9 |
| Spain | 17.0 | 21.6 | 19.1 | 18.8 | 17.7 | 21.7 | 18.3 | 19.8 | 15.8 | 21.3 | 20.2 | 17.2 |
| South Korea | 37.6 | 37.1 | 40.7 | 31.9 | 38.5 | 37.3 | 39.8 | 32.0 | 33.7 | 36.5 | 44.9 | 31.6 |
| Thailand | 27.2 | 24.0 | 29.0 | 40.2 | 28.3 | 25.7 | 29.0 | 40.8 | 24.5 | 20.3 | 29.0 | 36.8 |
| United Kingdom | 26.1 | 26.2 | 26.8 | 26.0 | 25.6 | 26.0 | 27.0 | 26.5 | 27.2 | 26.7 | 26.3 | 24.8 |
| United States | 10.4 | 8.7 | 9.1 | 10.5 | 10.7 | 9.4 | 10.4 | 11.1 | 10.2 | 7.9 | 7.4 | 9.9 |
| West Germany | 28.7 | 30.2 | 29.0 | 33.2 | 28.7 | 29.7 | 27.8 | 32.1 | 28.5 | 31.3 | 31.8 | 36.4 |

Note: *The concept of domestic market is represented by the GDP minus exports plus imports of goods and services.
Source: IMF, *International Financial Statistics*, several issues.

## Table 6
## Technical Import Coefficients by Industry*

| Sector | 1974 | 1977 | 1980 | 1983 | 1987 |
|---|---|---|---|---|---|
| Non-metallic Minerals | 3.16 | 1.82 | 1.43 | 0.66 | 0.71 |
| Metallurgy | 8.04 | 3.96 | 5.54 | 3.22 | 3.43 |
| Mechanics | 10.34 | 5.76 | 5.70 | 3.21 | 3.48 |
| Electrical Material | 18.90 | 11.03 | 9.03 | 8.07 | 5.50 |
| Transport Material | 6.89 | 4.79 | 5.50 | 4.57 | 6.25 |
| Wood | 1.17 | 0.64 | 1.22 | 1.36 | 1.07 |
| Furniture | 0.56 | 0.24 | 0.38 | 0.06 | 0.04 |
| Paper and Cardboard | 7.41 | 3.27 | 2.44 | 1.16 | 1.38 |
| Rubber | 7.54 | 6.17 | 4.43 | 2.85 | 5.53 |
| Hide and Skin | 3.19 | 1.42 | 1.57 | 1.37 | 3.10 |
| Chemical | 16.97 | 16.00 | 14.03 | 8.33 | 4.87 |
| Veterinary and Pharmaceutical Products | 15.53 | 10.77 | 13.51 | 11.87 | 12.43 |
| Perfumery, Soaps, Candles | 6.38 | 1.98 | 2.84 | 1.74 | 1.14 |
| Plastic Products | 9.23 | 3.62 | 2.50 | 1.72 | 1.63 |
| Textile | 4.69 | 1.27 | 1.23 | 0.76 | 0.93 |
| Apparel, Footwear and Textile Products | 1.23 | 0.76 | 0.7 | 1.57 | 0.33 |
| Food Products | 2.10 | 1.06 | 1.68 | 0.88 | 1.42 |
| Beverage | 6.58 | 4.02 | 3.91 | 5.45 | 3.64 |
| Tobacco | 2.16 | 3.17 | 2.13 | 0.46 | 0.25 |
| Publishing and Editing | 4.65 | 1.94 | 3.07 | 2.66 | 1.88 |
| Miscellaneous | 13.09 | 7.22 | 7.76 | 5.18 | 3.16 |
| Total | 8.14 | 5.04 | 5.58 | 3.86 | 3.70 |

Note: * The import coefficient was obtained by dividing the total value of foreign products purchases by the total value of sales, multiplied by 100.
Source: Ministério da Fazenda, *IPI-Informações Tributárias*, several years.

In 1990, the foreign trade policy reform was expanded with the following objectives:

1. To replace the minidevaluation system with a system of market exchange rates;

2. To eliminate all special import regimes (with the exception of "drawback," the Manaus Free Trade Zone [Zona Franca de Manaus], and international agreements) as well as administrative controls on imports; and

3. To introduce a generalized reduction in legal tariffs until the year 1994, with the objective of reaching an average tariff of 14.2 percent at the end of that year, with a small standard deviation (about 7.9).

These changes represent an important transformation in Brazil's international trade policy and have important impacts on the level of production of different segments of the economy. The country is reducing protection significantly for the first time on the domestic market and eliminating many administrative controls on imports.

On average, the nominal protection, which was about 32.2 percent in 1990, will decrease to 14.2 percent in 1994. The structure of import tariffs to be in place in 1995 has been defined by means of criteria based on an evaluation of the productive chain, comparisons of international prices, and tariffs on inputs.

The most frequently used nominal tariff is 20 percent, with a minimum of 0 percent for the following products: products for which Brazil has clear comparative advantages, products not domestically produced, and products with low value added and high international transportation costs. The highest tariffs were placed on durable consumption goods (30 to 35 percent), with the maximum nominal protection given to informatics (40 percent).

Certain basic parameters of the tariff structure that will be in place after 1990 are presented in Table 7.

### Table 7
### Import Tariffs
(percent)

| Years | Average | Standard Deviation |
|-------|---------|--------------------|
| 1989  | 41.0    | 19.1               |
| 1990  | 32.2    | 19.6               |
| 1991  | 25.3    | 17.4               |
| 1992  | 21.2    | 14.2               |
| 1993  | 17.1    | 10.7               |
| 1994  | 14.2    | 7.9                |

Significant reductions in nominal tariffs took place between 1989 (the year immediately before the reform) and 1994. The average tariff will be approximately one-third of the tariff in place in 1989, with a similar reduction in its dispersion, making the tariff structure much more homogeneous.

A nominal tariff determines consumption decisions, while an effective tariff (on the value added) determines the allocation of production. The figures for effective protection available until the year 1994 indicate the direction of changes in the level of protection that will be observed in the following years. Data provided in Table 8 show that the level of effective protection in the future will approach the levels of nominal protection, since there will be a dramatic reduction in the variance of protection. Changes in tariffs clearly will benefit certain sectors, particularly those that received minimal protection under the previous structure, and will have a positive effective protection after the reform. Such sectors include agriculture, mineral extraction, transport materials, food, beverages and tobacco. Among the sectors that will receive more protection after the reforms are implemented are mechanics, transportation, hides and leather, perfumes, soaps and candles, food, beverages, and tobacco.

## Table 8
## Effective Protection per Industrial Sector*

| Sector | Implicit | 1991 | 1992 | 1993 | 1994 |
|---|---|---|---|---|---|
| Agriculture | (15.30) | 13.10 | 11.50 | 10.40 | 9.60 |
| Mineral Extraction | (15.20) | 1.38 | 0.28 | (0.29) | (0.36) |
| Non-metallic Minerals | 30.80 | 17.32 | 14.85 | 9.95 | 8.82 |
| Metallurgy | 44.80 | 27.41 | 23.35 | 19.82 | 16.89 |
| Mechanics | 14.00 | 34.71 | 29.65 | 24.09 | 23.06 |
| Electrical Material | 48.50 | 44.76 | 38.67 | 31.96 | 25.45 |
| Transport Material | (9.80) | 72.60 | 56.52 | 45.48 | 39.66 |
| Wood | 35.20 | 10.80 | 10.50 | 10.20 | 10.00 |
| Furniture | 68.20 | 42.70 | 31.50 | 25.00 | 26.40 |
| Paper and Cardboard | 42.20 | 10.46 | 10.45 | 10.46 | 10.46 |
| Rubber | 92.90 | 44.60 | 34.60 | 22.80 | 15.70 |
| Hide and Skin | 23.70 | 13.30 | 11.90 | 10.20 | 8.40 |
| Chemical | 42.40 | 11.35 | 10.00 | 8.58 | 8.22 |
| Veterinary and Pharmaceutical Products | 69.90 | 19.10 | 16.20 | 13.10 | 13.10 |
| Perfumery, Soaps and Candles | 81.30 | 64.80 | 40.90 | 33.90 | 26.10 |
| Plastic Products | 77.80 | 46.13 | 38.47 | 25.53 | 22.44 |
| Textile | 125.60 | 47.40 | 35.21 | 29.23 | 19.21 |
| Apparel, Footwear and Textile Products | 164.40 | 55.89 | 44.87 | 32.00 | 23.76 |
| Food Products | (1.30) | 27.51 | 22.26 | 19.16 | 16.43 |
| Beverage | (6.50) | 108.00 | 89.30 | 51.50 | 24.80 |
| Tobacco | (80.10) | 133.30 | 117.60 | 98.70 | 54.70 |
| Publishing and Editing | 1.90 | 10.80 | 9.20 | 8.80 | 8.40 |
| Miscellaneous | 84.20 | 43.20 | 35.10 | 27.10 | 20.40 |
| Industry Average | 45.10 | 46.70 | 38.80 | 31.00 | 24.60 |
| Standard Deviation | 52.50 | 33.20 | 29.60 | 25.60 | 20.90 |

Note: * Average weighted by value of production.
Source: Hahn 1992, 39.

With this information in mind, it is possible to identify those sectors that could become the winners and the losers in the process of import liberalization. Agriculture, mineral extraction, lumber, chemicals, and publishing and editing are sectors that should expand their activities because of a reduction in the levels of protection of the domestic market and the anti-export bias of the international trade policy. Sectors currently receiving the highest levels of effective protection will be natural candidates for a reorientation of their activities and a reduction in their participation in Brazilian industry. The following sectors fall into this category: electrical material, rubber, perfumes, pharmaceuticals, plastics, textiles, apparel, and footwear.

Given the high degree of diversification and verticalization of industry in São Paulo and in Brazil in general, there is no doubt that some activities — those that will be unable to reach international levels of competitiveness in a short period of time — will tend to disappear or at least decrease in importance.

On the other hand, other industries will benefit from the country's higher international specialization through a rejuvenation of its traditional industries. Automation and microelectronics will make important technological advances available to industries such as textiles, paper and paperboard, apparel, and transportation materials, sectors in which both the state of São Paulo and the country lost their relative positions in the world market during the 1980s.

Such results will become reality if the liberalization program is implemented effectively. Results as of 1992 indicate that substantial progress needs to be made in order to signal economic agents of an irreversible change in Brazil's international trade regime. The main problem with the external sector's liberalization program relates to the "timing" of that process. Initially intended to be implemented after the country achieved considerable economic stabilization, the plan was implemented in the midst of another anti-inflationary plan. Hence, fluctuations in real exchange rates, which were already very high in 1990 (about 50 percent), tended to persist and failed to signal a change in relative prices in favor of tradeable goods (for details, see Graph 1 and Table 9).

A devaluation of the real exchange rate and a virtual elimination of any fluctuation are necessary conditions for the success of the liberalization program. There is no successful case in international experience of a program for liberalization of the external sector that was followed by valorization and fluctuations in real exchange rates. The overvalued exchange rate is one of the most critical elements of the Real Plan implemented in 1994.

An open conflict existed by 1992, when the exchange rate was being utilized either as an instrument of stabilization policy or as an instrument for liberalization of the external sector. Since the country had not advanced sufficiently in terms of economic stabilization by the early 1990s, there was a temptation to utilize the exchange rate as an instrument to control inflation. As a consequence, export growth, another important element of a liberalization program in the external sector, was viewed as difficult to obtain. (In 1991, the value of exports was lower than the 1988 level.)

Credibility of the liberalization program can only be obtained if administrative controls on imports are eliminated and if the exchange rate

## Table 9
## Real Exchange Rate Index

| Year | Real Exchange Rate Index[*] |
|------|------------------------------|
| 1970 | 87.3 |
| 1971 | 90.4 |
| 1972 | 93.4 |
| 1973 | 84.7 |
| 1974 | 77.1 |
| 1975 | 77.2 |
| 1976 | 74.2 |
| 1977 | 73.4 |
| 1978 | 83.4 |
| 1979 | 84.1 |
| 1980 | 94.4 |
| 1981 | 79.5 |
| 1982 | 74.1 |
| 1983 | 98.7 |
| 1984 | 100.0 |
| 1985 | 102.8 |
| 1986 | 103.9 |
| 1987 | 97.2 |
| 1988 | 93.4 |
| 1989 | 73.1 |
| 1090 | 64.7 |
| 1991 | 77.9 |

Note: [*] Real exchange rate is in U.S. dollars, taking the OECD GDP deflator as the world price index and the Brazilian GDP deflator as the domestic price index.

Sources: Banco Central do Brasil, *Conjuntura Econômica*, and author's calculations.

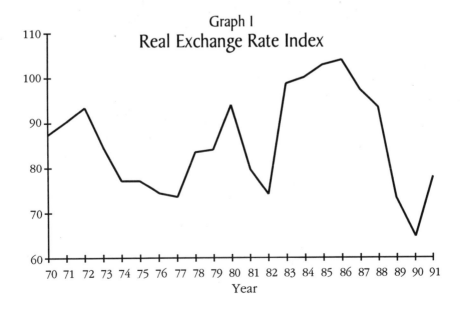

## Graph I
## Real Exchange Rate Index

signals a definitive change in favor of opening the external sector. This will be possible only at a later stage in the stabilization program.

## The Foreign Debt Problem

The foreign debt problem has its origins in two important developments. First, a drastic change occurred in U.S. economic policy at the beginning of the 1980s, when an expansionist fiscal policy and contractionist monetary policy raised international interest rates, appreciated the dollar, caused recession, and reduced the exports of debtor countries, ultimately forcing about 40 countries to default on their debts. Certain countries, particularly in Latin America, opted for an external adjustment strategy in the 1970s based on import substitution and foreign indebtedness, without considering an aggressive policy of export promotion. Such a strategy made these countries highly vulnerable to the shocks of international interest rates. In addition, a deterioration of public finances in these countries during the 1970s contributed decisively to recessive and inflationary outbreaks in the 1980s, making domestic adjustments impossible.

In the early 1990s, the problem of foreign debt continued to impose significant constraints on economic growth in four countries (Argentina, Brazil, Mexico, and Venezuela) and remained a problem of high exposure for the large North American banks.

A solution to this problem depended on at least three factors: 1) the evolution of the world economy, 2) the implementation of adjustments in domestic economies, and 3) a definition of some type of institutional reform at the international level that will make it possible to split the cost of external adjustment among private banks, governments of industrialized countries, and debtor countries.

In 1992, a consensus among debtor countries was that foreign debt (in accordance with the Brady Plan) should not be serviced in a conventional manner and that an ingress of new external funds is necessary for these countries to resume growth at rates compatible with those prior to the 1980s.

Regarding the evolution of the world economy during the coming years, much will depend on the way the United States deals with its domestic and external deficits and on the degree of cooperation of other Organization for Economic Cooperation and Development countries (particularly Germany and Japan) with respect to these problems.

Negotiation of Brazil's foreign debt should be analyzed within this context; this section first will examine its evolution. In 1974, immediately after the first oil shock, Brazil's net debt was approximately US$12 billion. The Brazilian strategy for adjusting to the external shock was to expand domestic supply (instead of constraining aggregate demand), increasing external indebtedness and resulting in an increase in the net debt to US$46 billion in

Table 10

## Evolution of Brazil's Balance of Payments

| | 1974 | 1979 | 1980 | 1982 | 1984 | 1986 | 1988 | 1990 |
|---|---|---|---|---|---|---|---|---|
| Trade Balance | (4,690) | (2,840) | (2,716) | 780 | 13,090 | 8,349 | 19,184 | 10,990 |
| Exports (FOB) | 7,951 | 15,244 | 20,234 | 20,175 | 27,005 | 22,394 | 33,789 | 31,414 |
| Imports (FOB) | 12,641 | 18,084 | 22,950 | 19,395 | 13,915 | 14,014 | 14,605 | 20,424 |
| Services | (2,433) | (7,920) | (10,152) | (17,083) | (13,215) | (12,912) | (15,103) | (14,025) |
| Profits and Dividends | (284) | (636) | (310) | (505) | (796) | (1,237) | (1,539) | (1,614) |
| Interest | (652) | (1,162) | (6,311) | (11,353) | (10,203) | (9,093) | (9,832) | (8,906) |
| Unilateral Transfers | 1 | 18 | 168 | (8) | 171 | 85 | 94 | 834 |
| Current Transfers | (7,122) | (10,742) | (12,807) | (13,311) | 41 | (4,476) | 4,175 | 1,777 |
| Capital | 6,254 | 7,657 | 9,679 | 7,851 | 253 | (7,340) | (8,685) | (3,450) |
| Investment | 887 | 1,685 | 1,487 | 992 | 1,077 | (109) | 2,270 | 380 |
| Borrowing and Financing | 7,355 | 11,228 | 10,596 | 12,515 | 10,401 | 3,096 | 2,845 | 3,425 |
| Amortization | (1,926) | (6,385) | (2,297) | (6,959) | (6,468) | (15,590) | (17,087) | (7,776) |
| Errors and Omissions | (68) | (130) | (343) | 360 | 402 | (540) | 833 | (31) |
| Superavit (+) Deficit (-) | (936) | (3,215) | (3,472) | (5,828) | 700 | (12,356) | (5,343) | (7,010) |
| Compensatory Capital | 936 | 3,215 | 3,472 | 5,828 | (700) | 12,356 | 5,343 | 7,010 |
| Short-term Assets | 784 | 3,325 | 3,507 | 3,083 | (7,168) | 3,504 | (1,332) | (481) |
| Gold | | | | 1,191 | | 352 | 83 | |
| Regularization Operations | | | 4,177 | 6,468 | 8,501 | 6,591 | | |
| IMF | (10) | (106) | (35) | 378 | | | | (741) |
| Short-term Debts | 162 | | | | | | 8,232 | |
| Reserves | 5,269 | 9,689 | 6,913 | 3,994 | 11,995 | 6,760 | 9,140 | 9,973 |
| Total Debt | 17,166 | 55,803 | 64,244 | 85,364 | 102,040 | 110,282 | 113,469 | 118,444 |

Note: The values expressed in parentheses are negative values.
Source: Central Bank of Brazil.

1979. Despite such extraordinary growth, the debt was not yet a matter of concern since export expansion guaranteed favorable conditions for servicing the debt at prevailing rates in the international market.

## Table 11
## Resource Transfers Abroad
### (US$ millions)

| Years | Real transfers[1] (A) | Financial transfers[2] (B) | GDP (C) | % (A/C) | % (B/C) |
|---|---|---|---|---|---|
| 1970 | (165) | (230) | 42.2 | (0.39) | (0.54) |
| 1971 | (831) | (901) | 49.1 | (1.69) | (1.84) |
| 1972 | (893) | (974) | 58.0 | (1.54) | (1.68) |
| 1973 | (958) | (1,003) | 79.6 | (1.20) | (1.26) |
| 1974 | (6,135) | (6,222) | 104.9 | (5.85) | (5.93) |
| 1975 | (4,978) | (4,827) | 124.3 | (4.00) | (3.88) |
| 1976 | (3,618) | (3,829) | 152.3 | (2.38) | (2.51) |
| 1977 | (1,132) | (1,479) | 175.8 | (0.64) | (0.84) |
| 1978 | (2,242) | (2,744) | 208.3 | (1.08) | (1.32) |
| 1979 | (4,523) | (5,938) | 234.2 | (1.93) | (2.54) |
| 1980 | (5,027) | (6,354) | 239.1 | (2.10) | (2.66) |
| 1981 | (710) | (2,402) | 263.0 | (0.27) | (0.91) |
| 1982 | (1,869) | (4,364) | 270.4 | (0.69) | (1.61) |
| 1983 | 4,902 | 3,368 | 205.9 | 2.38 | 1.64 |
| 1984 | 11,841 | 10,873 | 212.6 | 5.57 | 5.11 |
| 1985 | 11,499 | 10,325 | 227.9 | 5.05 | 4.53 |
| 1986 | 7,068 | 15,620 | 280.2 | 2.52 | 5.57 |
| 1987 | 8,819 | 10,583 | 323.6 | 2.73 | 3.27 |
| 1988 | 16,166 | 11,277 | 333.0 | 4.85 | 3.39 |
| 1989 | 13,334 | 11,910 | 336.3 | 3.96 | 3.54 |
| 1990 | 9,059 | 11,518 | 339.7 | 2.67 | 3.39 |

Notes: [1] Trade Balance plus non-factor services (freight, insurance, international travel, government services).
[2] Interest plus profits and dividends plus other services less net foreign capital inflows (including compensatory capital and unilateral transfers).
Sources: Baumann 1989 and Central Bank of Brazil.

The situation dramatically changed after 1980, with a rapid increase in interest rates, declining rates of export growth, and disappearance of the voluntary financing of the external debt after 1982. To highlight the significance of such dramatic changes, in 1979 interest rates on the net debt were 2.5 percent, export revenues grew 20 percent more than in the previous year, and the current account deficit (excluding interest) was US$9.58 billion. In 1982, however, the situation was completely different: export revenues were 13.5 percent lower than the previous year, interest rates on the net debt had reached 14 percent, and the current account deficit (excluding interest) was $4.59 billion.

One must also take into account the importance of risk capital inflow to Brazil during a period of intense growth and a gradual reduction of such inflows as political and economic instability increased during the 1980s (see details in Table 10). Generally, in recent decades, Brazil has concentrated its opening to the world capital market much more on borrowing capital than on risk capital, and this has had important consequences with respect to its capacity to honor payments as well as its economic growth.

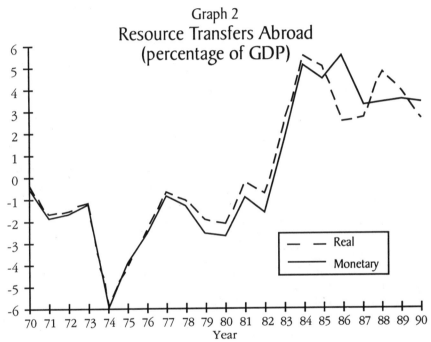

Graph 2
Resource Transfers Abroad
(percentage of GDP)

Data from Table 11 and Graph 2 show how the tendency to borrow constantly affected the Brazilian economy: when real interest rates became strongly positive in the world market during the first half of the 1980s, the country no longer had a positive net inflow of foreign capital (in real terms) but a real outflow of resources at a level nearly reaching 5.6 percent of GDP in 1984.

During the 1983-1985 period, the diagnosis of foreign debt problems in countries like Brazil was that these were problems of liquidity and not problems of insolvency. Therefore, once a network of financial support was in place, it would be possible for these countries to regain external equilibrium and voluntarily return, in the medium term, to the international private financial market to finance their development programs.

The stabilization programs implemented under IMF conditionalities became extremely detrimental to domestic growth since they resulted in a further reduction of investment. Table 12 provides an indication of the magnitude of such adjustments.

### Table 12
## Gross Fixed Capital Formation (I) and Balance of Payments' Current Account Balance Excluding Interest (X) as a Percent of GDP

| Periods | I/GDP | X/GDP |
|---|---|---|
| 1977/1982 | 22.3 | -2.1 |
| 1983/1985 | 18.5 | 4.9 |

Sources: *Revista Conjuntura Econômica*, May 1987; and IMF, *International Financial Statistics*, 1988.

During this period, investments fluctuated around 22.3 percent of GDP with a net inflow of foreign resources equivalent to 2.1 percent of GDP. The situation was reversed completely in the 1983-1985 period when investments fell to 18.5 percent of GDP, and the net flow of resources became negative.

Moreover, it became clear that the crisis was not short-lived and that protectionist trends in industrialized countries could place serious restrictions on the expansion of exports by debtor countries. It should also be noted that there was no possibility for the debtor countries to return to the private international financial market.

As debtor countries realized that they would have to transfer resources abroad for several years, they began to challenge such an alternative openly. It is apparent that all the actors involved (debtor countries, creditor banks, multilateral institutions, and governments of industrialized countries) are looking for an unorthodox solution. As of 1992, the situation is ambiguous and the spectrum of cases is quite extensive. For example, some countries, such as South Korea, have been able to service their debt in a conventional manner (that is, through substantial increases in exports), while other countries, including many in Africa, already have had their debt forgiven (concentrated in official banks). Large Latin American debtors are in an intermediary situation — they go through alternating periods of default and uneasy relations with creditors to periods when they follow conventional rules of debt service so that they may be granted concessions in terms of rescheduling the principal, reducing the spread, and obtaining additional credits from multilateral agencies.

Several solutions have been proposed to resolve the problem of the external debt of developing countries, including capitalizing overdue interest rates, converting debts into investment, securitizing, pegging the debt service to export revenues, buying back the debt at discount, voluntarily reducing the debt, and others. The most important elements in the debt renegotiation process are beyond the control of the main actors involved since interest rates depend on the macroeconomic policies of industrialized countries and since the rate of export expansion basically depends on the growth of world income. If international growth rates excel and international interest rates decline in the near future, debt renegotiation will be greatly facilitated. On the contrary, the problem will be to administer the distribution of the debt-reduction value among other debtor countries, creditor banks, multilateral institutions, and governments of industrialized countries.

Therefore, the crucial element in a favorable evolution of the debt problem is the positive performance of the global economy. In particular, if the United States reduces its trade and fiscal deficits and if other industrialized countries adopt an accommodative monetary policy and expansionary fiscal policies, a sustained growth of world income and lower interest rates could be achieved, and debtor countries could benefit significantly.

Outside this framework, consistent macroeconomic policies pursued by debtor countries would increase their bargaining power greatly at the international level and allow them to obtain lower spreads, new financing, and greater maturity periods, in addition to providing them with the possibility of implementing securitization programs and implementing programs for converting debt into investment.

Through the simultaneous use of these instruments, it will be possible to decrease the level of resource transfers from debtor countries to the rest of the world and to expand investments necessary for economic growth that suffered dramatic declines during the 1980s.

The Brazilian proposal concerning renegotiation of its debt should be similar to agreements recently signed by other countries (the Philippines, Mexico, and Venezuela) that contemplated a reduction of the value of the principal and service. A variety of instruments are included in these agreements, ranging from zero coupon bonds (bonds in which interests are capitalized until the end of the term) to conversion of debt into investments for the purpose of reconciling the interests of both debtors and creditors.

From the point of view of Brazil, which aims at achieving greater insertion in the world economy, the sooner such an agreement is reached, the easier it will be for the country to reach its objective of external market liberalization. A conflicting, antagonistic stance toward the world financial community would complicate dialogue between the governments of debtor countries and multilateral agencies and ultimately would have a negative effect on Brazil's foreign trade.[3]

# Notes

———

1.   It should be noted that the "Index of Comparative Advantages" reflects not only the competitive advantages of countries but also the distortions in international trade resulting from government policies (export subsidies, import tariffs, non-tariff restrictions, and so forth).

2.   For more information, see Kume 1990.

3.   It is worth mentioning that at the time of this printing, many of the changes suggested and outcomes predicted in this chapter have occurred.

# References

Baumann, R. 1989. *Comportamento Recente do Capital Estrangeiro - Algumas Considerações Gerais*. Discussion Paper no. 5. Brasília: IPEA/IPLAN/UnB.

Braga, C.P., and C.L. Martone. 1987. *Trade Policies and the Performance of the Export Sector*. São Paulo: Fundação Instituto de Pesquisas Econômicas/The Rockfeller Foundation Conference on Brazil and the Uruguay Round (mimeo).

Carvalho, J.L. 1985. "Liberación de las restricciones comerciales en Brasil." *Comércio Exterior*. (Mexico: Banco Nacional de Comercio Exterior): 1141-1152. (1st part).

Cavalho, J.L. 1986. "Liberación de las restricciones comerciales en Brasil." *Comercio Exterior* (Mexico: Banco Nacional de Comercio Exterior) 36(1). (2nd part).

Finger, M., and Olechowski. 1990. *The Uruguay Round*. Washington, D.C.: The World Bank.

Hahn, L.M.M. 1992. "A Reforma Tarifária em 1990." *Revista Brasileira de Comércio Exterior* 8(30): 35-41.

International Monetary Fund (IMF). *International Financial Statistics*, 1960-1990. Washington, D.C.

Kume, H. 1990. *A Política de Importação Recente e a Reforma Tarifária*. Ph.D. dissertation, University of São Paulo, FEA.

Luque, C., G. Dias, R. Macedo, and S. Silber. 1988. *Sair da Crise*. São Paulo: IBCB.

Ministério da Fazenda. *IPI- Informações Tributárias*, 1960-1990.

Moreira, H.C., and A. Barboza. 1984. *Política Brasileira de Importações: Uma Descrição*. Série Estudos de Política Industrial e de Comércio Exterior, no. 1. Rio de Janeiro: IPEA/INPES.

Nunnenkamp, P., and Fasano Filho. 1986. *Manufactured Export Performance of Brazil: Analysis of Determinants and Prospects*. Kiel: Working Paper no. 269.

Silber, S.D. 1983. *The Export Performance at the Firm Level*. Ph.D. dissertation, Yale University.

Silber, S.D. 1991. *Brazilian Trade Policies*. Paper presented to the Second Florida Brazil Institute Conference on U.S.-Brazil Trade Relations (mimeo).

Silber, S.D., et al. 1990. *Livre para Crescer*. São Paulo: Cultura Editores Associados.

The World Bank. 1983. *Brazil: Industrial Policies and Manufactured Exports*. Washington, D.C.

United Nations. *Commodity Trade Statistics*. Several issues. New York.

United Nations. 1967. *Standardized Input-Output Tables of Economic Commission for European Countries for Years Around 1965*. New York.

SEVEN

# Brazil's Exchange Rate Regime

## Álvaro Antônio Zini, Jr.

## Introduction

The exchange rate is one of the basic relative prices of market economies. Its importance stems from the use of this particular price in all transactions between the domestic economy and the rest of the world. By examining general analytical equilibrium models, a given exchange rate can be interpreted to be appropriate when it reflects 1) the country's external competitiveness and 2) economic agents' confidence in certain fundamental macroeconomic factors. The concept, however, conceals important difficulties regarding its empirical application.

This chapter focuses on an analysis of the exchange rate regime in Brazil as of the early 1990s and discussion of the possibility of making it compatible with the opening of Brazil's economy to the international market launched in 1990. Additionally, the text conceptualizes basic terms used in the literature for exchange rate regimes, with special attention to the system that has governed the exchange rate in Brazil.

Brazil's exchange rate regime operates under a monopoly; that is, only the Central Bank can deal legally with foreign exchange in the country or authorize other agents to operate in the market under its supervision. The determination of foreign exchange prices (exchange rates), however, should not be misconstrued as being determined within a monopolistic market. The exchange rate is established by market forces and by Central Bank interventions. Regulation of the exchange rate is guided by Laws 4131/62, 4330/64, and 4594/67.

Three exchange rates coexist within the market. The official exchange rate to the U.S. dollar is used in all transactions of goods and services as well as in capital transactions. It is established by the so-called floating exchange rate system. Before March 1990, it was established by the Central Bank under a "mini-devaluation policy" based on the movements of an index of domestic prices. The second type of exchange — the tourism exchange rate — is used for transactions of foreign currencies related to international travel. Finally, the "parallel" or black market rate is used in all transactions not authorized by the two official market rates.

The interventionist feature of the Brazilian exchange rate regime is quite old. Its origins can be found in the foreign exchange crises caused by fluctuations in revenues derived from coffee exports at the beginning of the twentieth century. This regime operated under several schemes of exchange rate determination before the adoption of the mini-devaluation policy, which began in 1968 and lasted until February 1990. In response to demands for a progressive liberalization of the exchange rate policy, a tourism exchange rate was authorized in 1989, marking the beginning of a period with a more flexible exchange rate market. In March 1990, a final important change was applied when the Ministry of Economy announced the adoption of a floating exchange rate. The Central Bank's intervention was restricted to the licensing of agents to operate in the market. Since then, a floating exchange rate system has been in place. Technically it could be regarded as a "dirty" floating scheme since the market is free to determine the relationship between the dollar and the *cruzeiro* (the Brazilian currency prior to the *real* in 1994), while it is subject to Central Bank interventions that smooth out fluctuations and establish a price for the dollar.

The mini-devaluation exchange rate policy existing in the 1970s and 1980s also could be regarded as a "dirty" floating scheme, although there was less freedom during these years than in the 1990s. The exchange rate during the 1970s and 1980s was not fixed; that is, the nominal exchange rate fluctuated. Nor was it freely determined by market forces since only transactions authorized by the government could be carried out. What existed and continues to exist is an administered floating exchange rate, with high levels of intervention in early years, aimed at maintaining the currency at a certain real parity level. The difference between the floating system of the 1990s and the mini-devaluations of the earlier period is that the Central Bank was no longer obligated to make daily adjustments to the exchange rate, and its obligation to maintain a certain fixed parity became more flexible. The relevant question posed at the beginning of the 1990s was whether the current regime will permit a realignment of the exchange rate with the country's external competitiveness so that the external sector may play its designated role, allowing a vigorous insertion of the Brazilian economy into the current trend of modernization in the international economy.

In order to adapt the exchange rate to the objective of opening the economy to the external market, three alternative approaches to exchange rate policy recently proposed in Brazil are discussed in this chapter. The first proposal contemplates a return to the mini-devaluation system under the administration of the Central Bank, which introduces corrections in exchange rules. The second proposes a system of dual exchange rates, keeping one rate under control while allowing the other to be determined by the market (floating rate). The third proposal defends the adoption of a free market system for the determination of exchange rates.

This chapter is organized into four sections following the introduction. The first explains the sector's institutional organization and presents the evolution of recent practices and norms adopted by the exchange rate system in Brazil. The second discusses three proposals for modifications to exchange rate rules and also appraises the costs and benefits associated with each of these propositions. The third section provides a critical evaluation of the exchange rate policy at the end of the 1980s and the beginning of the 1990s, analyzing the real exchange rate indicators during the period. The fourth section offers some conclusions.

## The Exchange Rate Markets and the Institutional Organization

Using general equilibrium models, it is possible to demonstrate that the exchange rate is adequate when it reflects the external competitiveness of a country and confidence of economic agents in fundamental macroeconomic factors. Though relatively easy to understand, this statement conceals important practical difficulties that are revealed only by determining empirically the "equilibrium" exchange rate for an economy. In practice, this question has been approached from two different angles: either the market has to find the equilibrium as in a floating system, or the government itself arbitrates the exchange rate in an administered system. Between the two positions, there are variations on the types of transactions that are allowed 1) when the system is a "clean" or "dirty" floating system (in which government's interventions are disguised) or 2) when the system follows the administered scheme with a fixed or indexed exchange rate (that is, whether the government pursues a given nominal exchange rate or a real exchange rate). Both solutions, however, involve many problems and limitations. The decision to adopt either alternative must be based on hypotheses concerning how the economy works and on societal preferences.

Brazil's exchange rate regime, as indicated earlier, functions under a monopolistic exchange market. The country's residents, including the national financial system, are obliged accordingly to submit all transactions in foreign currencies to the Central Bank for approval. Three exchange rates coexist in the current market: an official exchange rate, which is the basic rate in the whole system, established by the floating system, discretely controlled by the government, and used in a majority of foreign exchange transactions; tourism exchange rate, which is used in transactions for which the dollar price is determined by the demand and supply of foreign exchange by tourists; and the black market, in which all transactions not authorized by the Central Bank are performed. From a legal point of view, the black market's operations are ambiguous, as transactions carried out in foreign currency outside the legal markets are not allowed by the country's laws, yet the possession of foreign currency is. In practice, the black market is tolerated by the government.

During the 1980s, as new external financing became unavailable, the official market operated under the restriction of having to supply the foreign exchange necessary to honor the foreign debt. The country was left with a negative external balance of payments (liquid reserves less payments overdue) on two or three occasions. In July 1989, for instance, with the non-concession of new loans established during the external debt renegotiation with creditor banks, the Ministry of Economy suspended interest payments to foreign commercial banks and centralized all foreign exchange transactions within the Central Bank. Based on reviews of the country's priorities for external payments, international payments could be made only after receiving authorization from the Central Bank. Although those banks that were operating in the external sector were able to continue their operations through their own foreign subsidiaries or correspondents abroad, all operations had to wait for approval, and all foreign exchange surpluses were subject to withdrawal from the market by the Central Bank. The main effect of this centralization process was that all external payments were subject to scheduling by the Central Bank. The regime then included the rationing of foreign exchange.[1]

The foreign exchange monopoly on which the Brazilian exchange system rests has been eroded partially by the creation of alternative mechanisms on parallel markets for overcoming official controls over foreign exchange. An expressed increase in the use of the extra-official mechanisms of purchase, sale, and remittance of foreign currencies was observed during the 1980s. From an operational point of view, these mechanisms indicated that there were a number of foreign exchange transactions performed in the country that were not carried out through the Central Bank, thereby creating a sort of parallel balance of payments in the economy. This balance, by definition, must be in "equilibrium" as the exchange rate adjusts freely to clear the market. The notion of equilibrium, in this context, refers to the short-run equilibrium rate established in a specific market. The rate should not be confused with what economists refer to as "fundamental equilibrium." The supply and demand of foreign currencies in the black market originate from several sources. The following factors can be cited as demand-side sources:

- Portfolio investments of the country's residents in foreign currency;
- Smuggled imports, particularly of products whose legal import is not allowed;

- Payments to services, such as tourism, and to factors of production and others when restricted in the official market due to laws or administrative controls; and
- Repatriation of capital not registered in the Central Bank.

On the supply side, the main sources are the following:

- Underinvoicing of exports and overinvoicing of imports;
- Smuggled exports (coffee, soybeans, gold, and others);[2]
- Inflow of capital not registered in the Central Bank; and
- Receipts of payments for services performed, primarily from tourism.

A basic difference between the two official markets and the black market is that the former are legal and therefore authorized to operate within the banking system. All operations performed in these two markets are subject to Central Bank inspections and recorded in the balance of payments. Operations within the black market are not registered in the balance of payments account, due to market characteristics and, consequently, do not affect the country's position in terms of international reserves.

Another important development in recent years was the emergence of several market arbitrage and hedge mechanisms. Among these mechanisms, the following are the most important:

1. Future market and gold options, with the Central Bank exerting arbitrage on international prices;
2. Foreign currency deposits in the Central Bank by exporters and importers;
3. Dollar-indexed federal bonds;
4. Exchange market for *cruzeiros* in Montevideo, Uruguay, particularly important for "tourism dollar" transactions;
5. Financial market in dollars, invested abroad, based (ballasted) on assets of Brazilian residents, estimated at around US$35 to US$40 billion in 1990;
6. Exchange of dollars for gold and vice-versa among licensed financial institutions and the Central Bank; and
7. Authorization to issue dollar-indexed debentures to exporters (bonds with three or more years of maturity) and short-term export notes of up to 90 days' maturity.

The tourism exchange market, in contrast, was authorized by Resolution 1557 in 1988. Its organization is very specific: banks, tourism agencies, and hotels must be licensed by the Central Bank to operate in the market. The market buys foreign currencies from tourists and sells them to Brazilian tourists with valid passports and proof of international travel. The sales limit is US$4,000 per person. The system began its operations in January 1989, and the exchange rate in this market soon was pegged to the black market rate. An almost perfect arbitrage is observed in these two markets.[3]

Information provided by the Central Bank for the first two years of operation in the tourism market shows that the system expanded rapidly and has consolidated. There are 573 authorized agents with 1,427 sales offices. In 1989, a total of US$7.2 billion was negotiated — US$3.7 billion in purchases and US$3.5 billion in sales. Commercial banks were responsible for about 80 percent of operations, and travel agents accounted for approximately 12 percent of the total. It is important to mention that a large part of the dollars channeled into this market came from the black market, which relieves the Central Bank from having to maintain liquidity to operate. The item "International Travel" in the balance of payments showed a deficit of US$600 million in 1988, followed by a surplus of US$474 million in 1989, and a small deficit of US$122 million in 1990.

Operations in the "tourism market" did not destabilize other markets, in part because of a specific regulation issued for this sector whereby all operations are registered with regional agencies of the Central Bank on the same day. In addition, operators cannot function without a match or "overbooked" when they accumulate assets in foreign currency. Nor can they operate "underbooked," accumulating liabilities.

Regarding the official exchange rate market, the sector's organization has been consolidated for many years. Its objectives are to allow a reasonable degree of control by the Central Bank, the agency responsible for supervision; to facilitate the rationing of foreign exchange when necessary; and, in a broader sense, to allow the public sector to transfer income from the export sector to other sectors. In spite of its consolidation, the system is not immune to fraud. As occurs in any rationing system, it is vulnerable to corruption during periods of high rationing, especially in the case of the concession of quotas by the old Cacex (Caixa Amortizadora de Comércio Exterior). The need to resort constantly to explicit rationing measures during the 1980s created a diversity of superimposed rules that ultimately eroded the system. The instability and arbitrariness of many of these rules stimulated a search for alternative mechanisms, which resulted in the black market.

The organization of the official market involves several elements. There is a meticulous system of accounting for banks that are authorized to operate the system and every type of operation and remittance allowed. There is a system of verification of all commercial transactions to check the validity of foreign exchange operations and the accuracy of practiced prices. It involves the old Cacex in the concession of import permits and verification of import and export prices and the customs authorities for the inspection of merchandise being loaded and unloaded. Only banks and exchange brokers authorized by the Central Bank can operate in the system, and all transactions must follow specific regulations in place in these institutions.

It is also necessary to mention that the exchange rate control system in Brazil is one of the most efficient among developing countries. The logic behind the system is to manage the shortage of foreign exchange, when necessary, or to permit sectoral income transfers. Accordingly, there are periods in which the rationing of foreign exchange takes precedence over other considerations or over more general rationality criteria and allocative efficiency. The centralization of foreign exchange is an example of such a practice. The system, however, operates with reasonable ease due in large part to the system's well-consolidated structure. In fact, the concept that the state must intervene in international payments is old, its origins found in the 1906 Taubaté Agreement established to protect coffee producers following a large drop in international coffee prices. The intervention system was expanded in the 1930s when the external shocks and impacts of the Great Depression caused export revenues to drop. This same system permitted the transfer of income from the export sector to the import sector during the period from 1940 to 1970.

## Alternative Policies and Their Implications

There are three sets of proposals to change the rules that govern the exchange rate regime in Brazil. The first maintains that exchange rates be determined by monetary authorities according to mini-devaluation policies, although with the incorporation of additional criteria into the policy. The second proposes a larger dual system of exchange rates. The third supports the determination of exchange rates through market forces aimed at total market freedom. All three proposals have appeared in the debate on the Brazilian exchange rate system. Their positive and negative implications will be examined in this section.

### Proposal I

The first proposal consists of readopting mini-devaluation policies, maintaining the exchange rate under the control of monetary authorities, and incorporating additional criteria to maintain real parity. There are three additional criteria for this proposal. The first is to index the exchange rate to fluctuation in the wholesale price index, WPI (Indice de Preços por Atacado), which better reflects fluctuations in production costs. The second is to adopt the 1985 parity, which was reasonably aligned with the economy's international competitiveness and cannot be considered too high. Third, the policy needs to incorporate factors such as changes in the terms of trade and the income effects on trade. In periods of expansionary domestic demand or deterioration in the terms of trade, it is necessary to adjust the exchange rate to maintain its real value and preserve the equilibrium in the current account.[4]

## Proposal 2

Some analysts defend a more ample system of dual exchange rates as a transitional step toward the regime's complete liberalization. Accordingly, a given proportion of export revenues would be exchanged at the price established in free auctions, while the remaining revenues would be transacted at the official rate, which would be established by a mini-devaluation policy. There are a variety of alternative forms of the dual exchange rate system, differing with respect to the proportion of export revenues that go into auction (between 10 and 30 percent) or with respect to the types of transactions that are allowed at the free exchange rate. For instance, the proportion of export revenues could be fixed at 30 percent, while all imports, including superfluous goods, are transacted at a market rate, including, of course, all pertinent taxes. A more cautious alternative would allow 10 percent of export revenues plus the inflow of risk capital to be sold at auction, stipulating a list of products and items that could be acquired at the free market rate.

## Proposal 3

A free exchange regime (or a regime with a greater degree of fluctuation than the present one) is defended by other analysts who profess the need to let the market freely reflect the forces existing in it. The Central Bank would continue to exercise controls over the forms of payment authorized during the system's initial years but would not establish exchange rates. Exchange rates would be determined through exchange auctions, for which access would be restricted to authorized agents. To minimize the impact on public sector accounts, in case of a real devaluation, taxes may or may not be imposed on export revenues and import disbursements.

The views regarding the advantages and disadvantages of these different proposals vary according to the response of each analyst to the following questions:

1. How would a real exchange rate devaluation be prompted that could liberalize trade without overburdening the financing of the public sector?

2. What is the impact of the above measure on inflation?

3. Who performs the job of determining an adequate exchange rate for the economy better, the government or the market?

4. How stable is the system?

Proposal 1, a return to mini-devaluations, presupposes that foreign exchange restrictions and the potential capacity to prevent speculative attacks on the currency justify control over the exchange rate. Moreover, supporters of this proposal believe that the system results in smaller devaluations than would occur under the alternative of open auctions. This is true because controls over the exchange rate are maintained at the same time that the potential speculative demand for dollars is contained as a hedge against inflation. The alternative of dual exchange rates, Proposal 2, does not represent an advantage over the first proposal in regard to real devaluation, since the administered segment of the system would have to adopt a significant real devaluation in order to compensate for delays in exchange rate adjustments. Proposal 3, a free exchange rate, implicitly assumes that a strong real devaluation of the exchange rate will be needed in order to satisfy the potential demand for dollars. It does not, however, address the inflationary impact imposed by such a strong devaluation.

On the issue of who better determines the adequate exchange rate — the market or the government — the experience gathered in Brazil and elsewhere does not indicate clearly one or the other. During the 1970s, management of exchange rates in Brazil was adequate. In the 1980s, however, the government utilized exchange rate controls as an instrument to fight inflation. Little success was obtained with this strategy, however, and the exchange rate became overvalued. As the real exchange rate distanced itself from its market value, strong pressure to devalue the official exchange rate emerged. Under the floating exchange rate system, the Central Bank was released from the obligation to establish the exchange rate.

The virtue of having the market determine the price for currency is that it becomes responsible for all good and bad performance. There is sufficient evidence, however, that the market establishes exchange rates that are not in line with the country's competitiveness. Well-known examples of this situation are the exchange rates between the U.S. dollar and the Japanese yen and between the U.S. dollar and the German mark during the 1980s, at which time the United States accumulated large trade deficits. International experience has shown that when countries follow consistent macroeconomic policies, and particularly when they minimize the rigidity of prices in the goods and factor markets, the difference between a floating and fixed exchange rate is insignificant.

Regarding the system's stability, the mini-devaluation rule, by definition, yields more stability than the free market system. In fact, one of the characteristics of the free market foreign exchange system is its high volatility. The results of historical experience demonstrate that the floating exchange rate may be subject to drastic, rapid changes, depending on the expectations built into the economy. The advantage of the first proposal is its greater potential for long-run stability of the real exchange rate, an important element in expanding exports.

The dual exchange rate system also may have various potential advantages or benefits. This type of system makes it possible for the market to play a role in the determination of the exchange rate while maintaining a good portion of the inflow of foreign exchange under the supervision of the Central Bank. Second, it permits immediate trade liberalization for goods subject to the free exchange rate rule. Third, as the system allows for varied fluctuations in the rate, this mechanism reduces the need for any devaluation of the real exchange rate. This proposal, therefore, results in a smaller impact on the financing of the public sector, especially on the purchase of foreign exchanges to service the official external debt. Fourth, it is expected that the dual exchange rate also will reduce capital flight and fraudulent actions against foreign exchange controls to the extent that it will speed up a market mechanism. It should be made clear, however, that the proposal for a dual system does not eliminate the existing controls over the exchange rate, although it does allow the market to play a more significant role in the determination of exchange rates.

On the negative side, a dual exchange rates system gives rise to instability and speculation, generating several problems. First, it requires that additional bureaucracy be in place in order to administer and keep the two market segments separate. Second, the system represents a subsidy to the group that benefits from the preferential exchange rate, thereby increasing pressure to expand the list of privileged products. Third, it may be conducive to an appreciation of the controlled exchange rate since this rate applies to all government payments related to the external debt and critical imports. Fourth, by maintaining both a controlled and a free exchange rate, the system becomes vulnerable to speculative incursions aimed at a devaluation of the controlled rate.

The advantages of proposal three, the floating exchange rate, are very attractive from a theoretical point of view. In addition to allowing the market to determine foreign currency prices, the system is expected to preserve the balance of payments equilibrium (external equilibrium) since the supply and demand for foreign exchange must match at a certain price. It is also postulated that the floating exchange rate insulates the economy, stimulating the adoption of consistent domestic policies (internal equilibrium). Finally, the regime grants more efficacy to the monetary policy in the presence of capital mobility, since the effects of such a policy are perceived fully in the economy, as shown by the Mundell and Fleming model.

Past experiences have demonstrated, however, that free exchange rates may also create problems. During the 1970s, for instance, when industrialized countries first adopted the system, capital mobility received much attention, causing exchange rates to be highly volatile. Several signs of serious misalignment among the main international currencies became evident. To avoid such volatility, many countries chose to avoid the floating exchange rate system. In 1987, for example, 90 of 151 state members of the International Monetary Fund (IMF) had fixed exchange rates — 34 were pegged to the dollar, 14 to the franc, and 42 to other currencies. Thirty-three states adopted a limited system with administered fluctuations, and only 28 countries maintained the floating system — 21 of them in a dual exchange rate system. These figures reveal that the majority of countries were so cautious that they connected their exchange rates to some point of reference in order to avoid speculative behavior.

In Brazil, specific factors discourage the adoption of a free exchange rate system. First, the higher volatility of a real exchange rate brought about by frequent fluctuations discourages exports. Second, the lack of a strong, credible capital market would transform the U.S. dollar into an asset to protect against inflation, creating a strong speculative demand for this currency. Third, problems associated with this kind of exchange rate system would affect the economy as a whole and influence the current inflation rate.

Therefore, the adoption of a free exchange rate would make the macroeconomic policy highly vulnerable in an economy that is suffering from the chronic problem of a large external debt. The truth is that the nominal exchange rate is difficult to determine, and its stability depends on a certain degree of confidence in economic fundamentals. If economic agents believe that there will be a devaluation, the resulting run against the domestic currency will determine this depreciation despite the effects of real economic conditions, and the system will become unstable. This is known as the "problem of the weight": lack of confidence in fundamental factors destabilizes the exchange rate system, leaving the price system without "anchors." Therefore, because of the problem of foreign currency restriction and the lack of freedom in terms of macroeconomic policy and inflation control, the adoption of the free exchange rate in Brazil seems to be an inappropriate alternative.

## The Exchange Rate in the 1990s

This section presents the main aspects of the exchange rate adopted in Brazil during the latter part of the 1980s and the early 1990s. Two institutions participate in the exchange rate policy in Brazil: the Finance Ministry decides the basic criteria to be followed, while the Central Bank administers the policy on a daily basis, deciding on devaluations, arbitrage operations, and supervision of the overall system.

From August 1968 to March 1990, exchange rate policy in Brazil followed the principle of mini-devaluations. Zini (1993) presents a detailed analysis of this period. In this chapter, the focus will be on the elements that are important for an understanding of the evolution of such a policy in recent years. The mini-devaluation policy consisted of frequent, small changes in the nominal exchange rate with the objective of adjusting for the difference between domestic and international inflation, also known as the relative purchase-power parity criterion. The key aspect of this policy was to administer small changes in the exchange rate to avoid abrupt changes in the domestic currency value.

International literature on this issue shows that the relative purchase power parity criterion fails when it is the only criterion used to adjust exchange rates in the long run. In the short run, however, this rule seems to be appropriate, especially when high inflation or other perturbing monetary phenomena are present, as is the case of hyperinflation in Brazil.

The main aspects of the exchange rate policy during the past several years are summarized below. With the exception of the exchange rate freeze imposed during the first four months of the Summer Plan (1989), mini-devaluations were used throughout 1988 and 1989 on a daily basis to make adjustments in the exchange rate based on the expected variation of the consumer price index (CPI) during the month. However, this policy created a large gap in the real exchange rate indexes since the actual inflation was higher than expected. The economic plans adopted during this period eventually validated the previously developed gap by not devaluing the exchange rate. In comparative terms, the results were the following: in 1988, inflation during the period measured 934 percent according to the CPI and 1,053 percent according to the wholesale price index (WPI), while the exchange rate devaluation was only 967 percent; in 1989, inflation was 1,765 percent according to the CPI and 1,750 percent according to the WPI, while the exchange rate devaluation was only 1,384 percent or approximately 25 percent below the CPI.

In March 1990, the new administration adopted the floating system, according to which banks and authorized brokers would determine the daily exchange rate by buying and selling U.S. dollars. The Central Bank renounced its daily obligation to announce the new exchange rate. This change was followed by an announcement that the maintenance of desirable levels of international reserves would determine possible interventions in the market. Instead of having the obligation to buy and sell U.S. dollars at the rate imposed by mini-devaluation criteria, the Central Bank gained flexibility to buy and sell foreign currencies as desired.

At the very beginning of the period, the exchange rate dropped significantly due to a liquidity crisis stemming from the expropriation of assets in *cruzados*. The Central Bank acted as a buyer in March to avoid a further drop in the exchange rate. As time progressed, market agents learned how to operate in the new system, and the Central Bank began to carry out interventions based on other motives (Souza 1990).

During 1990 and 1991, the market operated in a manner in which the exchange rate paralleled the expected monthly inflation. Between October and December 1990, however, the Central Bank accelerated devaluations to correct the real exchange rate and to reverse the trend of declining exports. The same occurred in the third quarter of 1991 when the devaluation reached 17 percent in one day during September.

In theory, Central Bank interventions in the floating market would be limited to smoothing out the fluctuations in exchange rates in the short run and, in the meantime, storing international reserves in accordance with established targets. In this case, the floating exchange rate would free the Central Bank from the onus of an unplanned expansion or contraction in the monetary base due to the closing of exchange rate operations. In practice, however, Central Bank interventions are derived from more complex motives.

Between May and September 1990, the Central Bank was very active in reducing the margin of difference between official and black market rates by selling gold at the black market rate and buying U.S. dollars at the official rate. As a result, the margin of difference between the two markets was reduced to between 5 and 15 percent. Beginning in September, Central Bank interventions aimed to adjust the real exchange rate because of a drop in international reserves and poor export prospects. In other words, the Central Bank began to consider the need for domestic currency real parity without ignoring export competitiveness.

Under the new system, the need and function of a future market for exchange rates became evident because both exporters and importers could perform an exchange rate hedge more adequately. Currently, this market is still very restricted in Brazil and works only with future contracts instead of future exchange rates.[5]

Before proceeding with an analysis of the evolution of real exchange rate indicators, certain definitions are worth clarifying. The real exchange rate index (r) is the relative price between a foreign price index (P') and a domestic price index (P), both expressed in the same currency: $r = eP'/P$ (where e is the exchange rate). This concept may be used to calculate the bilateral exchange rate — that is, cruzeiro/dollar — or to deal with a currency basket. In the latter case, the concept is known as effective real exchange rate. The concept of a currency basket weighs the participation of a country's main trade partners, in the calculation of an effective exchange rate and of the international price index. This is the most appropriate indicator for evaluating exchange rate policy because each country trades with several partners and the discussion of the exchange rate should take into account the price relationship between these partners.

There are several factors to consider when deciding which price index should be used to compare real exchange rates. On the one hand, the WPI reflects the prices practiced by producers and follows the prices of industrial goods and tradable agricultural goods. This price shows the evolution of prices of goods that can be characterized as "tradable." The CPI, on the other hand, follows the prices paid by consumers for final goods. One problem with this index, however, is that it includes several of the goods and services of particular countries that are not internationally exchanged (nontradable goods). These types of goods and services, therefore, should not be included in the comparison of the competitiveness of these economies.

Another indicator that may be used is the exchange rate/wage ratio, though this index is the most problematic of all. It only emphasizes one element on the cost side. Available indexes of average wages paid by industry are collected on a lenient, voluntary basis. Calculation of the average wage is at best deficient because it is measured as the simple average of all wages received in a given period divided by hours worked, without taking into consideration the type of work performed nor the occupational structure of industrial employment over the years. The resulting index is an average of an ambiguous total. One final problem with this indicator is that the usual comparisons do not take labor productivity into consideration. Altogether, these problems make this index inappropriate for use in Brazil. They may result in more problems than solutions. Alternately, real exchange rate indicators generate more consistent and more reliable information.[6]

Table 1 shows some real exchange rate indicators in Brazil between 1988 and 1991, using 1985 as the base year. Although there are several arguments that may be presented to justify using 1985 as the base year, the main reason is that all of the evidence indicates that the exchange rate during that year was relatively well aligned with the country's foreign competitiveness. The country's balance of payments in 1985 was stable, the margin between the official and black markets was small, and studies on Brazil's effective protection showed little distortion. Table 1 figures indicate a real currency depreciation when the indicator increases and real currency appreciation when the indicator decreases.

The indicator Dol_WPI, depicted in Table 1, deflates the average exchange rate (cruzado/dollar) for each period with relative prices between Brazil's wholesale price index (WPI) and the same index in the United States. Data show a large gap in relation to the dollar. The index drops from 100 points in 1985 to 46.2 points by the first quarter of 1990, hampering Brazil's efforts to export to the North American market. A slight recovery is observed beginning in mid-March 1990, while at the end of 1991, the index had reached 68.9 points.

The use of the currency basket concept reduces this gap to some degree since the dollar devalued in relation to the mark and the yen between 1985 and 1990. The e_WPI indicator deflates the exchange rate using wholesale

Table I
# Brazil: Real Exchange Rate 1988–1991
(1985 = 100)

| | | | Dollar | | Currency Basket | |
|---|---|---|---|---|---|---|
| | | | Dol_WPI | e_WPI | e_NCPI | e_TNT |
| 1988 | 1st | quarter | 79.4 | 99.2 | 106.2 | 99.5 |
| | 2nd | quarter | 77.3 | 96.0 | 106.1 | 99.8 |
| | 3rd | quarter | 75.6 | 90.6 | 100.4 | 94.7 |
| | 4th | quarter | 73.8 | 91.1 | 102.4 | 95.7 |
| 1989 | 1st | quarter | 72.7 | 89.0 | 96.5 | 90.7 |
| | 2nd | quarter | 68.0 | 78.7 | 75.0 | 71.9 |
| | 3rd | quarter | 64.0 | 74.8 | 79.2 | 75.3 |
| | 4th | quarter | 58.0 | 69.3 | 73.7 | 69.0 |
| 1990 | 1st | quarter | 46.6 | 56.6 | 61.3 | 57.1 |
| | 2nd | quarter | 50.1 | 61.9 | 65.3 | 59.9 |
| | 3rd | quarter | 51.0 | 64.9 | 66.8 | 60.8 |
| | 4th | quarter | 60.8 | 79.2 | 80.3 | 72.9 |
| 1991 | 1st | quarter | 64.2 | 82.3 | 81.7 | 73.5 |
| | 2nd | quarter | 62.6 | 78.0 | 78.1 | 68.9 |
| | 3rd | quarter | 61.4 | 76.3 | 75.8 | 66.4 |
| | 4th | quarter | 68.9 | 87.0 | 89.7 | 68.4 |
| 1990 | JAN | | 52.4 | 63.3 | 68.4 | 63.8 |
| | FEB | | 49.5 | 59.9 | 64.6 | 60.4 |
| | MAR | | 43.2 | 52.6 | 57.4 | 53.1 |
| | APR | | 49.8 | 61.1 | 64.1 | 59.1 |
| | MAY | | 49.4 | 61.3 | 66.1 | 60.7 |
| | JUN | | 51.1 | 63.1 | 65.8 | 60.1 |
| | JUL | | 52.7 | 66.5 | 69.0 | 62.7 |
| | AUG | | 51.3 | 65.5 | 68.1 | 62.2 |
| | SEP | | 49.4 | 63.3 | 64.2 | 58.4 |
| | OCT | | 55.5 | 71.7 | 72.6 | 66.3 |
| | NOV | | 60.2 | 78.9 | 81.3 | 73.8 |
| | DEC | | 65.0 | 85.1 | 85.3 | 76.9 |
| 1991 | JAN | | 67.8 | 87.5 | 87.7 | 78.6 |
| | FEB | | 63.7 | 83.3 | 84.1 | 75.7 |
| | MAR | | 62.0 | 77.4 | 76.0 | 67.7 |
| | APR | | 60.7 | 76.4 | 78.1 | 69.4 |
| | MAY | | 63.5 | 78.7 | 79.2 | 70.6 |
| | JUN | | 63.3 | 78.0 | 77.1 | 67.7 |
| | JUL | | 62.0 | 76.6 | 76.1 | 66.6 |
| | AUG | | 60.6 | 75.4 | 75.2 | 65.7 |
| | SEP | | 61.6 | 77.0 | 76.4 | 67.0 |
| | OCT | | 66.7 | 83.1 | 86.6 | 76.0 |
| | NOV | | 67.6 | 85.4 | 88.5 | 77.5 |
| | DEC | | 71.2 | 91.2 | 93.0 | 81.0 |
| 1992 | JAN | | 70.1 | 89.7 | 92.6 | 80.4 |

Source: Author, based on Central Bank and IMF data.
Note: Dol_WPI, exchange rate cruzeiro/dollar deflated by the respective WPIs; e_WPI, currency basket of 15 most important trade partners deflated by the respective WPIs; e_NCPI, basket deflated by the consumer price indexes.

## Table 2
# Real Exchange Rate Indicators in Brazil
## 1960–1991
### (1970 = 100)

|        | e_WPI | e_NCPI | e_TNT |
|--------|-------|--------|-------|
| 1960   | 81.1  | 81.0   | 92.5  |
| 1961   | 88.1  | 95.4   | 107.3 |
| 1962   | 99.2  | 108.1  | 119.7 |
| 1963   | 86.1  | 100.3  | 107.2 |
| 1964   | 104.8 | 112.1  | 123.1 |
| 1965   | 120.8 | 119.5  | 131.4 |
| 1966   | 102.6 | 103.1  | 111.2 |
| 1967   | 92.9  | 93.8   | 97.6  |
| 1968   | 96.3  | 100.1  | 102.2 |
| 1969   | 100.7 | 103.0  | 103.6 |
| 1970   | 100.0 | 100.0  | 100.0 |
| 1971   | 101.5 | 103.2  | 101.4 |
| 1972   | 104.7 | 109.0  | 106.5 |
| 1973   | 110.1 | 116.0  | 116.0 |
| 1974   | 108.8 | 108.0  | 115.9 |
| 1975   | 113.9 | 113.5  | 119.8 |
| 1976   | 109.9 | 110.7  | 116.6 |
| 1977   | 109.2 | 111.1  | 114.9 |
| 1978   | 115.3 | 119.5  | 120.3 |
| 1979   | 127.7 | 133.2  | 136.1 |
| 1980   | 135.2 | 156.0  | 162.7 |
| 1981   | 114.8 | 135.4  | 139.6 |
| 1982   | 107.1 | 123.9  | 127.4 |
| 1983   | 127.0 | 163.6  | 167.0 |
| 1984   | 116.9 | 171.4  | 174.0 |
| 1985   | 114.8 | 176.4  | 172.1 |
| 1986   | 116.7 | 183.9  | 171.2 |
| 1987   | 118.8 | 176.9  | 162.4 |
| 1988   | 105.8 | 160.9  | 147.3 |
| 1989   | 83.2  | 125.5  | 115.9 |
| 1990   | 77.9  | 112.9  | 100.7 |
| 1991*  | 92.2  | 130.9  | 114.7 |

Source: Author, based on data from *International Financial Statistics.*
Note: e_WPI uses wholesale prices in Brazil as deflator, and the rest of the world prices as
    numerator; e_CPI uses consumer price index (CPI-RJ) as deflator; e_TNT uses the CPI-RJ
    as deflator and WPI in the rest of the world as numerator.
*Figures for 1991 are based on average indicators for the first five months of the year.

prices in Brazil and the same price indexes for its 15 largest trade partners, all
converted into dollars and weighted by the relative importance of these
countries in Brazil's international trade during the 1985-1988 period (weighted

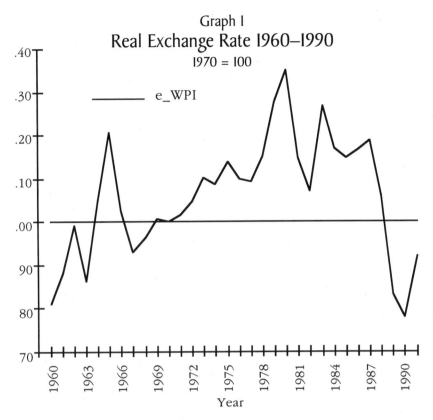

Graph I
## Real Exchange Rate 1960–1990
1970 = 100

e_WPI

average). The e_NCPI indicator uses the weighted CPI of trade partners as a numerator and deflates the currency basket with the national consumer price index (NCPI) computed by the Brazilian Statistical Bureau (IBGE — Instituto Brasileiro de Geografia e Estatística). The e_TNT indicator uses the NCPI as a deflator for Brazil's prices and the weighted index of wholesale prices for the trade partners as a numerator.[7] The three indicators are shown in Table 1. The 15 trade partners included in this index are listed in order of importance: the United States, Germany, Japan, the Netherlands, Italy, France, Argentina, United Kingdom, Canada, China, Belgium, Spain, Chile, Venezuela, and Switzerland. Table 2 shows the evolution of the e_WPI, e_CPI, and e_TNT for the period 1960-1991, using 1970 as the base year (weighting mechanism adjusted every five years).

Graph 1 shows the evolution of the real exchange rate in Brazil for the same period, 1960-1991. The graph shows that in 1980 and 1983, there were real devaluations in the domestic currency, with the last devaluation maintained until 1987. After 1988, however, there was a strong appreciation of the Brazilian currency; the index dropped from 118.8 in 1987 to 78.5 in 1990 (Table 2). In three years, there was a real appreciation of 40 percentage points,

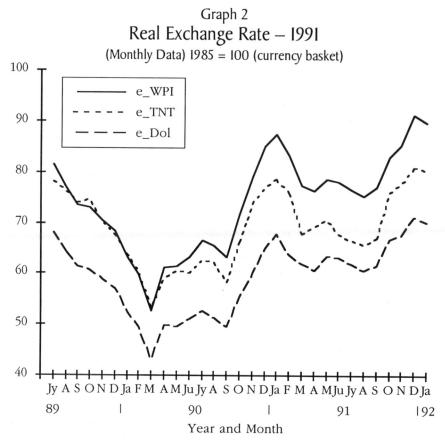

Graph 2
## Real Exchange Rate – 1991
(Monthly Data) 1985 = 100 (currency basket)

while the e_WPI reached its lowest value. This unbearable appreciation, compounded with pressure from exporters, led the Central Bank to seek a recovery of the real exchange rate parity at the end of 1990.

Graph 1 illustrates further lessons. For instance, during the 32 years under study, despite the large number of different exchange rate policies, the real exchange rate tended to reach toward a certain level, in this case between 105 and 110 points. It also shows that even though short-run policies may use exchange rate manipulation as an anti-inflationary instrument, allowing the exchange rate parity to lag behind, there are real forces in the economy that increase the exchange rate to a minimally competitive level. Moreover, Graph 1 clearly demonstrates that those who believed that the floating exchange rate adopted in 1990 would keep the real exchange rate constant were completely wrong. The truth is that the concept of a real exchange rate gap not only remained valid (and it has been utilized in countries with free exchange rate systems), but it also showed that further developments imposed its adjustment.

## Graph 3
# Real Exchange Rate 1984–1991
### (Quarterly Data) 1985 = 100 (currency basket)

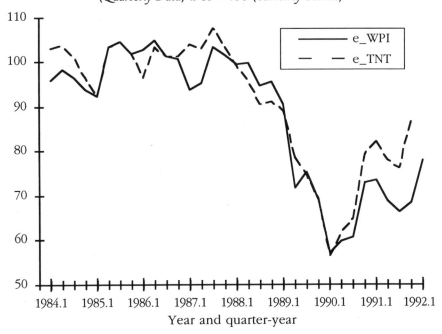

Year and quarter-year

The course of recovery can be seen in the monthly data from 1989 to 1991 in Graph 2 and the quarterly data from 1984 to 1991 in Graph 3. These data show that the exchange rate gap began to accumulate after the first quarter of 1988. Until that time, the real exchange rate as measured by the currency basket concept was aligned reasonably with the 1985 real parity. In Graph 2, one can see that the real exchange rate reached its minimum level in March 1990, recovering about ten points by September and with another strong "push" between October 1990 and January 1991. This big push was not engendered by the market alone. Rather, it was aided by the active intervention of the Central Bank, which was concerned with declining exports and declining international reserves. Collor Plan II caused a new gap of ten points in the real parity between January and March 1991. Real parity recovered by the end of 1991, however, once again due to a Central Bank intervention.

Another negative aspect of the exchange rate policy in recent years is that it has widened the real exchange rate variance. Empirical evidence clearly shows that export revenues are negatively affected by unstable real remuneration by exporters and international trade flourishes under stable exchange rates.

The data in Table 3 portray the increasing stability of exchange rates in Brazil. Based on quarterly data for the e_WCP, the coefficient of real exchange rate fluctuation increased from 6.5 percent in the 1970s to 11.5 percent in the 1980s.

## Table 3
## Real Exchange Rate: Basic Statistics

|                      | 1957-68 | 1969-79 | 1980-84 | 1985-89 | 1980-89 |
|----------------------|---------|---------|---------|---------|---------|
| Number of observations | 46    | 44      | 20      | 20      | 40      |
| Average              | 84.3    | 82.2    | 91.9    | 83.3    | 87.6    |
| Standard deviation   | 11.8    | 5.3     | 9.3     | 9.1     | 10.1    |
| Coefficient of variation | 13.9 | 6.5    | 10.1    | 10.9    | 11.5    |
| Minimum value        | 57.4    | 74.5    | 77.7    | 60.7    | 60.7    |
| Maximum value        | 117.3   | 97.7    | 113.7   | 93.1    | 113.7   |
| Skewedness           | 0.31    | 0.64    | 0.66    | -1.21   | 0.2     |

Sources: Author.

Note: The statistics refer to the evolution of the "e_WPI" index (base 1980 = 100). The columns refer to the following periods: 1st quarter of 1957 to 2nd quarter of 1968; 1st quarter of 1969 to 4th quarter of 1979; 1st quarter of 1980 to 4th quarter of 1984; 1st quarter of 1985 to 4th quarter of 1989; the decade of the 1980s.

## Conclusions

Discussions on the institutional framework of the Brazilian exchange rate regime, as well as an analysis of the real exchange rate indicators, lead to certain conclusions about the performance of the floating exchange rate regime in Brazil. The adoption of the floating exchange rate regime was supported by exporters and economic analysts before and after March 1990. Agents expected that the adoption of the new system would lead to a significant depreciation of the exchange rate, bringing it closer to the black market rate, which was about 80 percentage points above the official rate. This would have happened under normal conditions, but the proponents of this type of exchange rate system ignored the effects of a liquidity contraction that follows anti-inflationary programs. These effects brought about a lower exchange rate — an appreciation of the Brazilian currency — the opposite of what otherwise might be expected.

In Brazil's case, the floating system has the unique feature of being monitored closely by the Central Bank, in what can be described as an oligopsonistic system. The Bank's relative size and varied mechanisms give it power to determine the exchange rate. In addition to purchasing foreign currency directly to honor the external debt services and performing arbitrage operations, the Bank also indirectly oversees official banks and purchases of foreign exchange by state-owned companies. In practice, therefore, the floating system in Brazil resembles the old mini-devaluation regime. Daily devaluations of the exchange rate have followed the indexation of bonds but with slight fluctuations. In 1990, for instance, these devaluations closely followed the fluctuation of the Fiscal Treasury Bonds (BTNF) and, in 1991, followed the Referential Daily Rate (Taxa de Referência Diária — TRD). The main difference is that under the new regime, the Central Bank is not obliged to establish the exchange rate publicly on a daily basis.

It is also necessary to consider the evolution of the black market exchange rate. Until 1990, the dollar suffered large fluctuations in the black market due to unstable expectations. The Central Bank realized that it could perform profitable arbitrage between the gold market (selling gold at the dollar black market rate) and the official floating market (buying dollars at the floating rate). Therefore, after March 1990, the Central Bank actively operated in the market, buying dollars in the official market and selling gold at black market rates. This intervention reduced the margin between the black market and the official market from 90 percent to between 5 and 15 percent, which was a positive accomplishment in itself. At the end of 1991, with the heavy inflow of foreign resources, the margin fell to negative values without further intervention by the Central Bank. The result of the Central Bank intervention, which is difficult to evaluate, is that billions of dollars in public sector bonds were transformed into investments in gold between March 1990 and March 1991. It is important to keep in mind that the arbitrage operations performed by the Central Bank constituted one of the new system's innovations.

Taking stock of the performance of the floating system, it is possible to conclude that the system adopted in Brazil, which can be called a dirty floating system, has produced results that are very similar to a well-administered mini-devaluation system. The new system expanded the market/Central Bank relationship, and after Central Bank officials changed their perception of the exchange rate gap, it allowed for significant, necessary adjustments in the real exchange rate. There is also greater approval for the new system since the market prefers to operate through a floating system. At the same time, the system confers a greater degree of freedom to the Central Bank. The results obtained with the adoption of the floating system, therefore, can be considered positive. It should be pointed out that since the system is similar to the regime of full indexation, it may become more difficult to control inflation.

Finally, it seems that at the moment the best alternative to the exchange rate regime in Brazil is a careful transition to a regime with more freedom, without renouncing a certain degree of control. The main implication of this alternative is that the Central Bank has to monitor the market carefully in order to maintain the real exchange rate in line with the country's international competitiveness. This also seems to be the Central Bank's understanding, which should be maintained in the near future, while the country proceeds with the strategy of gradually liberalizing exchange rate operations.

# Notes

1. The centralization of foreign exchange was canceled in the second half of 1990, when the country opted to suspend temporarily interest payments accrued on the official foreign debt. The suspension was lifted at the beginning of 1991.

2. Some observers from the private sector estimate that the Brazilian export market operated at the end of the 1980s under the rule of 80/20; that is, for each US$100 exported on average, US$80 was registered in the official market. Payment of the remaining US$20 was made through the black market. Other analysts believe that the underinvoicing of agricultural products reached 30 percent of the reported export price in 1988-1989. In view of these estimates, one can speculate that the effective surplus in Brazil's trade balance would probably be 20 or 30 percent higher than the official figures.

3. Given the characteristics of gold, the value of which varies with the exchange rate, the same arbitrage can be noticed in relationship with the gold market. That is, since gold is internationally accepted, investors pay special attention to the possibility to perform arbitrage between the internal and external price of this metal. For practical purposes, one can say that there are only two exchange rates in Brazil: the official rate and the black market rate.

4. A fourth proposition would be to fix the exchange rate. This proposal, however, cannot be sustained until the country's inflation is overcome.

5. See H.S. Gonzales in Zini, Jr., 1993, 171-177.

6. Monetary authorities could calculate some more specific indexes on foreign trade. In particular, there are two indicators that could be computed on a regular basis. One is the index of tradable goods prices. This is not the unitary price of exports, which is the ratio between the value of total exports and the quantity of exported goods. The IPEA (Instituto de Pesquisas Econômicas Aplicadas) is working on a methodology for Brazil, but the indicators are not yet published regularly (Pinheiro and Motta 1990). The other index is the unitary cost of labor, not average salary. The two indicators are very useful for evaluating the economy's external competitiveness.

7. This index divides the wholesale prices in the rest of the world by Brazil's consumer price index. The objective of such an index is to portray the evolution of the price relationship between tradable and nontradable goods (T/NT), which is a critical relative price in the discussion of changes in the real exchange rate. The relative hypothesis is that the domestic consumer prices reflect the price evolution of nontradable goods, while the index of international wholesale prices shows the price evolution of tradable goods.

# References

Gonzales, H.S. 1993. "O Mercado futuro de Taxas de Câmbio no Brasil" (Apêndice Especial). In *Taxa de Câmbio e Política Cambial no Brasil*, ed. A.A. Zini, Jr. São Paulo, S.P.: EDUSP/BM&F.

Pinheiro, A.C., and R.S. Motta. 1990. "Indices de Exportação para o Brasil." *Anais do XVIII Encontro Nacional de Economia*, v. 2. Brasília, D.F: ANPEC.

Souza, F.E.P. de. 1990. "O Regime de Câmbio Flutuante numa Etapa de Transição." *Anais do XVIII Encontro Nacional de Economia*, v. 2. Brasília, D.F.: ANPEC.

Zini, Jr., A.A. 1993. *Taxa de Câmbio e Política Cambial no Brasil.* São Paulo, S.P.: EDUSP/BM&F.

# Population, Labor Force, and Labor Market in Brazil, 1960-1990

## José Paulo Zeetano Chahad

## Introduction

This chapter focuses on the evolution and main aspects of Brazil's population, labor force, and labor market during the 1960-1990 period. Its objective is to uncover the principal facts and evidence associated with these variables and their impact on the labor market.

The chapter is arranged in three sections. The first section presents the evolution of the Brazilian population and discusses the implications of an observed reduction in population growth. The second section deals with the urbanization process and ensuing labor force movements, as well as changes in the economic, demographic, and educational characteristics of the labor force. The third section focuses on the performance of the urban/industrial labor market, viewed as representative of the emergence of salaried work, and also discusses the phenomenon of open unemployment.

## Evolution of Brazil's Population

As implications of population issues go beyond the economic sphere, reaching the social, political, and cultural realms of society, they are among Brazil's most important structural problems. This chapter deals only with the evolution of the population and its relationship to the labor force.

### Population Changes between 1960 and 1988

According to information provided by the National Household Survey (Pesquisa Nacional por Amostra de Domicílios — PNAD), Brazil's population doubled in size between 1960 and 1988, increasing from about 70 million to about 140 million inhabitants (see Table 1). The annual population growth

Table 1

Population Characteristics
1960-2000

| Variables | Year | | | | | | | | | |
|---|---|---|---|---|---|---|---|---|---|---|
| | 1960 | | 1970 | | 1980 | | 1988 | | 2000[b] | |
| | n°* | % | n°* | % | n°* | % | n°* | % | n°* | % |
| **1. Sex** | | | | | | | | | | |
| Male | 35.1 | 49.9 | 46.3 | 49.7 | 59.1 | 49.7 | 68.4 | 49.08 | 86.5 | 49.2 |
| Female | 35.1 | 50.1 | 46.8 | 50.3 | 59.9 | 50.3 | 72.0 | 50.92 | 83.7 | 50.8 |
| **2. Geographic Area** | | | | | | | | | | |
| Urban | 31.3 | 44.8 | 52.15 | 55.9 | 80.4 | 67.7 | 104.1 | 73.73 | 134.8 | 79.2 |
| Rural | 38.8 | 55.2 | 41.1 | 44.1 | 38.6 | 32.2 | 37.3 | 26.27 | 35.3 | 20.8 |
| **3. Age Group** | | | | | | | | | | |
| 0 - 9 | 21.4 | 30.4 | 27.3 | 29.2 | 31.2 | 26.2 | 33.9 | 21.77 | 33.4 | 19.6 |
| 10 - 59 | 45.4 | 64.7 | 61.0 | 65.5 | 80.5 | 67.6 | 111.6 | 71.65 | 132.9 | 72.2 |
| 60 + | 3.4 | 4.9 | 4.9 | 5.3 | 7.3 | 6.2 | 10.2 | 6.58 | 14.0 | 8.2 |
| **4. Education**[a] | | | | | | | | | | |
| Literate | 24.3 | 60.3 | 35.6 | 66.2 | 54.8 | 74.5 | 74.0 | 81.09 | - | - |
| Illiterate | 16.0 | 39.7 | 10.1 | 33.8 | 18.7 | 25.5 | 17.3 | 18.91 | | |

Notes:  *Millions of people.
   [a] Population 15 years of age and older.
   [b] Projection by Camarano (1986) and Baltar assuming a fall in the fertility of a level that will guarantee the replacement of existing population, that is, at a net rate of replacement of children born during the reproduction cycle equivalent to the unit.
Sources: IBGE-Anuário Estatístico do Brasil, several issues; Pesquisa Nacional por Amostra de Domicílios (PNAD) 1988.

rate is still relatively high (around 2.5 percent in 1980) but is experiencing a steady decline. According to various hypotheses on migration, the geographic expansion of economic activity, and fertility rates, it is expected that the annual population growth rate will vary between 1.7 and 2.5 percent during the 1980-2000 period.[1]

Population growth has been accompanied by a dramatic migration to urban areas. Throughout the 1960s and into the mid-1970s, there was a strong rural to urban migratory trend. With 45 percent of the total population living in urban areas by the 1960s, this percentage rose to 73.4 percent in 1988. By the end of the century, total population living in urban areas is expected to reach almost 80 percent. Table 1 indicates that the reduction in population growth rates is more accentuated in rural areas and could be expected to drop to negative levels after 1980.

Another change in the population's composition has been a relative decrease in the infant population, accompanied by an increase in the population of people over ten years of age and of older people (above 65 years of age). Camarano, Beltrão, and Neupert (1989, 33) show that by the end of the twentieth century, the 65-and-older group will experience the highest growth rate among the Brazilian population, and if the composition of the population does not change in the near future, as will be discussed later, the impact of current trends on the welfare system will be negative.

Additionally, although the quality of education and statistical methods officially used to measure literacy remain questionable, the proportion of literate people in the total population has also increased (see Table 1).

## Causes of Lower Population Growth

Since international migration has been negligible, lower population growth rates have been attributed to changes in both fertility and mortality rates.[2]

*Declining Fertility Rates.* A decline in fertility rates is the main factor causing a reduction in population growth rates. According to Table 2, the drop in the fertility rate between 1960 and 1980 was approximately 30 percent. The average number of children conceived by a woman from either a rural or urban area fell during her lifetime from 6.3 to 4.4 for the same period. Current rates in urban areas may be considered low, however.

There are a number of different factors that affect fertility rates. One is an improvement in living standards among the urban population and a related change in the ideas about family size. Given the access to land and economies of scale, children in rural areas are more important as producers than as consumers, whereas the cost of maintaining a child increases with urbanization. Moreover, the advancement of capitalism has forced many families to

Table 2

## Main Demographic Indicators of Population Movements 1960-1980

| Variables | Years | | | | | | | | |
|---|---|---|---|---|---|---|---|---|---|
| | 1960/1950 | | | 1970/1960 | | | 1980/1970 | | |
| | T | U | R | T | U | R | T | U | R |
| 1. Annual geometric rate of population growth (per 100 inhabitants) | 3.0 | 5.2 | 1.6 | 2.9 | 5.2 | 0.6 | 2.5 | 4.4 | 0.6 |
| 2. Infant mortality rate (%) | 118.1 | - | - | 116.9 | 115.3 | 118.5 | 87.9 | 85.2 | 92.9 |
| 3. Dependency rate (%)[a] | 83.2 | 71.7 | 93.6 | 82.6 | 73.2 | 65.4 | 73.2 | 65.4 | 92.1 |
| 4. Life expectancy at birth | 52.4 | - | - | 52.7 | - | - | 60.1 | - | - |
| 4.1 Male | - | - | - | 51.6 | 52.0 | 51.2 | 59.6 | 60.0 | 58.8 |
| 4.2 Female | - | - | - | 55.9 | 56.2 | 55.5 | 64.1 | 64.7 | 63.2 |
| 5. Fertility rate | 6.3 | - | - | 5.8 | 4.6 | 7.7 | 4.4 | 3.6 | 6.4 |
| 6. Net emigration rate | 12.6 | - | - | 14.3 | - | - | 15.5 | - | - |
| 7. Net immigration rate | 12.3 | - | - | 14.2 | - | - | 15.3 | - | - |
| 8. Population Density (inhab/km²) | 8.3 | - | - | 11.1 | - | - | 14.7 | - | - |

Note: [a] Population younger than 15 and older than 64 years of age.
    T = Total; U = Urban; R = Rural
Sources: IBGE-Anuário Estatístico do Brasil, several issues; Censos Demográficos, several years.

abandon the countryside to a greater or lesser extent and forgo subsistence production; as a result, the average family size has been significantly reduced.

Another explanation for declining fertility rates, particularly in urban areas, is the encouragement of social, cultural, and economic aspirations, whose fulfillment implies a reduction in family size. Moreover, the increasing participation of women in the labor force, especially in urban areas, has resulted in lower rates.

These factors have had a heavy impact on the levels of fertility and are accompanied by easier access to modern means of birth control as well as diffusion through the media of new values and aspirations regarding family size. It is necessary, however, to mention that reduction was not uniform among and within regions. Magno de Carvalho (1988, 43) has shown clearly that a reduction in fertility rates in the South was much higher than in the North and the Northeast. Specifically, fertility rates declined 35.3 percent in the South, compared to 21 percent and 18.4 percent declines in the Amazon region and the southern portion of the Northeast, respectively.

*Declining Infant Mortality Rates.* The impact of a reduction in fertility was partially offset by a decline in the infant mortality rate. According to Table 2, there was a significant decline in infant mortality in both urban and rural areas. However, despite significant variations in rates across regions, current infant mortality levels are still extremely high. According to the Brazilian Statistical Bureau (Fundação Instituto Brasileiro de Geografia e Estatística — FIBGE), the infant mortality rate in the South was approximately 60.9 per thousand during the 1970-1980 period, compared to the Northeast where it was twice as high at 124.5 per thousand for the same period.

Overall, the gross mortality rate during the 1970s declined continuously, partially offsetting the impact of lower fertility. The end result was a decline in the rate of population growth. According to Camarano (1985, 7), if there had been no decline in the fertility rate, the reduced infant mortality rates between 1970 and 1980 would have led to an annual population growth rate of 3.1 percent — or 24 percent higher than the actual rate. On the other hand, if there had been no decline in the infant mortality rate, the reduction in fertility rates would have resulted in a population growth rate of 2 percent a year for the same period.

## Consequences of Reductions in Population Growth Rates

The decline of fertility and mortality rates has also resulted in higher life expectancies for both males and females. In fact, between 1960 and 1980, there was an increase in the life expectancy of approximately 8 years for males and 8.2 for females in both urban and rural areas. The discrepancy in life expectancy across regions, as with other variables, is very wide. At the beginning of the 1980s, individuals in the South were expected to live 68 years, while individuals in the Northeast were not expected to live more than 57 years.

Changes in the principal demographic variables have caused a significant shift in the composition of age groups in the population, subsequently affecting the size and participation rate of the labor force as well as the demand for public goods and services, particularly the social security system. The reduction in the dependency rate (ratio of nonproductive individuals to total labor force) from 83.2 percent in 1960 to 73.2 percent in 1980 (Table 2) is significant. It was the result almost exclusively of decreasing dependency rates in urban areas.

While declines in fertility rates imply lower growth rates for young populations, greater life expectancy results in an increase in the number of older citizens within the population. Therefore, there will be a dramatic shift in the age pyramid, decreasing at the base and increasing at the top. The dependency ratio, consequently, will be around 52.7 percent by the end of the twentieth century.

Some of the main consequences of changes in the age composition of the Brazilian population are as follow:

1.  A need for better planning of urban areas, including more efficient use of natural resources.

2.  A need for more jobs since the participation of older groups in the total population will increase. This need will be accentuated by labor-saving technological progress, a phenomenon that will become stronger in urban areas where 80 percent of the Brazilian population will live by the end of the century.

3.  Increased demand for social security services because of the larger older population. Moreover, changing expectations about social security will demand better services in this area.

4.  A reordered demand composition for public services, especially in the areas of education, housing, transportation, sanitation, leisure, and health. Although fewer services will be required by a smaller young population, there will be greater demand for equal opportunity in education.

In the case of health services, the pressure on obstetric services will decrease as a result of a lower fertility rate. By the same token, there will be less demand for child care and gynecologic services. The pressure on cardiovascular and geriatric services, in contrast, will increase, as will the demand for treatment of typical urban diseases, including degenerative illnesses. Due to a high concentration of population in urban areas, there will also be a greater demand for transportation, housing, sanitation, and leisure services.

The crucial question regarding the population issue in Brazil involves the duration and characteristics of the ongoing transition process. Due to cultural factors, disorganized settlement in urban areas, and the high levels of poverty found in many regions of Brazil, the trend of declining mortality rates will persist into the final stages of the demographic transition and will take longer to complete than the trend of declining fertility rates.

Another aspect that ought to be considered is the relative difficulty with any prediction regarding the direction, pattern, or duration of the demographic transition period in Brazil. In a country with such a large expanse and so many regional disparities, each region tends to follow its own path with its distinct characteristics that make projections very difficult.

# Urbanization and the Labor Force

The urbanization process in Brazil that began at the end of the 1930s, when agriculture started to lose its relative importance, stepped up its pace after the 1960s. Table 1 indicates that about 74 percent of the population lived in urban areas in 1988 and almost half in large metropolitan areas. Table 3 shows that about 11 percent of the total population in 1970 was concentrated in the cities of Rio de Janeiro and São Paulo. Despite a strong growth rate, the rate of growth in urban areas between 1960 and 1980 was less intense, attributable primarily to two major factors. First, along with a drop in mortality rates, there was a drop in fertility rates that led to a reduction in population growth. Second, urban growth rates slowed down as migrations from rural areas lost momentum. Another characteristic of urban growth in the 1960s was a change in spatial distribution involving higher growth in the Southeast, especially in São Paulo. During the 1970s, the pattern changed significantly; high urban growth rates shifted to the frontier regions of the North and Center-West, for example.

## Changes in the Composition of the Labor Force: Gender and Age

The urbanization process consolidated a change in the composition of the labor force that had been initiated in the 1940s. The growth rate of the economically active population (EAP) has increased every decade, varying according to specific population segments and economic sectors. In regard to the latter, such changes are an indication of a new direction toward greater participation in secondary (manufacturing) and tertiary (services) economic sectors. The EAP growth rate in non-agricultural sectors, particularly manufacturing and civil construction, has increased consistently.[3] On the other hand, during the 1970s, agricultural activities, now of less importance, experienced negative growth. The result of these trends was a radical change in the EAP composition by the end of 1988, at which point the industrial and service sectors became the primary economic sectors (see Table 4).

## Table 3
# Urbanization Indicators, Evolution, and Remuneration of Labor Force 1960–1980

| Variables | 1960 | 1970 | 1980 |
|---|---|---|---|
| **A. Urbanization** | | | |
| 1. Share of population living in urban areas | 45.1 | 55.9 | 67.7 |
| 2. Share of population living in metropolitan areas | 21.5 | 25.5 | 29.9 |
| 3. Share of population living in cities with more than 500,000 inhabitants | 16.2 | 28.6 | 24.4 |
| 4. Share of population living in the cities of São Paulo and Rio de Janeiro | 10.2 | 11.0 | 11.4 |
| 5. Annual geometric growth rate of urban population (%) | 6.2 | 5.4 | 4.8 |
| 6. Urbanization rate (%) | 3.1 | 2.4 | 2.3 |
| 7. Differential between urban and rural growth[a] | 3.4 | 3.7 | 11.0 |
| **B. Labor force[b]** | | | |
| 1. Annual growth rate of total labor force | 2.7 | 2.5 | 3.9 |
| 2. Annual growth rate of male labor force | 2.3 | 2.2 | 3.0 |
| 3. Annual growth rate of female labor force | 4.9 | 4.1 | 6.6 |
| 4. Annual growth rate of labor force in non-agricultural sector | 4.4 | 4.6 | 6.2 |
| 5. Annual growth rate of labor force in agriculture | 1.8 | 0.5 | -0.3 |
| 6. Annual growth rate of labor force in industry | 1.9 | 6.1 | 7.3 |
| Manufacturing industry | 2.0 | 5.2 | 7.8 |
| Civil construction | 2.9 | 8.2 | 6.2 |
| 7. Annual growth rate of labor force in the service sector | 5.4 | 4.0 | 6.0 |
| **C. Remuneration of labor force** | | | |
| 1. Professional IDs issued as percentage of | | | |
| Total labor force | 2.6 | 8.7 | 11.7 |
| Industrial labor force | 19.3 | 48.5 | 48.5 |
| 2. Salaried workers outside agriculture[c] | 58.4 | 63.0 | 62.2 |
| 3. Share of salaried workers outside manufacturing | 7.3 | 7.5 | 8.5 |
| 4. Share of salaried workers in labor force[c] | 32.4 | 34.8 | 42.3 |

Notes: [a] See Martine et al. 1988, 21.
   [b] Information up to 1980 from Médice 1988.
   [c] See Paiva 1984.
Sources: IBGE, *Censos Demográficos*, several years; *Anuários Estatísticos*; and PNAD.

In reference to the gender composition of the labor force, Table 3 shows a higher growth rate for females than males in the EAP, a situation that was particularly true in the 1970-1980 period when the economy was growing rapidly. Although these changes can be attributed to the growth of those sectors in which the female labor force is better accepted, such as the service sector and certain industrial segments, for example, they are due mainly to the acceptance of the female labor force as a necessary condition for economic growth. It is also interesting to note that the increase in female participation

Table 4

Labor Force by Economic Sectors
1960–1988

(percentages per 1,000 inhabitants)

| Sector | Year | | | | | | | |
|---|---|---|---|---|---|---|---|---|
| | 1960 | | 1970 | | 1980 | | 1988 | |
| | nº | % | nº | % | nº | % | nº | % |
| 1. Agriculture and fishing | 12,278 | 54.0 | 18,087 | 44.3 | 12,661 | 29.3 | 14,233 | 24.23 |
| 2. Industry | 2,940 | 12.9 | 5,296 | 17.9 | 10,772 | 24.8 | 18,955 | 32.47 |
| 3. Commerce | 1,478 | 4.5 | 2,247 | 7.6 | 4,088 | 9.3 | 6,789 | 11.56 |
| 4. Service[a] | 5,341 | 23.5 | 7,775 | 26.3 | 34,043 | 32.6 | 21,152 | 36.02 |
| 5. Public administration | 713 | 3.1 | 1,152 | 3.9 | 1,782 | 4.0 | 2,845 | 4.85 |
| 6. Total labor force | 22,750 | 100.0 | 29,557 | 100.0 | 43,236 | 100.0 | 61,048 | 100.00 |
| 7. Population 10 years of age and older | 48,840 | – | 65,867 | – | 87,805 | – | 107,487 | – |
| 8. Participation rate (6/7) | 46.6 | – | 44.9 | – | 49.2 | – | 55.7 | – |

Note: [a] Includes other activities.
Sources: IBGE, *Censo Demográfico*, several issues; *Anuário Estatístico* 1987; PNAD 1988.

in the labor force has been accompanied by a reduction in fertility rates as well as an expansion in the supply of domestic appliances.

In the Brazilian case, increased participation has been eased by the relatively low cost of female labor. As a result, the participation rate of females in the labor force increased from between 16.6 to 17.7 percent in 1960 (sources vary) to 35.1 percent in 1988, while the ratio for males decreased slightly (see Table 5).

Table 5

# Characteristics of Labor Force 1960 and 1988

(percentages per 1,000 inhabitants)

| Variables | 1960 n° | % | Participation Rate[b] | 1988 n° | % | Participation Rate[b] |
|---|---|---|---|---|---|---|
| **1. Sex** | | | | | | |
| Male | 18,672 | 82.1 | 77.2 | 39,632 | 64.92 | 75.94 |
| Female | 4,077 | 17.7 | 16.4 | 21,415 | 35.08 | 38.72 |
| **2. Age** | | | | | | |
| 10 – 19 | 4,708 | 20.7 | 39.8 | 19,318 | 27.90 | 36.53 |
| 30 – 59 | 16,759 | 73.7 | 74.6 | 47,075 | 68.00 | 70.52 |
| 60 + | 1,283 | 5.6 | 56.8 | 2,831 | 4.10 | 27.66 |
| **3. Education**[a] | | | | | | |
| Less than one year of school | 9,697 | 42.6 | 61.3 | 20,458 | 19.06 | 50.31 |
| More than one year of school | 13,053 | 57.4 | 53.6 | 87,002 | 80.94 | 58.32 |
| **4. Income**[c] | | | | | | |
| 10- | - | 1.9 | - | - | 1.0[d] | - |
| 50- | - | 17.4 | - | - | 13.5[d] | - |
| 10+ | - | 39.6 | - | - | 47.5[d] | - |
| Gini coefficient | 0.497 | - | - | 0.595[d] | - | - |

Notes: [a] Active labor force, 10 years of age and older.
[b] Ratio of active labor force to Population 10 years of age and older.
[c] From Médice 1988a, 142; and Médice 1988b, 150; excludes people "without income."
[d] 1986 data.
Sources: IBGE, *Censo Demográfico*, 1960; and PNAD 1988. Due to difficulties with the 1960 data, and also because data originate from different sources, the information above should be taken not as absolute figures but as an indication of changes in the variables.

Part of this decline in male participation may be attributed to a lower participation by the youngest and oldest age groups among males. In the case of younger males, the change was due to an increase in school registration, primarily because of the scarcity of job opportunities that would permit workers to reconcile conflicts between studies and work. In the case of the elderly, improvements in retirement plans allowed more males to retire sooner than in the past. Table 5 shows changes in activity rates for selected age groups.

Since the absorption of female labor outweighed a reduction in the participation of other groups (young and old people), the end result was an increase in the total EAP rate during the 1960-1980 period. At the end of 1988, for instance, about 50 percent of the total population ten years and older was economically active. In urban areas, participation of the male population in the labor force, especially for the youngest and oldest population age groups, is higher than rates for developed countries.

Within the 15-19 age group in Brazil's urban areas in 1980, the male participation rate in the labor force was 59.2 percent, compared to 53.7, 23.7, 52.4, and 39.3 percent in Spain, France, the United States, and Sweden, respectively (Baltar 1988). Female participation in urban areas has been lower than in developed countries for all age groups; in Brazil, the rate was 35.8 percent, compared to 25.3, 50.9, 55.8, and 63.9 percent in the above mentioned countries, respectively. Only Spain has a lower female participation rate than the one observed for Brazil's urban areas.

The main factor affecting the pattern of male participation is the high level of poverty that forces the male population to enter the labor force at a very early age. By the same token, elderly males postpone their departure from the labor force until much later than they would otherwise. An explanation for the inverse situation in the case of female participation is that only recently has female work begun to be accepted in the labor market.

## The Labor Force and Salaried Work

Changes in the production structure, characterized by a higher growth in sectors where capitalist labor relations are present, have accentuated the trend toward the adoption of salaried labor, primarily in the industrial sector. In fact, about one-half of the industrial EAP was officially registered as employed at the end of 1985.[4]

An increase in employment on a salaried basis took place in rural areas, and even more so in urban areas. Between 1960 and 1985, the proportion of workers "employed" in agricultural activities rose from 26 percent to 38.1 percent, and in non-agricultural activities from 74 to 75 percent. It was evident that capitalist labor relations of production had expanded more quickly in rural than in urban areas during the period. In fact, the lack of dynamism in the leading urban sectors, the existence of constant crises, and rural-urban migration movements brought about a revival of independent forms of production characterized by non-capitalist labor relations.

## Education and Earnings

Another important change in the period was the increasing rate of literacy in the labor force. While in 1960 only 57.4 percent of the labor force had more than one year of formal education, this share increased to 80.9 percent in 1988. It should be emphasized that the intention here is not to challenge the quality of education provided workers or even the accuracy of information regarding workers' education, but to point out that the literacy rate in the labor force for the period was much higher.

The higher level of education, however, does not mean that the Brazilian labor force has achieved educational levels that are compatible with those observed for more developed countries or with those countries that share similar characteristics with Brazil. There are several factors that make the supply of unskilled labor absolutely elastic, therefore reducing the likelihood of higher salaries. Though a necessary condition for such an enhancement, the solution to the problem of lower salaries certainly does not come from an improvement in labor force education only. The country must also resume economic growth, and important structural changes such as better income distribution must take place.

Table 5 shows a pattern in the evolution of the labor force that indicates a dangerous — if not contradictory — path toward the concentration of labor income. According to the table, between 1960 and 1986, the Gini coefficient[5] increased from 0.497 to 0.595, indicating a concentration of income distribution. This phenomenon apparently occurred despite the source of income, be it capital or labor. While the poorest 10 percent of the EAP had its share of total income reduced between 1960 and 1986, the share of total income received by the richest 10 percent of the EAP increased from 39.6 to 47.5 percent.

In short, several trends developing in the labor force after World War II gained strength after the 1960s. Among them, the following are worth citing:

1. Changes in the composition of the EAP, with a clear predominance of urban occupations;

2. Dramatic increases in female participation, not only through the expansion of certain so-called "female" occupations, but mainly through cultural changes that definitively incorporated female labor into the new work environment;

3. Reduction in the participation levels of younger and older male age groups, having serious implications for the future of the social security system;

4. Greater monetarization of the labor force followed by an expansion of salaried work, leading to more homogeneous and stable labor relations;

5. A progressive trend toward higher concentration of income;

6. An increase in total labor participation, mainly due to the expansion of female participation; and

7. An improvement, although precarious, in the educational level of the labor force.

# Industrial Relations and the Performance of the Urban Labor Market

An intense urbanization process characterized by a predominance of secondary and tertiary activities and subsequent greater utilization of salaried labor created a new reality for Brazilian workers. It also brought with it new demands and new sources of concern for the Brazilian government.

This new reality has several different facets, the most visible of which relates to the emergence of open unemployment. A characteristic of a capitalist economy defined as the inability of the productive sector to absorb all workers who are willing to work at current salaries, this phenomenon gradually developed during the growth process in Brazil and increased in size as the population migrated from rural to urban areas. The intense and disorganized growth of large cities caused by large migration movements makes informal labor markets more apparent. The informal sector is no longer simply a source of income for the poor and unskilled, but a functional instrument in filling job opportunities during open unemployment crises.

In the early 1960s, for reasons that are beyond the scope of this work, there was strong government intervention in various spheres of capital-labor relations, especially with respect to wage policies and union movements.

The following sections will evaluate the urban labor market with most of the emphasis placed on the private sector, where industrial relations are more intense. The final section of the chapter briefly examines the public sector as well.

## The Urban-Industrial Labor Market

During the 1960-1990 period, the industrial sector was mainly responsible for the process of economic growth and ensuing structural transformations. Although the labor force in the service sector had the highest growth rate, the analysis here will concentrate on the evolution of a labor force absorbed by the industrial sector. Changes in the industrial sector were the most significant; the dynamic element determining changes in capital-labor relations is usually present in this sector.

*Production and Employment in Brazilian Industry.* Table 6 presents the main indicators in the evolution of the industrial labor market in Brazil.[6] The main observations derived from that table are the following:

1.  Continuous growth of physical production in the industrial sector, consisting of breaks only during periods of crises at the beginning of the 1980s and the 1990s;

2.  Stagnation of employment opportunities at levels lower than those in the mid-1970s (employment, as mentioned, also suffered cyclical changes due to a drop in activity level); and

3.  Strong gains in productivity when measured in terms of physical production and employment, with evidence that productivity gains did not result in better salaries.

## Table 6
## Physical Production and Employment in the Industrial Sector 1975–1990
### (1975=100)

| Year | Physical Production | Employed People | Real Wage* |
|------|--------------------|-----------------|------------|
| 1975 | 100.0 | 100.0 | 100.0 |
| 1976 | 110.9 | 105.4 | 106.6 |
| 1977 | 113.1 | 106.4 | 115.5 |
| 1978 | 121.9 | 108.5 | 126.0 |
| 1979 | 130.8 | 112.3 | 109.2 |
| 1980 | 139.9 | 112.4 | 98.7 |
| 1981 | 127.7 | 108.1 | 100.4 |
| 1982 | 127.7 | 100.3 | 108.6 |
| 1983 | 117.9 | 93.1 | 70.9 |
| 1984 | 126.8 | 88.8 | 63.6 |
| 1985 | 136.5 | 93.6 | 70.0 |
| 1986 | 152.4 | 103.9 | 120.1 |
| 1987 | 153.8 | 105.2 | 70.2 |
| 1988 | 148.8 | 100.9 | 46.5 |
| 1989 | 153.4 | 102.7 | 37.4 |
| 1990 | 139.5 | 97.3 | 54.6 |

Sources: FIBGE, *Indicadores Conjunturais da Indústria* and FIESP. Deflator: IGP-DI/EGV.
* (labor cost in percent).

Even though some rationalization of production may explain part of the mismatch between production and employment growth, one can infer from this information that the absorption of the labor force by industry was below the desirable level. The growth of all other sectors (mainly the service sector), however, was not attributable to the supply of "good jobs" and, therefore, could neither compensate for the low level of absorption of labor into the industrial sector nor for the growing labor force population. In recent years, as cyclical crises have been occurring more frequently, these trends have characterized the consolidation process of the urban labor market.

*Evolution of Real Salary in Industry.* In terms of real wage gains for industrial workers, the following conclusions can be drawn from the data presented in Table 6:

1.  There have been strong fluctuations in the level of real wages (here treated as labor cost) that have shown a clear tendency toward lower real wages (by 1990, real wages were 50 percent less than in 1975).

2.  During the recession of the early 1980s, real wages increased, while the opposite occurred during the stagnation/recession of the late 1980s and early 1990s when real wages were already at very low levels.

As a result of attempts to compensate for real salary losses, the period is marked by an interminable succession of nominal wage indexations that very rarely contributed to the preservation of real wages.[7] Within the context of an economy plagued by profound disequilibria, the indexation system ended up feeding inflation, directly or indirectly, via a wage indexation based on past inflation rates. Moreover, the presence of oligopolies has transformed wage adjustments into recompositions of the industry's mark-up, thereby intensifying the redistributive conflict.

Using as an example a labor market that emerged with the Brazilian industrialization and urbanization processes, it is possible to conclude that it was unable to generate salaried work and maintain the purchasing power of wages through nominal indexation adjustments. Another implication is the appearance of a new form of unemployment — open unemployment — typical of societies that are expanding salaried work, albeit slowly.

## Open Unemployment: The New Face of the Urban Labor Market

To approach this new feature of the labor market, the nature of open unemployment and its evolution will be discussed.

*The Nature of Open Unemployment.* It was not until the end of the 1960s that Brazil began to produce statistics (although precarious) on open unemployment through the PNAD, under the administration of the FIBGE. Before that time, salaried work did not receive the attention it deserved. There were relatively low levels of unemployment in Brazil during the post-World War II period when the country was experiencing high levels of labor utilization. Another explanation may be the cultural heritage of the Brazilian state that has always been dominated by an elite concerned with its own interests and that always placed secondary importance on social issues, including those related to the labor market, and more specifically, the issue of unemployment.

Open unemployment, which makes its introduction into the labor market along with salaried work, may be evaluated more accurately by comparing the impact of an economic crisis occurring during a time when the agricultural sector was dominant with present-day crises led by the industrial and service sectors.

During the earlier agriculture-dominated crisis, there was no open unemployment. The relationship between worker and employer had not been completely disrupted. The agricultural worker quite often continued to maintain some sort of relationship with a landlord or employer and, consequently, was able to work at least at a subsistence level. In contrast, in more recent times, when crises are more frequent and the presence of an urban-industrial productive segment is significant, the nature of labor relations is such that a reduction in labor demand is followed almost immediately by open unemployment with no guarantees of subsistence.

This situation is compounded by the fact that structural transformations have been conducive to stronger interindustrial relations, which help the crises to spread rapidly from sector to sector. Although not the most labor-intensive sector in the economy, the industrial sector (and part of the service sector) has played a crucial role in determining unemployment levels as a result. The dynamism of these activities combined with their location in urban areas turn unemployment crises into periods of substantial social tension, a phenomenon that never occurred in Brazilian society prior to economic changes.

In the context of the Brazilian labor market, it remains necessary to develop an interpretation of the open unemployment phenomenon. As mandated by a need to honor foreign obligations and to attack the persistent inflation that has plagued the country, it is the result of contractionist policies implemented to adjust the economy. In this sense and in light of the crises of the early 1990s, the following considerations are made.

Labor underutilization is not a new phenomenon in the Brazilian economy. History demonstrates that unemployment and underemployment have always existed in Brazil. However, current unemployment differs from previous forms of unemployment because the former not only encompasses the structural unemployment typical of growth processes but also a cyclical unemployment resulting from frequent, conjunctural crises. Large numbers of workers have been expelled from the productive process due to a recurrence of conjunctural crises on a previously unimagined scale.

Within the economic growth process created by circumstances that go beyond the scope of this chapter, labor absorption has excluded a portion of the population. A significant number of workers have always been deprived of the benefits brought about by growth. They constitute the so-called "structurally unemployed," an unemployment category typical of countries with dependent growth within a capitalist sphere of production. The adoption of capitalist production, accompanied by strong growth, was incorporated with increasing levels of participation by the population in the labor force, particularly in the 1970s. It was not only a result of the growth process's increasing need for labor, but also of changes in labor force participation. The urban labor market in particular was affected by changes in habits and tradition, especially regarding the role of women in the labor market.

Brazil's urban unemployment must be understood within the context of the industrialization of a capitalist production system, whose features are typical of a developing country. Thus, what becomes important is the level of unemployment and, even more so, the nature of unemployment encompassing workers in the formal market.

As the country advances into the industrialization and urbanization processes, this "natural" unemployment and underemployment level is expanded to those segments of the population who were at one time incorporated into the labor market, but who were expelled later during the crises. This type of unemployment is, therefore, not a *structural* unemployment characteristic of underdevelopment, but *cyclical* unemployment generated by frequent crises that result from external or domestic disequilibria.

## Table 7
## Rate of Open Unemployment[a]
## 1968–1990

| Year | Rate (percent) |
|------|----------------|
| 1968 | 2.3 |
| 1969 | 2.4 |
| 1970 | 2.5 |
| 1971 | 2.3 |
| 1972 | 3.1 |
| 1973 | 2.6 |
| 1974 | n.a. |
| 1975 | n.a. |
| 1976 | 1.8 |
| 1977 | 2.3 |
| 1978 | 2.3 |
| 1979 | 2.7 |
| 1980 | 2.0 |
| 1981 | n.a. |
| 1982 | 5.8 |
| 1983 | 6.8 |
| 1984 | 7.1 |
| 1985 | 5.3 |
| 1986 | 3.6 |
| 1987 | 3.7 |
| 1988 | 3.8 |
| 1989 | 3.5 |
| 1990 | 4.4 |

Notes: [a] PNAD up to 1981 corresponds to total of Brazil; PME corresponds to the average of the six largest metropolitan areas.  n.a. = not available
Sources: IBGE, PNAD, and PME.

Stated differently, the unemployment crises of the early 1990s were characterized by a combination of structural problems typical of a poor yet urbanized society with the conjunctural problems inherent in a capitalist form of economic development — the distinctive mark of urban unemployment in Brazil at that time. It must be acknowledged again that this was a relatively new situation in the Brazilian labor market: facing the cyclical problems of unemployment common to industrialized countries without the institutional apparatus typically maintained by industrialized countries. Moreover, the situation was exacerbated by political instability generated by a need for social development that could complement economic achievements.

## The Level of Open Unemployment

This new dimension of open urban unemployment changed the attitude of Brazilian authorities who, after 1980, began to produce a more refined unemployment rate statistics for the six main metropolitan regions using the Monthly Survey of Employment (*Pesquisa Mensal de Emprego* — PME — under the administration of FIBGE). Prior to the survey's development, unemployment was measured only from information obtained by the PNAD (see Table 7).

Compared to the PNAD's data, PME statistics beginning in 1981 show much higher unemployment rates. Several reasons have been given. First, unemployment levels are naturally much higher in the six metropolitan areas (measured by PME) than the national level of unemployment (measured by the PNAD). This significantly higher level of unemployment in metropolitan areas represents a new socioeconomic phenomenon in the current Brazilian labor market that has developed because of changes in the production structure and urbanization process.

Second, a transformation in production and the incorporation of new segments of the population into the labor force have taken place. Once economic policies designed for advanced capitalist nations were applied to Brazil's developing economy, these changes would ultimately increase the level of open unemployment. In other words, the recessive adjustments imposed during the 1980s displaced a significant number of workers who had entered the labor force during the 1970s. The same phenomenon is still present because of the stagnation and recession that the economy faced at the beginning of the 1990s.

Third, the highest unemployment rates exhibited in the PME indicate advances in the method of data collection since the PME was created specifically to capture this new phenomenon. The PNAD, in contrast, emphasized household information, where unemployment was treated as an "additional" item without the appropriate methodology to capture the "status" of the labor force.

## Open Unemployment and the Informal Sector

In a society whose productive activities possess heterogeneous characteristics and, consequently, whose labor market possesses certain peculiarities, open unemployment must be understood as a level of minimum labor underutilization. As the urbanization process developed, a large segment of the labor force moved to occupations whose labor relations were unclear. The old form of underemployment persisted, and its new features were invigorated by continuously low levels of labor absorption and the creation of spaces to be filled by new informal productive activities.[8]

An evaluation of the informal sector's dimension, nature, features, and possible solutions to control its expansion has been at the center of Brazilian studies of the labor market (see note 7). The fundamental characteristics of this labor market as it relates to the question of urban unemployment are the following:

1. The extent of the informal market during recessions has been approximately 35 percent of the total labor market (see Table 8).

2. The "informality" of labor relations has been much greater in poor and less dynamic regions of the country. During the most recessive periods, the informal sector of the Northeast has represented up to 50 percent of the total labor market.

3. Recessions increase urban open unemployment as well as the size of the informal sector. This is true for both rich and poor regions.

4. The impact of crises on open unemployment has been much greater in more developed regions, such as the Southeast, for example, where industrialization is more intense and where the largest share of the labor force is located. During a recession, the expansion of the informal labor market has been equally large in poor and rich regions.

## Table 8
## Urban Unemployment and
## Labor Market Segmentation (percent)

| Variables | Region | | | | | |
| | Northeast | | Southeast | | Brazil | |
| | 1981 | 1983 | 1981 | 1983 | 1981 | 1983 |
|---|---|---|---|---|---|---|
| 1. Rate of urban unemployment | 6.5 | 6.9 | 6.4 | 7.4 | 6.1 | 6.9 |
| 2. Labor market | | | | | | |
| Formal | 52.8 | 49.9 | 72.3 | 69.1 | 67.9 | 65.5 |
| Informal | 47.2 | 50.1 | 27.7 | 30.9 | 32.1 | 34.5 |

Note: Informal market is defined as comprising salaried workers without social security protection, receiving up to two minimum wages; plus employers with income lower than five minimum wages; plus self-employed with income up to two minimum wages, and family members without remuneration.

Sources: Jatobá 1989. Primary data from IBGE/PNAD, elaborated upon by the author.

Cyclical movements of open unemployment and of informality in labor relations may be observed in the new data on the labor market for metropolitan regions. The State Foundation for Data Analysis (Sistema Estadual para Análise de Dados Estatísticos — SEADE), in agreement with the Inter-Union Department of Statistics and Socioeconomic Studies (Departamento Intersindical de Estatísticas e Estudos Sócio-econômicos — DIEESE), made this data available after 1985.

A summary of data for the São Paulo metropolitan area is presented in Table 9, which shows a decline in open unemployment and in precarious employment (underemployment) between 1985 and 1988 derived from economic growth spurred by the "New Republic" (the administration following military rule) and the Cruzado Plan. The economy then went through a period of economic stagnation and recession during which unemployment levels began to rise once again.

Since precarious employment is experienced by a subset of workers in informal activities, it should be noted that the levels of precarious employment in this study may be used to approximate the levels of informal employment even though the former is not a direct measure of the latter.

## Table 9
## Open Unemployment and Precarious Jobs in Greater São Paulo 1985–1991 (percent)

| Unemployment topology | 1985 | 1986 | 1987 | 1988 | 1989 | 1990 | 1991 |
|---|---|---|---|---|---|---|---|
| Total unemployment | 12.2 | 9.6 | 9.2 | 7.7 | 8.7 | 10.3 | 11.6 |
| Open | 7.6 | 6.0 | 6.3 | 7.0 | 6.5 | 7.4 | 7.9 |
| Disguised | 4.6 | 3.6 | 2.9 | 2.7 | 2.2 | 2.9 | 3.7 |
| Precarious jobs | 2.9 | 2.0 | 1.7 | 1.8 | 1.5 | 2.0 | 2.8 |
| Discouraged | 1.7 | 1.4 | 1.2 | 0.9 | 0.7 | 0.9 | 0.9 |

Source: *PED.*

Ultimately, open unemployment and the informal sector — a new form of traditional underemployment — were integrated into the Brazilian labor market during the urbanization and industrialization processes. It should be emphasized that these two categories of labor expanded not only as a result of changes in the production structure and in labor relations but also because of the government's passive attitude toward social issues. Until only recently has the Brazilian state adopted an unemployment compensation program.[9]

In periods of crisis, the informal sector expands significantly because former salaried workers displaced by reduced production cannot find any other means to subsist. Even if the benefits and limitations of universal unemployment programs are considered, during periods of recession unemployed workers are left with the option of penetrating the informal market and competing for a share of the declining income resulting from recession or stagnation.

## Economic Cycle, Open Unemployment, and Employment in the Brazilian Public Sector

The increase in open unemployment during recessions has been followed simultaneously by an increase in employment in the informal sector. The informalization of the labor market has been a powerful means of easing labor in an economy with such a highly heterogeneous productive sector. Informality has even served as a buffer to pressures caused by disorganized state finances resulting in taxes unacceptable to the productive sectors.

In addition to the informal sector, the state has emerged as an employer seeking to minimize the social severity of a crisis. That is, employment in the public sector, which naturally tends to increase with economic growth and the expansion of the state's role in the economy, has also exhibited an anti-cyclical pattern in the Brazilian case. This pattern is illustrated in Table 10.[10]

### Table 10
## Determinants of Public Sector Employment[a]
## 1979–1989

| Areas | Constant | Explanatory Variables[b] | | R²(%) | n |
| | | Population | GDP *per capita* | | |
|---|---|---|---|---|---|
| 1. São Paulo | -0.65170 | 0.55650 | -0.48030 | | |
| | (-0.52800) | (7.33300)* | (-3.78900)* | 93.7 | 11 |
| 2. Brazil | -1.0688 | 1.17782 | -0.62690 | | |
| | (-2.69158)* | (10.37890)* | (-2.57790)* | 93.3 | 11 |

Notes: [a] Public sector employment relative to total employment in the formal sector. Logarithmic form.
　　　[b] Values in parentheses refer to "t" Student statistics.
　　　* Statistically significant at a 5% confidence level.
　　　R² = Explanation power.
　　　n= Number of observations.
Sources: Chahad 1990 and 1991.

Taking into consideration the limitations of assessments, the results presented in Table 10 clearly show that public sector employment tends to cushion the unemployment crisis in periods of negative GDP growth rates. Accordingly, public sector employment performs a role similar to that of the informal sector.

Although there are enormous distortions in the labor market of the Brazilian public sector, the issue of labor absorption in the country's interior is more complex than often is diagnosed. While the results of this study indicate that the state has played an important role in shielding employment in periods of crisis, several studies on the topic have emphasized the eminently political character of employment in the public sector.

# Notes

1. Several authors have written about this theme. See, among others, Camarano 1986; Camarano, Beltrão, and Neuper 1989; Baltar 1988; and Magno de Carvalho 1988. In the present text, the change will be dealt with on the basis of observed behavior of the most important demographic variables, without much consideration of the demographic transition experienced by the country.

2. Fertility rates show the average number of children per woman during her reproductive cycle, given a current fertility pattern. See Camarano, Beltrão, and Neupert 1989, 9.

3. For more information on changes in the production pattern, see, among others, Chahad 1987 and Médice 1988.

4. The precarious nature of the information provided in Table 3 is well known, especially the percentage of work ID cards issued, since the same individual may have more than one card simultaneously. In spite of the problems with data, it is difficult to believe that these duplicated documents are the main factor in determining the trends toward the increase in salaried workers.

5. The Gini coefficient is a measure of inequality based on the income distribution of the population. A coefficient equal to one (1) indicates perfect inequality, and a coefficient equal to zero indicates perfect equality.

6. The availability of data determined the time period covered in the table.

7. See, among others, Chahad and Luque 1990.

8. There is vast literature on the informal sector, exploring its several relationships with other aspects of the labor market and of society. Among others, those by Jatobá 1988 and 1989, Souza 1980, Cacciamali 1993, and Camargo 1989 are good sources of information on the informal sector.

9. The unemployment compensation program was introduced in Brazil in March 1986, when the Cruzado Plan was implemented. Its coverage, however, does not encompass more than 5 percent of the unemployed workers from the formal sector. This is a very small proportion of the workers in need of such assistance.

10. A more detailed presentation of this argument can be found in Chahad 1990 and 1991 and in Rezende 1974. In what follows, the possible links between the public deficit and public employment will be omitted.

# References

Baltar, P.E.S. 1988. "Evolução Demográfica, Emprego e Demandas Sociais Urbanas no Brasil." In *Transição Demográfica: Anais do VI Encontro Nacional de Estudos Populacionais, ABEP*, 1. Olinda, Pernambuco, October 16-20.

Cacciamali, M.C. 1983. *Setor Informal Urbano e Formas de Participação na Produção.* Série Ensaios Econômicos 26. São Paulo: IPE/USP.

Camarano, A.A., K. Beltrão, and R.P. Neupert. 1989. *Século XXI: A Quantas Andará a População Brasileira?* Discussion Paper 5. Brasília, D.F.: IPEA/IPLAN.

Camarano, A.A., K. Beltrão, and R.P. Neupert, eds. 1986. *Dinâmica Demográfica e Crescimento da Força de Trabalho no Brasil: 1980/2000.* Recife: Fundação Joaquim Nabuco.

Camargo, J.M. 1989. "Informalização e Renda no Mercado de Trabalho." In *Mercado de Trabalho e Distribuição de Renda: Uma Coletânea.* Série Monográfica 35. Eds. Guilherme Sedlacek and Ricardo P. de Barros. Rio de Janeiro: IPEA/INPES.

Chahad, J.P.Z. 1987. *Seguro-Desemprego: Lições da História, Aspectos Teóricos e Perspectivas para o Brasil.* Série Ensaios Econômicos 64. São Paulo: IPE/FEA/USP.

Chahad, J.P.Z. 1990. "Emprego e Salários na Administração Pública Brasileira: Evidências da Década de Oitenta." *Revista Brasileira de Economia* 44, 4: 551-573.

Chahad, J.P.Z. 1991. "Emprego Público e Ciclo Econômico no Estado de São Paulo." *Revista São Paulo em Perspectiva* 5 (1): 59-63.

Chahad, J.P.Z., and C.A. Luque. 1990. "Salário Real e Oferta de Alimentos Básicos no Brasil." *Revista de Economia Política* 10(3): 40-61.

Jatobá, J. 1989. "A Dimensão Regional da Pobreza Urbana e os Mercados de Trabalho: O Caso Brasileiro, 1970-1984." In *Mercado de Trabalho e Distribuição de Renda: Uma Coletânea.* Série Monográfica 35. Eds. Guilherme Sedlacek and Ricardo P. de Barros. Rio de Janeiro: IPEA/INPES.

Jatobá, J. 1988. *Latin America's Labor Market Research: A State of Arts.* Discussion Papers, Dp/9/1988. Geneva, Switzerland: IILS.

Magno de Carvalho, J.A. 1988. "O Tamanho da População Brasileira e sua Distribuição Etária: Uma Visão Prospectiva." In *Transição Demográfica: Anais do VI Encontro Nacional de Estudos Populacionais, ABEP*, 1. Olinda, Pernambuco, October 16-20.

Martine, G., et al. 1988. "Urbanização no Brasil: Retrospectiva, Componentes e Perspectivas." In *Urbanização e Processo de Transformação da Sociedade Brasileira: Anais do VI Encontro Nacional de Estudos Populacionais, ABEP*, 2. Olinda, Pernambuco, October 16-20.

Médice, A.C. 1988a. "A Mensuração da Subjetividade: Notas sobre a Variável Renda." In *PNADS em Fóco Anos 80.* Ed. Diana Sawyer. ABEP.

Médice, A.C. 1988b. "Urbanização e Transformações Estruturais na Força de Trabalho no Brasil: Notas para uma Discussão." In *Urbanização e Processo de Transformação da Sociedade Brasileira: Anais do VI Encontro Nacional de Estudos Populacionais, ABEP*, 2. Olinda, Pernambuco, October 16-20.

Merrick, T., and E. Berquó. 1983. *The Determinants of Brazil's Recent Rapid Decline in Fertility*. Washington, D.C.: National Academy Press Committee on Population and Demography.

Ministério do Trabalho. 1987. "Transição Demográfica e Força de Trabalho." In *O Mercado de Trabalho Brasileiro, Estrutura e Conjuntura*. Brasilia, D.F.: Ministério do Trabalho.

Paiva, P.T.A. 1984. *Cinqüenta Anos de Crescimento Populacional e Absorção de Mão-de-Obra no Brasil: de 1950 a 2000*. Discussion Paper 19. Belo Horizonte: CEDEPLAR/UFMG.

Rezende, F., et al. 1974. *A Avaliação do Setor Público na Economia Brasileira: Estrutura Funcional da Despesa*. Coleção Relatórios de Pesquisa. Rio de Janeiro: IPEA/INPES.

Wong, L.R., R. Hakkert, and R.A. Lima. 1987. *O Futuro da População Brasileira: Projeções e Técnicas*. São Paulo: ABEP, Seminário Técnico sobre Projeções Populacionais.

# NINE

# Obstacles to Human Capital Formation in Brazil

## Eduardo Giannetti da Fonseca

From almost any angle of inquiry, one can conclude that the 1980s were a true watershed in contemporary economic development. It is premature to believe at this point, however, that the changes that took place are irreversible or conclusive, for a prognosis of the surprises of the last decade and the speed with which they occurred need to be evaluated with caution. The matters that cannot be left unquestioned are the depth and extent of the transformations now in course.

For a majority of middle and low income countries, the 1980s marked a sharp reversal of expectations. After a period of optimism and fast growth during the post-war period, when the distance between developing and developed countries seemed to be decreasing progressively, the 1980s witnessed a process of polarization in the world economy. On the one hand, developed countries were able to overcome stagflation and initiate a new series of technological innovations and growth. On the other hand, the Soviet bloc collapsed, suffocated by its own inefficiency. Third World countries, with few exceptions, were faced with the economic problems of chronic inflation, external disequilibrium, and prolonged stagnation.

From the viewpoint of the developing world, and Latin America in particular, the 1980s did not find a solution to the difficulties and uncertainties that faced the world economy in the 1970s but rather an exacerbation of these problems. Between 1982 and 1989, the inflation rate in Latin America and the Caribbean increased from 56 to 1,023 percent per year, while the region's per capita gross domestic product (GDP) fell 8.9 percent (CEPAL 1990, 20). Certainly, this poor economic performance of the great majority of middle and low income countries over the last decade has led, as expected, to serious questioning and revision of the growth models adopted by these countries and to a reexamination of economic development theory in general.[1]

In accordance with the theoretical trends of the early post-war period (Keynesian thought and the apparent success of central planning in Eastern Europe), the traditional literature on development viewed market imperfections as signals for investment needs, proposing government planning and coordination of economic growth as a corrective mechanism. The basic conclusion was that in order to promote economic progress in middle and low income countries, it was essential that the state's role be comprehensive in implementing a fast-growth strategy based on strong protection of the domestic market, accumulation of capital in the industrial sector, and manipulation of macroeconomic aggregates (such as domestic savings, balance of payments, and supply of exchange rate and credit).

The experience of the 1980s, however, has brought to light some of the most serious limitations of the "great developmentalist consensus." Among the basic problems of this directed approach to development, as practiced mainly in Latin America, two are of utmost importance: 1) the rules of the game — the lack of adequate recognition of the importance of disciplinary action exerted by the market in the promotion of allocation efficiency; and 2) the quality of the players — the weak performance of human capital formation, which has become indispensable for the modernization of production and per capita production increases.

Regarding the rules of the game, contrary to what happened in the post-war period, the consensus of development scholars is that the export promotion model adopted by the so-called Asian Tigers is much more efficient and promising in terms of growth than the import-substitution model followed by countries such as Brazil and India. While industrialization via import substitution paddled against the tide, generating true "greenhouse plants" that survived to a large extent in a symbiotic or parasitic relationship with the state, the export promotion strategy worked in favor of the market, allowing for technological innovation and productivity gains associated with the division of labor and specialization.

As Bardhan (1990,6) accurately observes in his discussion of the contrast between these two development strategies:

> One important aspect of the quality of state intervention that the recent East Asian success stories highlight is something that the critics of neoclassical theory, in their eagerness to emphasize the highly interventionist nature of the East Asian state, often overlook. . . . The intervention schemes have worked closely with the market, and the state's alertness in using the signals emanating from world markets to judge dynamic efficiency has helped keep firms on their

toes and prevented infant industries from turning into inefficient geriatric protection lobbies. However convinced one may be of the pervasiveness of market failures in developing countries, one must recognize the vital disciplining function of competition in encouraging quick learning and cost and quality consciousness.

In terms of development, any recovery program for Brazil should redefine the role of the external sector as an inducer of competitiveness and as a source of gains in productivity and efficiency compatible with those of countries that are more integrated with world trade. The closing of the Brazilian economy to international trade facilitated the concentration of market power in firms already established in the country, generated an excessive verticalization of production, and inhibited the diffusion of new technologies that are essential for economic development. The liberalization of imports and an increase in foreign capital and technology inflow represent, in this perspective, fundamental measures leading to an increase in competitiveness and modernization and specialization of production activities that can generate higher growth rates for exports.

The purpose of this chapter, however, is not to identify the most adequate rules of the game for development. Rather, the goal here is to analyze the obstacles to an improvement in the quality of the players that perform in accordance with those rules. The importance of skilled labor and organization and specialization of productive activities has become clear, especially in light of an increase in the speed of scientific and technological innovation in the 1980s; the rapid diffusion of new processes, equipment, and possibilities that affect the entire productive base of economies (microelectronic, biotechnology, new materials, artificial intelligence, and so on); the growing integration of international markets for goods and services; and the increasing competition for capital in the world economy. The question now becomes how to recover the time lost and how to accelerate the formation of human capital stock needed to face this new reality.

The basic premise of this discussion is the notion that abundant natural resources and cheap labor have lost importance as determinants of international competitiveness. The world trend clearly is converting "brain power" (as opposed to "muscle" or "natural endowments") into the key element for increasing per capita production and standards of living. From this perspective, economic performance not only will depend on the capacity to absorb, adapt, and create new technologies but also will depend on the ability to explore the opportunities presented in the domestic market and in foreign markets quickly and competently. Human capital as well as stable and adequate rules — microeconomic efficiency — are the bases for high production per capita and wealth. Without these elements, no macroeconomic plan will resolve the serious problems of the material deprivation and backwardness of Brazilian society, no matter how brilliantly conceived and well implemented the plan may be.

The argument put forth in this chapter is organized in the following manner. First, an examination is made of the Brazilian educational system in the 1980s, its main deficiencies, and its relationship to poverty, the condition of a large portion of Brazil's population. A profile of the public sector's expenditures on social programs follows, especially those related to education, which highlights the need to improve the profile of public spending and create non-monetary incentives for the formation of human capital. Final considerations related to the state and the market's roles in the process of human capital formation will be offered.

## Poverty and Educational Opportunities

More careful, empirical studies of the magnitude of absolute poverty and the evolution of the main social indicators in Brazil during recent decades reveal that, despite some progress, the results achieved thus far have been modest and the present social conditions represent a serious problem. Considering the fact that 42 percent of the Brazilian population is less than 18 years of age, socioeconomic conditions and relative access to essential goods for children living in low income families deserve special attention.

First of all, a reduction in absolute poverty indicators between 1970 and 1980 is observed. Hoffmann (1984), who defined the "poverty line" as those households whose total monthly income was less than the minimum monthly salary (of August 1980), estimated that the proportion of poor families in Brazil dropped from 42.2 to 21.9 percent from 1970 to 1980. Similar results were obtained by Pastore and Pagotto (1983), who defined the "poverty line" as those household monthly per capita incomes that were less than one-fourth of the minimum wage. Their study concludes that the proportion of families in "extreme poverty" had declined from 43.9 to 17.7 percent from 1970 to 1980. (It should be noted that there was a slight growth in the real minimum wage during the period, especially in the country's poorest regions.) More recent data show that 14.7 percent of Brazilian families live on an income below one-fourth of the minimum wage per capita (extreme poverty), while 34.6 percent of the families live in "poverty," earning less than US$300 per year, a monthly income below one-half of the minimum wage per capita (Jaguaribe et al. 1989).

Some social indicators point toward an amelioration in the quality of life for Brazilians in the last decade. Life expectancy at birth increased from 54.7 years in 1960 to 65.6 years in 1990. The infant mortality rate (children five years of age and younger) decreased from 159 per 1,000 births in 1960 to 85 per 1,000 births in 1989. The literacy rate for the population (15 years of age and older) increased from 66 to about 79 percent from 1970 to 1985.

The proportion of the total population with access to drinking water jumped from 62 percent in 1975 to 96 percent in 1988 (United Nations 1991). These statistics, however, should not obscure the persisting severity of Brazil's social conditions.

The basic fact is that, despite the decreased proportion of families living in conditions of severe poverty (per capita household income less than US$150 per year) and poverty (less than US$300 annually), the extent of the problem in absolute terms continues to be massive. Even worse, the incidence of poverty among children and adolescents (ages 17 and younger) is particularly alarming. For such a large sector of the population, the extraordinary performance of the Brazilian economy between 1960 and 1980 (ranking number one in the world with a per capita income growth rate of approximately 5.1 percent per year) represented very little in terms of socioeconomic advances.

By the end of the 1980s, about 4.7 million families were living in conditions of extreme poverty, and more than 11 million were living in poverty. Based on an average of 4.8 individuals per poor family — compared to the national average of 4.1 and the "non-poverty" average of 3.7 — approximately 53.2 million Brazilians lived in poverty, which represented 41 percent of the total population. The most disturbing aspect of this whole picture is that approximately 26 million children (or about one-half of Brazil's children under 14 years of age) live in poor households.

Two crucial aspects related to the formation of human capital should be stressed when discussing Brazil's poverty profile. First, the data on poor families show a more than proportionate participation of the following types of households: 1) families comprised of young members (heads of households younger than 29 years), 2) families in their final life cycle (heads of households older than 60 years), and 3) single-mother families. Regarding the latter, although only 18 percent of all Brazilian families are headed by a single mother, this same proportion increases to 22 percent among poor families and to 25 percent among families living in extreme poverty. Combining the first and third categories of families mentioned above, it is apparent that 59 percent of all families headed by single women younger than 29 years of age are living in poverty. From the set of households headed by two parents in the same age group (under 29 years), 37 percent live in poverty, while only 29 percent of families headed by persons between 50 and 59 years live in poverty (Jaguaribe et al. 1989).

Moreover, it is important to note that the massive income transfers promoted by the Brazilian government did not accomplish their objective of helping targeted groups. Of the 55 million poor people in Brazil, at least 60 percent live without any kind of social security protection. The same is true of the benefits provided by labor legislation, such as vacation, thirteen months of salary, and maternity leave. Of the families living in extreme poverty, 75 percent were headed by men and women working without legal worker registration. Even in metropolitan areas, about 50 percent of the population living in extreme poverty failed to have proper registration. This large number of low income workers working without the necessary legal requirements are excluded from all benefits provided by labor legislation and other social benefits provided by the government.

The most alarming element concerning the Brazilian social condition, however, is the precarious socioeconomic situation of the great number of children (ages zero to 14) and adolescents (ages 15 to 17) living in low income households, indicating a continuation of a vicious cycle of poverty and incompetence under which a large portion of the Brazilian population has lived for centuries. The main challenge for social policy in the next decade is to reverse this situation.

Although the proportion of children and adolescents in the total population in Brazil has declined from 44 to 42 percent in the 1980s and is expected to continue its decline in the current decade, the number of children in absolute terms increased from 53 to 59 million between 1981 and 1989.[2] Of this total, about 70 percent live in urban areas and 30 percent live in rural areas. Compared to the averages of developing countries worldwide, Brazil's population is quite young: children and adolescents (ages zero to 17) compose 42 percent of the Brazilian population, compared to the 26 percent average in all developing countries. Younger children (ages zero to 14) constitute 36 percent of the Brazilian population, compared to the 22 percent average in developing countries (World Bank 1980). These proportions bear great economic importance to the extent that they affect the following: 1) the dependency rate of children on the economically active population (EAP); 2) the future growth rate of the EAP; 3) the stock of capital per worker; and 4) the rate of human capital formation per capita, that is, the average investment in health and professional training for each child or adolescent.

Table 1 presents data on the distribution of children among households classified according to different categories of monthly household per capita income in 1986. In 1986 — with no significant change since — 43 percent of the population in the zero to 17 age bracket (or about 25 million children and adolescents) were living in poor households with a monthly household income per capita lower than one-half the monthly minimum wage, while this proportion was 32 percent in urban areas and 68 percent in rural areas. The exceptionally high incidence of poverty among the young population becomes evident if one realizes that 28 percent of the poorest households in the country consist of approximately 45 percent of all Brazilian children younger than 14 years of age.

Table I

Households and Individuals Living in Private Housing
According to Monthly Household Per Capita Income and Age Groups, Brazil, 1986

| | Absolute figures (1,000s) | Total | Classes of per capita monthly household income (minimum wage) Relative numbers (%) | | | | | | |
|---|---|---|---|---|---|---|---|---|---|
| | | | Up to 1/4 | More than 1/4 to 1/2 | More than 1/2 to 1 | More than 1 to 2 | More than 2 | Without income | Undeclared |
| Households | | | | | | | | | |
| Total | 33,059.9 | 100 | 9.7 | 17.2 | 24.1 | 22.4 | 24.2 | 1.5 | 0.8 |
| Urban | 25,088.2 | 100 | 5.3 | 13.5 | 23.7 | 25.2 | 29.8 | 1.5 | 0.9 |
| Rural | 7,971.6 | 100 | 23.6 | 28.6 | 25.3 | 13.7 | 6.7 | 1.5 | 0.6 |
| Households with persons 0–17 years old | | | | | | | | | |
| Total | 23,170.0 | 100 | 12.5 | 19.6 | 25.8 | 21.9 | 17.7 | 1.8 | 0.7 |
| Urban | 17,109.5 | 100 | 6.8 | 15.9 | 26.8 | 25.4 | 22.5 | 1.8 | 0.8 |
| Rural | 6,060.5 | 100 | 28.3 | 29.8 | 23.2 | 12.0 | 4.3 | 1.7 | 0.6 |
| Persons | | | | | | | | | |
| Total | 134,438.3 | 100 | 13.1 | 19.2 | 24.8 | 21.3 | 19.7 | 1.0 | 0.8 |
| 0–17 years | 57,482.3 | 100 | 18.7 | 23.1 | 25.4 | 17.9 | 13.0 | 1.3 | 0.7 |
| Less that 1 year old | 3,238.1 | 100 | 20.0 | 23.1 | 24.6 | 15.7 | 12.0 | 4.1 | 0.5 |
| 1–3 years | 9,966.0 | 100 | 20.8 | 23.4 | 23.4 | 16.4 | 13.2 | 2.3 | 0.5 |
| 4–6 years | 10,541.7 | 100 | 21.1 | 22.8 | 23.9 | 16.5 | 13.7 | 1.5 | 0.5 |
| 7–9 years | 9,973.7 | 100 | 20.9 | 23.8 | 24.7 | 16.4 | 12.7 | 0.8 | 0.6 |
| 10–14 years | 15,321.5 | 100 | 17.8 | 24.1 | 26.6 | 18.2 | 12.1 | 0.5 | 0.6 |
| 15–17 years | 8,441.0 | 100 | 11.6 | 20.6 | 28.6 | 23.5 | 14.1 | 0.6 | 0.8 |
| 18 years and older | 76,954.0 | 100 | 8.9 | 16.3 | 24.4 | 23.9 | 24.6 | 0.8 | 1.0 |
| Age unknown | 2.0 | 100 | 63.6 | 12.5 | — | 11.3 | 12.5 | — | 1.0 |

Notes: Rural population of the North Region excluded.
Individuals living in houses as roommates, servants, and their relatives are excluded.
Source: IBGE-*Pesquisa Nacional por Amostra de Domicílios (PNAD)*.

This particular phenomenon is the result of two basic conditions. First, as previously discussed, the incidence of poverty is proportionately greater among families headed by men and women younger than 29 years of age. At this early stage of their life cycle, couples pass through their reproductive phase and bear children with more frequency, causing the presence of children to be substantially higher in these families. Second, there is a strong inverse relationship between family size and income level. Whereas 33 percent of households living in extreme poverty (those with less than one-fourth of minimum wage income per capita) in Brazil have more than four children, only 1 percent of the wealthiest households (income per capita equal to or greater than ten times the minimum wage) and 11 percent of all households in Brazil have more than four children. To illustrate the plight of poor children in Brazil further, statistics reveal that at least 60 percent of Brazilian children less than one year old (and 45 percent of those in urban areas) continue to live in houses that lack adequate sanitation, despite significant improvements during the 1980s.

One should also note that more recent evidence indicates a visible trend in the 1980s toward women becoming mothers at an earlier age, especially in low income families. The large disparities in fertility rates among mothers with different levels of schooling and income also persist. These data suggest that the number of deprived children in Brazil continues to increase, helping to expand further the incidence of poverty beyond the current level, which is already disproportionate for the youngest age groups. Moreover, the implications of this phenomenon are not yet well understood. As noted by the World Bank (1980, 40), "studies performed in developed countries (even after controlling for socioeconomic status) reveal that children born and raised in smaller families tend to be more developed physically, more intelligent, and have a longer life expectancy."

From an economic viewpoint, the main consequences of this situation in Brazil are its harmful effects on the professional ability, initiative, and productivity of large segments of the population. These effects take place when the absolute deprivation or lack of competence in poor families causes them to forgo any investment in the formation of human capital for younger generations. Therefore, a great number of children and adolescents who are receiving an insufficient quality and quantity of food and education exhibit precarious academic performance and hence enter the labor market prematurely. Their economic horizon is blocked, and the cycle of poverty and incompetence is ready to begin anew. Illustrative of this cycle, evidence in 1989 shows that 70 percent of illiterate adolescents (ages 15 to 17) in Brazil had illiterate mothers.

There are several methods that empirically demonstrate this vicious circle in Brazil during the 1980s. One way is to examine what happens with school attendance, academic performance, and participation in the labor market of children (ages ten to 14) and adolescents (ages 15 to 17) from low income families. Although school attendance is compulsory for children between seven and 14 years of age, and although labor legislation prohibits children under 14 from participating in the labor market, the reality of the situation is quite the opposite.[3]

In general, family strategies for generating income and the extent of other family members participating in the EAP besides the head of the household differ according to income levels. Families in the lowest income bracket (per capita income below two minimum wages) depend much more on work performed by their children (ages ten to 17) and show less participation by spouses in the EAP. Families with per capita income above two minimum wages predominantly rely on work by both parents to increase their income, keeping their children from prematurely entering the labor market. In 1986, 23.8 percent of children (ages ten to 14) from low income families worked, compared to only 6.1 percent of children from wealthier families.

At the same time, 51 percent of all adolescents (ages 14 to 17) and an estimated 46 percent of urban adolescents were working in Brazil in 1989. For all children in Brazil between ten and 14 years of age, this percentage was estimated at 20 percent. Working mostly in unskilled and badly remunerated jobs and for 40 or more hours per week, the great majority of these children essentially were not covered under labor legislation. Only 25 percent of adolescents (ages ten to 17) had worker identification cards. The average salary for these children was about 0.9 of the minimum wage in urban areas and 0.4 in rural areas.

In addition to examining the participation levels of children in the work force, it is also necessary to consider school attendance and academic performance of children in specific age groups. Of all Brazilian children between the ages of ten and 17 in 1986, only 59 percent had the privilege of attending school without having to work (65 percent in urban areas). Of the remaining population in this age group, 12 percent worked and attended school; 18 percent worked but did not attend school; 8 percent were responsible for housekeeping chores but did not work nor attend school; and 3 percent were not engaged in any of these activities. Such data show that about 7 million children between the ages of ten and 17 (3.8 million of whom were living in urban areas) did not participate in the formal education system. For children between ten and 14 years of age, 72 percent (80 percent in urban areas) attended school, but at least 19 percent, or 2.9 million of these children (1.4 million in the cities), did not attend school. During the 1980s, percentages changed slightly: there was a small increase in the proportion of children and adolescents attending school and a minor reduction in the proportion who only worked.

In the age group subject to compulsory school attendance, school attendance increased in 1989 from a little less than 50 percent of the target population (ages seven to 14) to about 85 percent (about 70 percent in rural areas and 88 percent in urban areas). Although certainly an impressive improvement, these statistics reveal that more than 4.5 million children in this age group still do not attend school, of which 2.6 million have never gone to school.

As expected, the lack of schooling is much higher in low income families than in other income levels. Whereas 97 percent of children (ages seven to 14) in wealthier families attend school, only 71 percent of children in poor families (with per capita income lower than one-fourth of the minimum wage) attend. Among 14-year-olds in poor families, the absenteeism rate reaches 40 percent. Furthermore, strong regional and sectoral disparities are also noticed. While 89 percent of all children between seven and 14 living in urban areas of the Southeast region attended school, only 67 percent of this same age group living in rural areas of the Northeast attended school. For the category of children between the ages of 15 and 17, attendance rates were lower than those of the younger groups and did not show any significant improvement during the last decade. In the 1980s, school attendance among this group only increased from 53 percent in 1981 to 55 percent in 1989, while the school attendance of the seven to 14 age group, who are required to attend elementary and middle school, increased much more during this time period.

Finally, another important source of information on problems that affect children's basic education in Brazil is the level of academic/intellectual performance per level of schooling. It should be noted that initial school attendance rates for the general population increase for children between five and ten years of age, and the peak attendance rate of 89 percent is reached at ten years of age. By the age of 14, this rate drops to 69 percent; and by the age of 17, to 44 percent. Part of the reason for this sharp decline in school attendance during the teenage years is the lack of motivation associated with poor academic performance (such as repeating the same grade) and mismatch between age and school level expected for particular age groups and grade levels. For example, 70 percent of seven-year-olds perform at their expected level of education (first grade), whereas only 10 percent of 14-year-olds perform at their expected level (8th grade). Children from poor families at this age who are still in school already have fallen an average of four years behind the expected level of education. A bottleneck in the system develops primarily during the first year of elementary school. The performance rate, based on age and level of academic performance, drops tremendously between the ages of seven and eight.

In light of these statistics, it is easy to understand why the illiteracy rate among Brazilian children (ages seven to 14) has increased in recent years, from 32 percent in 1981 to 34 percent in 1989, despite significant increases in the rate of school attendance by this same age group. Basically, it may be concluded that the quantitative increase in elementary education during the 1980s has been achieved at an enormous cost to the quality and utility of education. Thus, Brazil's education problem is not so much the lack of schools but the inadequate extension of educational opportunities to older children (very low levels of schooling for the population over 15) and the extremely low levels of progress achieved by students in general, due not only to the lack of support from their low income families but also due to the poor quality of the educational system (only one-fourth of all children who enter elementary school will complete it).

## Social and Education Policies

D ata on the structure of the government's social expenditures at three levels (federal, state, and local) suggest that, although the total level of benefits and income transfers promoted by the public sector in Brazil is impressive, the results obtained are meager because of strong distortions in terms of misallocation and inefficient use of these resources.[4]

Total social expenditures, including disbursements from the public sector and from households in the areas of health, education, sanitation, housing, nutrition, and social security, are estimated to be around 25 percent of Brazil's GDP — approximately 7 percent from the private sector for education and health and 18 percent from the public sector for all social programs. Public sector disbursements are divided further into 9 percent of GDP for the federal government and the other 9 percent among the 24 states and 4,000 municipalities. This division in public sector social expenditures among the various levels of government was altered by the 1988 Constitution, which transferred some of the federal government's resources to states and municipalities. Decentralization of government expenditures is expected to decrease the overall level of public sector waste in disbursements for social programs.

Taking into consideration the relative size of government budgets and GDP levels, international comparisons indicate that the magnitude of social expenditures in Brazil is comparable to those of other countries, such as Mexico and South Korea, with similar income levels. On the other hand, the quality of these expenditures and their effects on the main social indicators (life expectancy at birth, infant mortality, illiteracy, educational levels) have been much lower than desired.

The main reasons for poor results are 1) misdirected expenditures — the fact that social expenditures by the public sector do not reach their targeted groups, such as the most deprived groups, the more vulnerable, and those with higher economic potential; and 2) inefficiency — administrative waste and resources poorly allocated to social programs. According to the data provided above, about 60 percent (nearly 31 million people) of all poor people (53 million) in Brazil do not benefit from the social security system; less than one-half of all Brazilian workers are covered by social security. In contrast to the trend in the previous decade, the number of workers without social security increased twice as fast as the number of workers entering the labor force. The same trend is occurring with the growing number of workers without other benefits associated with labor legislation (vacation, thirteen month salary, maternity leave).

This information helps to explain the surprising results obtained by the World Bank regarding the public sector's distribution of social expenditures according to different income levels. While only 20 percent of all public sector social expenditures is allocated to the poorest 41 percent of the population (monthly household per capita incomes lower than one-half the minimum wage), 34 percent is allocated to higher income groups (more than two minimum wages), even though the latter group represents only 16 percent of the total population.

Such statistics show that the level of public sector social expenditures per household is not inversely related to household income levels, as expected. In 1986, expenditures were equivalent to an annual sum of US$110 per capita for the poorest households (monthly household income per capita lower than one-fourth of the minimum wage), compared to an annual sum of US$737 per capita for wealthier households (monthly per capita income higher than two minimum wages). Thus, using the set of social programs maintained by the public sector as a basis, it is evident that government assistance related to benefits and income transfers tends to be about seven times greater for those who are closer to the top of the income pyramid than for those at the bottom.

The distribution of the public sector's social expenditures by age group follows a pattern similar to that of expenditures according to income level: younger population groups receive proportions of social expenditures comparable to the poorest income groups, while older population groups receive expenditures comparable to wealthier income groups. Instead of prioritizing investments in children and younger age groups who have yet to realize their economic potential and have not yet had the chance to become responsible parents, the government prioritizes age groups at the opposite end of the spectrum. Children who are younger than five years of age and account for 13 percent of the population receive only 7 percent of government social expenditures. At the other extreme, citizens older than 55 years of age receive about 44 percent of total public disbursements in social programs, despite the fact that they represent only 9 percent of the population. The group of citizens between the ages of 55 and 64, who account for only 5 percent of the total population — a small portion of whom take advantage of old-age pensions for time of service and receive at least one-third of total government disbursements for pensions — receive about 16 percent of government expenditures on social programs.

How can these results be explained? What can be done to reduce such distortions? A complete and systematic analysis of the inappropriateness of the allocation of the public sector's social expenditures is a task beyond the scope of this chapter and would require a detailed discussion of all social area sectors in which the government operates (health, education, sanitation, housing, nutrition, and social security). It would be necessary to show 1) how the distribution of total expenditures among these sectors takes place and 2) how the allocation distortions affect each of them in particular. An analysis could reveal explicitly how the misallocation of social expenditures is, in fact, another example of the Brazilian state's great vulnerability to pressure from interest groups (otherwise known as a "privatization of the state"). This phenomenon reflects the greater capacity (monetary and otherwise) of the richest groups and elderly to capture the benefits of the government's social programs.

Although a complete analysis of this sort cannot be accomplished here, it is worthwhile to examine in more detail one particular area in which the government functions: the education system. Distortions observed in this area are useful in explaining the misallocation of social expenditures, and they clearly illustrate the nature of the problems affecting the government's social policy. Obviously, a decision to examine this area is justified by the important role that expenditures on education play in the formation of human capital and in the distribution of opportunities for economic and social advancement for the most deprived and vulnerable groups in the population.

Brazil's public sector expenditures on education and culture amount to approximately 4 percent of the GDP or US$11 billion (1986). This total is slightly above the 3.8 percent average (non-weighted) for 20 Latin American countries. However, these expenditures for education are significantly lower than those of developed countries and of middle income countries in East Asia, such as South Korea. No country in the developed world invests less than 4.5 percent of its GDP in public education.

One must not forget that, unlike Brazil, these advanced industrialized countries have populations that are much more equally balanced in terms of age distribution (with smaller proportions in the youngest categories), and they do not have one-half of their total infant population living in households with extremely low income, that is, households that are completely deprived of resources and are unable to invest in the education and professional training of their children. Considering the higher levels of GDP per capita and smaller proportions of children in their populations, it is easy to conclude that public expenditures per child on education in developed countries are substantially higher than those to be expected by simply comparing public expenditures in terms of percentages of GDP allocated to education.

A more serious aspect of this disparity in education expenditures is the funds that are disbursed ineffectively in Brazil. Statistics reveal the existence of distortions in education policy that seriously endanger the results of government actions to reduce poverty, improve the distributive profile, and speed the formation of human capital in the country.

The first element to be noted is the distribution of expenditures on education by levels of schooling. According to World Bank estimates, about 68 percent of the government disbursements for education are allotted to elementary schooling, 23 percent to the university level, and only 9 percent to high school education. In comparison, the South Korean government spends about 37 percent of its education expenditure on high school education, while the university level receives only 11 percent, even though the number of young adults between the ages of 20 and 24 attending college is exactly twice as many as in Brazil (see the comparisons made by Knight and Wasty 1989). Neglect of high school education in Brazil endangers the development of intermediate levels of professionals in the EAP and leads to a misuse of resources at the university level.

The regressive character, in distributive terms, of benefits provided by the government to university students becomes clearer if one realizes that some 50 percent of students registered in federal and state public universities are from families with monthly incomes higher than 10 minimum wages; 6 percent are from families with incomes lower than two minimum wages; and only 1 percent are from families with monthly incomes lower than one minimum wage. Thus, families with higher incomes benefit from a subsidized free university education. At the same time, the cost of this subsidy (an average of US$2,500 per student/year) for society as a whole is 18 times greater than the cost of an elementary education (US$149 per student/year) or for a high school education (US$144 per student/year).

The poor quality of elementary and high school education in the public system completes the circuit, guaranteeing families with higher incomes a virtual monopoly on the benefits of a university-level education. Higher income families are the only ones who can pay for better private elementary and high school educations, which prepare students to compete effectively for access (via entrance examinations) to state and federal universities. Reduced public expenditures on high school education perpetuate the quasi-monopoly of higher income families on a higher education subsidized by the government.

As a result, students who are successful in passing entrance examinations for admittance to Brazil's public universities are primarily from the richest households. After graduating from universities, they are professionally qualified to become members of the economic elite, which will allow them to earn much higher incomes than those denied the same educational opportunities. What is the justification for providing them a generous government subsidy to finance their educations, given the advantages they already have? Paradoxically, family members with lower incomes attend — and pay for — private universities, many of which do not have the qualifications to provide such services. Sixty percent of university students in Brazil attend private universities.

The result of such a perverse system of public outlays on education, and particularly the inequity associated with higher education, is, therefore, that the poorest households in the country (with incomes below one-fourth the minimum wage), representing 19 percent of the total population, receive only 15 percent of the public sector's expenditures on education. In examining expenditure distribution among the three levels of education, it is evident that the wealthiest families receive twice as much as families with lower levels of income. Moreover, since the average size of a poor household is larger than the average size of a wealthy household, a child from a wealthy family receives an average of four times the amount of education subsidies from the government as a child from a poor family.

Besides changing the expenditure profile (improving allocation) and increasing efficiency (reducing waste), there is much that the government can do to stimulate the formation of human capital in Brazilian society. First would be to enforce existing laws, which are numerous yet basically ignored. Two such laws deserve special attention: 1) mandatory school attendance for children between the ages of seven and 14 and 2) prohibiting children under 14 years of age from working (except for 12- and 13-year-olds who have authorization from the Juizado de Menores). As mentioned, both laws have been ignored almost totally throughout Brazil, reflecting a lack of interest by public authorities in protecting the welfare of poor children and in punishing adults who are responsible for breaking the laws. Putting an end to impunity for school evasion and putting an end to premature participation in the labor market would be important government contributions to protecting the welfare of poor children and adolescents.

Another important, relatively low-cost initiative would be to recover the integrity of public and private education at the elementary and high school levels. The basic idea is to establish a national unified exit examination for elementary school children and for high school seniors.

The benefits of such an initiative would be the following: 1) the examination would redeem the value of the grade a child has reached as evidence of real competence; 2) it would be an incentive for teachers and students to perform their responsibilities effectively — schools that do not perform well would be exposed through results of national exit examinations and would be forced to produce better results; and 3) it would be the beginning of a reliable system to monitor the quality of education across the country. Indices showing approval or failure and their evolution over the years would permit better evaluations and would allow for closer observation of public and private school performances in all regions. The information obtained through observation not only would help parents to select schools for their children but also would be of great importance in identifying weak points in the system and in devising an appropriate education policy for the public sector.

Regarding higher education, it would be necessary to withdraw the large numbers of academic degrees that are not legitimate. Currently, these degrees are only an indication that a student has met his or her financial obligations with the school. The objective of this proposal would be to convert many of the public and private universities into professional schools so that they can produce qualified graduates who can fulfill the positions demanded by the labor market. By cleaning up higher education, the value and importance of genuine university degrees would be recovered. Conversion of a part of the university system into a professional school system would gear human resource capabilities more adequately toward the needs of the labor market.

The objective of the proposals discussed here is to create non-monetary incentives that will stimulate the formation of human capital. Given the financial disarray of the public sector and given the need for fiscal adjustment that definitively could eliminate the public deficit, it is necessary to find ways to achieve the desired results while remaining consistent with the country's economic stabilization efforts. Above all, it is necessary to confront the harsh reality of Brazil's deteriorating educational system. The only way to transform this reality is to meet it face-to-face.

## Conclusions: State, Market, and Childhood

Human resources — initiative, professional competence, creativity, discipline, and acting in the present with a view to the future — are productive factors that are as important for the generation of wealth as any other type of capital. Contrary to the "great developmentalist consensus" theorists, who believed that the accumulation of physical capital in industrial and urban sectors was the main factor that could generate growth, modern consensus is shifting toward making the "human brain" the decisive factor for economic success.

In criticizing analytical flaws of traditional development theory, Datta-Chaudhuri (1990, 28-29) made the following claim:

> Later researchers in the field of economic growth seriously undermined the importance attached to capital formation in the growth process of an economy. Sollow's (1957) seminal contribution demonstrated that only a small part of the growth performance of an economy can

be explained by the increment in its stock of reproducible physical capital (or by the employment of a larger number of workers). Most of the economic growth seems to come from technical progress, which is essentially the ability of an economic organization to utilize its productive resources more effectively over time. Much of this ability comes from the process of learning to operate newly created production facilities in a more productive way or more generally from learning to cope with rapid changes in the structure of production which industrial progress must imply. Traditional development economics paid little attention to such learning processes and implicitly assumed that whatever technical progress was possible would automatically come with capital accumulation. The development experiences of the last three decades show that economies differ considerably with respect to their abilities to learn new techniques and how to adjust quickly to new lines of production.

However, the accumulated ability and capacity to learn — for a developing economy to be able to advance in the formation of human capital — require compatible investment efforts in the health and education of younger members of the population. It is necessary that individuals have the opportunity to develop their talents, abilities, and latent capacities, benefiting themselves (private return) and society as a whole (social return) in the process.

In Brazil, however, population growth, income concentration, and the profile of public expenditures in social areas have acted and continue to act as major obstacles to the formation of adequate human capital:

- Excessive population growth has increased the number of young in the population, thereby lowering investment in human capital per person. Children (age 17 and younger) represent 42 percent of the population in Brazil, compared to the 26 percent on average in developed countries.

- The concentration of income has kept a large number of families from obtaining a minimum level of available income for investing in their children's health and education. There are 25 million poor children and adolescents (per capita monthly income lower than one-half the minimum wage) in Brazil; 28 percent of the poorest households in the country account for 45 percent of all children under the age of 14.

- The government's social expenditures ultimately are captured by middle and high income families, thereby excluding the groups that need these benefits the most. The massive income transfers promoted by the welfare state in Brazil have not reached their target groups.

From an economic point of view, the main consequences of this picture are the undesirable effects on professional competence, initiative, and the productivity of large segments of the population. These result from the inability of poorer families to invest adequately in the formation of human capital in younger generations because of their absolute deprivation and unpreparedness. In sum, during the post-war period of fast growth, provision of adequate attention to the promotion of human capital formation failed. The somber picture of social conditions in Brazil fundamentally is a product of this lack of education. The poor qualifications of large numbers of Brazilian workers have caused them to produce little and have sentenced them to low wage earnings. In fact, the poverty of one generation is the main cause of low production per capita and of incompetence in the subsequent generation. The main challenge for Brazil is to break this cycle and to stop the enormous human and economic waste that it engenders.

The main challenge of any development strategy for the 1990s is to identify efficient ways to speed up human capital formation. It is necessary to mobilize a massive investment effort to develop economic competence, geared especially toward the younger population in order to raise their per capita production. Brazil will not belong to the modern world as long as prevailing illiteracy rates, extremely low levels of schooling, and the poor quality of basic education persist. A social policy aimed at full citizenship for a larger part of the population will concentrate available resources in basic education and in the preparation of the poor segments of the young population for professional livelihoods.

In a market economy, it is expected that individuals have the ability to defend their own interests. However, if there are tens of millions of children whose parents are poor, who lack proper nourishment and basic education or other opportunities to develop their economic potential, these children logically will not succeed in defending their interests — they will continue to live in poverty. Consequently, this continuous cycle, of which they are already victims, serves as the most obvious argument for legitimate government interference in the economy, especially when the interests of the younger generation clearly are being sacrificed because of the errors and omissions of prior generations. The British economist Lionel Robbins, citing an official report presented to the British Parliament in 1841, *Report on the Condition of the Handloom Weaver,* makes a clear and unequivocal argument:

> It is equally obvious that, if the state be bound to require the parent to educate his child, it is bound to see that he has the means of doing so. The voluntary system, therefore, the system which leaves to the ignorance, or negligence, or debauchery or avarice of the parents of one age to decide how far the population of the succeeding age shall, or shall not, be instructed beings, has been repudiated: and we trust that, in a matter of such importance, perhaps the most important of the many subjects requiring the attention of the Government, a system which has been repudiated in principle will not be permitted to continue in practice (Robbins 1965, 93).

Unfortunately, however, the need for government intervention to guarantee an education to newer generations continues to be ignored in Brazil.

Expressing a consensus among British liberals, Pigou, in *The Economics of Welfare*, reminds us:

> But there is an agreement that the State should protect the interests of the future *in some degree* against the effects of our irrational discounting and of our preference for ourselves over our descendants (Pigou 1932, 29).

There are sound economic reasons, in addition to humanitarian ones, to try to compensate for the disadvantages of children of destitute (or shortsighted) parents. One reason is that such children can realize their potential contributions to their communities and, at the same time, themselves benefit. Marshall (1919, 179) emphasizes this point:

> And the economic value of one great industrial genius is sufficient to cover the expenses of the education of a whole town, for one new idea, such as Bessemer's chief invention (the purification process of iron ore in the steel industry) adds as much to England's productive power as the labour of one hundred thousand men.

Certainly, although the government will never be able to replace private initiative as the innovative and propelling force for generating wealth, it does not imply a complacent posture on its part toward poverty. It is the government's duty to concentrate efforts in order to avoid the tremendous amount of human waste created by the "illiterate Shakespeare," the "incompetent Bessemer," and the "pick-pocket businessman." The government's legitimate responsibility is to prevent its citizens' talents and abilities from being suffocated by illiteracy, ignorance, and deprivation, and to prevent them from being carried to their graves without a trace of their existence.

Ignorance and low labor productivity are the main causes of the material deprivation in which Brazilians have lived for so many centuries. If these causes are not attacked now by concentrating efforts in the formation of human capital of the younger generations and by implementing an adequate family planning policy, the country will never break its cycle of poverty and incompetence. The main idea is not to redistribute the result — the income — that each individual obtains in the market derived from his or her efforts and talents but mainly to redistribute the initial endowment (the initial opportunity for individuals to develop their professional and economic abilities). It is essential to keep in mind that equality of results oppresses, while equality of opportunity emancipates.

# Notes

1. See, for instance, the works of Hirschman (1981), Sen (1983), Lal (1983), and the recent symposium on the state and economic development in *Journal of Economic Perspectives*.

2. Unless otherwise indicated, the sources of data presented in this section are from the 1981, 1983, 1986, and 1990 Pesquisa Nacional de Amostra Domiciliar, PNAD; and from the *Statistical Profile of Mothers and Children in Brazil*, IBGE/UNICEF 1988.

3. The only exception to the law is that children older than 11 years of age may receive written permission from the Juvenile Court (*Juizado de Menores*).

4. Unless otherwise indicated, all the data presented and discussed in this section are based on the World Bank's survey, reported in *Brazil: Public Spending on Social Programs 1988*.

# References

Arndt, H.W. 1987. *Economic Development: The History of an Idea*. Chicago: The University of Chicago Press.

Bardhan, P. 1990. "Symposium on the State and Economic Development." *Journal of Economic Perspectives* 4: 3-7.

Barreto, A., et al. 1990. "Sistema Educativo-Cultural: Uma Visão Prospectiva." In *Prioridades de Políticas Públicas para a Década de 90*. Brasilia: IDEA/IPLAN.

Bauer, P. 1984. "Market Order and State Planning in Economic Development." In *Reality and Rhetoric: Studies in the Economics of Development*. London: Weidenfeld and Nicholson.

Comisión Económica para Latin America (CEPAL). 1990. *Changing Production Patterns with Social Equity*. Santiago: CEPAL.

Dasgupta, A.K. 1988. *Growth, Development and Welfare*. Oxford: Blackwell.

Datta-Chaudhuri, M. 1990. "Market Failure and Government Failure." *Journal of Economic Perspectives* 4: 25-39.

Fonseca, E.G. da. 1992. "O Capital Humano na Filosofia Social de Marshall." *Revista de Economia Política* 12 (2): 64-87.

Hirschman, A.O. 1981. "The Rise and Decline of Development Economics." In *Essays in Trespassing: Economics to Politics and Beyond*. Cambridge: Cambridge University Press.

Hoffman, R. 1985. "Distribuição da Renda e Pobreza entre as Famílias no Brasil: 1980 a 1983." *Revista de Economia Política* 5: 50-61.

Hoffman, R. 1984. *A Pobreza no Brasil: Análise dos Dados dos Censos Demográficos de 1970 e 1980*. Paper presented at the 6th National Congress of Econometrics. São Paulo.

Hunt, J.M. 1969. *The Challenge of Poverty and Incompetence*. Champaign, Ill.: University of Illinois.

IBGE/UNICEF. 1988a. "A Situação da Fecundidade: Determinantes Gerais e Características da Transição Recente." Eds. C. da Silva Simões and L. Pinto de Oliveira. In *Perfil Estatístico de Crianças e Mães no Brasil*. Rio de Janeiro: IBGE/UNICEF.

IBGE/UNICEF. 1988b. "Sistema de Acompanhamento da Situação Sócio-econômica de Crianças e Adolescentes: 1981/ 1983/ 1986." Eds. C. da Silva Simões and L. Pinto de Oliveira. In *Perfil Estatístico de Crianças e Mães no Brasil*. Rio de Janeiro: IBGE/UNICEF.

Jaguaribe, H., et al. 1989. *Brasil, Reforma ou Caos*. Rio de Janeiro: Paz e Terra.

Knight, P., and S. Wasty. 1989. *Human Resource Development: Comparative Trends in Resource Allocation in Latin America, Asia, and Europe*. (mimeo)

Krueger, A.O. 1990. "Government Failures in Development." *Journal of Economic Perspectives* 4: 9-23.

Lal, D. 1983. *The Poverty of Development Economics*. London: Institute of Economic Affairs.

Marshall, A. 1949. *Principles of Economics*. London: Macmillan.

Neupert, R.F., S. Calheiros, and M.L. Theodoro. 1989. *Evolução da População Economicamente Ativa no Brasil até o Ano 2010*. Discussion Paper 12. Brasília: IPEA/IPLAN.

Pastore, J., H. Zylberstajn, and C.S. Pagotto. 1983. *Mudança Social e Pobreza no Brasil: 1970-1980*. São Paulo: FIPE/Pioneira.

*Pesquisa Nacional de Amostra Domiciliar* (PNAD) 1981, 1983, 1986, 1990. Rio de Janeiro: IBGE.

Pigou, A.C. 1932. *The Economics of Welfare*. London: Macmillan.

*Report on the Condition of the Handloom Weavers*. 1841. Official report presented to the British Parliament. Cited in L. Robbins, 1965.

Robbins, L. 1965. *The Theory of Economic Policy in English Classical Political Economy*. London: Macmillan.

Sen, A. 1983. "Development: Which Way Now?" *Economic Journal* 93: 745-762.

United Nations. 1990. *Human Development Report*. New York: United Nations.

World Bank. 1988. *Brazil: Public Spending on Social Programs*. Washington, D.C.

World Bank. 1980, 1986, 1988, 1989, and 1991. *World Development Report*. Washington, D.C.

Zockun, M.H., ed. 1990. *Livre para Crescer: Proposta para um Brasil Moderno*. São Paulo: Cultura Editores Associados.

# The Growing Inequality in Income Distribution in Brazil

## Maria Cristina Cacciamali

## Introduction

Among all the countries for which the World Bank publishes statistics on personal and household income distribution, Brazil distinguishes itself as having one of the highest income concentrations and by displaying large interregional and intraregional disparities.

Only one state in Brazil, Paraíba, ranks lower in the indices of human development than the average ranking of poor developing countries; seven Brazilian states have a human development ranking comparable to more developed countries; and the other states have values comparable to those of other countries. The same indices show that among Brazil's macroregions, three of them, the South, Southeast, and Center-West, exhibit a high level of development, while the other two regions, the Northeast and North, exhibit levels comparable to the average of other developing countries (Albuquerque and Vilella 1990).

The causes of increasing inequality in functional and personal income distribution in Brazil have been the focus of numerous studies in the past 20 years. Mainly centering on an explanation for the worsening of personal income inequality during the 1960s and 1970s, these analyses examine the 1980s when instability and stagnation were the norm.

The structural roots of disparities have received little attention from specialists in the field. In reality, the poor distribution of wealth and income in Brazil should be studied in light of the country's colonial past and history of slavery. Land tenure after the seventeenth century was characterized by high levels of concentration mainly because of the enormous difficulties faced by new tenants in gaining legal rights to the land. Although not the only important economic factor, Brazil's background does set the stage for a concentrated, authoritarian, and paternalist political structure that would remain in place until World War II with only brief periods of greater levels of political participation.

With the beginning of industrialization at the end of the nineteenth century, the Southeast region of Brazil was already the economy's dynamic export center. After the 1930s, when industry became the engine of economic growth, the region formed the center of the industrialization process and experienced the most important structural changes while absorbing the main economic benefits. Rapid industrialization led by state intervention 20 years later further intensified the high concentration levels of wealth in urban areas, especially during the so-called "economic miracle" period of the late 1960s and early 1970s.

Provision of mass public schooling, which started after the 1940s, failed to target the whole population in expanding educational opportunities; rather, large urban centers and the middle class were made priorities. The social policy implemented by leading elites was marked by clientelistic and paternalistic interests that sought to guarantee the status quo. As for the institutional aspects of the labor market after 1943, the state produced an extensive corporative body of legislation that was in opposition to any negotiation or interests originating from the practice of capital-labor relations that imposes restrictions on the accumulation of human capital in the labor market.

Regarding the existence and persistence of high concentrations of wealth and income in Brazil, not until the 1980s would specific concrete policies aimed at the deconcentration of income and wealth and at promoting greater political participation of the poorest segments of the population become part of political and economic policy.

Although the previous discussion is critical for understanding the current growth of inequality indices, it is beyond the scope of this work to investigate further the historic and structural elements of wealth and income concentration in Brazil. The causes of growing inequality in the distribution of personal income between 1960 and 1990 will remain the focus.

The next section discusses the main arguments and empirical evidence concerning the behavior of the personal income variable during the 1960s, and the next two sections will discuss this same phenomenon for the 1970s and 1980s. It is important to mention that even though there has been a movement toward concentration that has predominated during these three decades, the political and economic environment under which this phenomenon has developed is quite distinct from previous periods. The fourth section of this chapter will focus on recent studies and their conclusions concerning persistent differences in labor earnings in Brazil. Final considerations are presented in the last section.

## The Debate of the 1960s

The Gini coefficient, calculated from census data on the earnings of the country's Economically Active Population (EAP),[1] increased from 0.497 in 1960 to 0.565 in 1970 (Table 1). In this context, two interpretations for this phenomenon have been offered.

### Table I
### Distribution of Income of the Economically Active Population (EAP) Brazil - 1960-1980
(percent)

| Percentile | Share of total income | | |
| | 1960 | 1970 | 1980 |
|---|---|---|---|
| 10 - | 1.9 | 1.2 | 1.2 |
| 30 - | 5.9 | 6.2 | 6.2 |
| 50 - | 17.4 | 15.1 | 14.1 |
| 30 + | 66.1 | 71.7 | 73.2 |
| 10 + | 39.6 | 46.5 | 47.9 |
| Gini | 0.497 | 0.565 | 0.592 |

Source: Primary data from IBGE-*Censos Demográficos.*

The first claims that the increase in the degree of inequality observed in personal income is a direct consequence of high economic growth rates observed in the country during the period. This argument is sponsored, among others, by Langoni (1973), whose position was later supported by Senna (1976) and Castello Branco (1979).

The second interpretation links the greater inequality observed in the period to the economic policy employed by the first three military governments. Within this group, two distinct interpretations coexist. One group believes that the main cause of increasing income concentration is the institutional regulation of the labor market.[2] The second group argues that, in addition to this intervention, a more important cause of inequality was the import substitution-based industrialization conducted by the state during the 1950s, which was heavily based on strong stimuli to private national and international capital, including credit with subsidized interest rates, fiscal incentives, subsidized inputs, and others. This strategy led to a higher concentration of functional income that ultimately would affect inequalities in personal income indices.[3]

Langoni's study and its extensions during the Médici (1970-1975) and

Geisel (1975-1979) administrations constituted the official explanations for the increasing national inequality. It is important to emphasize that because they centered the argument on personal labor income distribution and on changes in the characteristics and sectoral distribution of the labor supply, the debate was restricted. Other important aspects were not approached, such as the demand structure of the labor market, the institutional framework, government policies, and distortions in the functioning of the labor market as well as cultural and historical factors transcending the period.

To explain growing inequality, Langoni's work postulated that two transitory and self-correcting mechanisms were at play during the process of economic growth. The first mechanism, which was inspired by Kuznets (1955), referred to changes in the composition of the labor force (across regions, economic sectors, industries, and age and educational levels) that took place during the period, with special emphasis on the distribution of educational levels.[4] The second mechanism involved an increase in the demand for skilled labor that evolved as a consequence of the complementary relationship between capital and labor during periods of economic growth. In conjunction with an inelastic supply of skilled labor in the short run, this latter factor would have provoked a disequilibrium in the labor market, with skilled labor commanding higher salaries relative to the salaries of unskilled labor. In the long run, the expansion of skilled labor supply would eliminate the quasi-rent appropriated by this class of workers.

Langoni's work was based strictly on human capital theory; education was considered the most important factor in explaining an increase in personal income disparities. According to Langoni, despite the fact that the overall average level of labor force schooling had increased, the tremendous rise in the number of college and high school students between 1960 and 1970 (96.25 and 79.28 percent, respectively) compared with the increase observed in elementary and junior high schools (5.34 and 55.62 percent, respectively) was the main cause of this phenomenon.[5]

Using the same data base as the Lagoni study but with different methodologies, Fishlow (1972) and Bacha and Taylor (1978) questioned Langoni's arguments. According to Fishlow, in order to explain the high increase in wage differentials between skilled and unskilled workers, the demand for highly skilled labor initially should have been much greater. Second, as to the composition effect, Fishlow estimated that changes in relative earnings were much more important than changes in the distribution of education. Finally, Bacha and Taylor found the results to be significantly fewer for composition effects in both relative earnings and those related to distribution of schooling.

It should be emphasized that the debate concerning the existence of composition effects dismisses the most important aspect of this phenomenon, that is, that the magnitude of changes occurring in the structure of production, labor force, and labor market during the period caused an emergence of composition effects (Cacciamali 1988). No one doubts this. The relevance of this question is that if these effects were strong enough, they then offer a satisfactory explanation for the expressed deterioration in the income distribution indices for the period.

Fishlow (1972), for instance, presented an inverse causal explanation to the one offered by Langoni. According to Fishlow, the government's intervention in the labor market and the ensuing salary control enabled workers at the top of the occupational hierarchy to appropriate relatively more income, thereby widening the gap in the salary structure. In this case, education would only reflect the previous concentration of high levels of this group's schooling.

Without ignoring the importance of composition effects and education on income distribution, interpretations parallel to, and in combination with, Fishlow's work introduced new elements that could explain the phenomenon as it related to economic policy, institutions, and the functioning of the labor market.

These studies highlight at least four important elements in explaining the relative deterioration of incomes of those groups in the lowest ranks during the period: 1) the salary policy adopted by military administrations after 1965, which was an important instrument of anti-inflationary policy; 2) the elimination of job security (tenure) and an incentive for greater labor turnover; 3) the dismantling of unions; and 4) distortions in the labor market and its segmentation.[6]

Between 1965 and 1973 primarily, the official salary indexation systematically underestimated adjustment rates for the salaries of registered workers in the economy's formal sector, while taxes were correctly indexed, and massive subsidized credits and fiscal incentives were given to private investments.[7] In accordance with the Lewis model, these measures favored functional income concentration as a means to stir economic growth in the direction of capital income instead of labor income.

Intervention impacted income distribution in at least two ways. First, capital income recipients and workers in managerial and executive positions who were already (and still are) positioned at the higher strata benefited the most from these policies. Second, wage policy had a more pronounced effect on less skilled workers, who are relatively abundant in supply, have weaker bargaining power, and can be recruited and trained at a very low cost.

The incentive for labor turnover, on the other hand, became an obstacle to the creation of more stable labor relations. It also became an impediment in training unskilled labor at both the individual and business levels. There was a strong stimulus on the part of workers to quit jobs and supplement their low salaries with resources from the Time Service Guarantee Fund (Fundo de

Garantia por Tempo de Serviço — FGTS).[8] For employers, labor turnover acted as a disincentive to training programs, since the initial employer would lose his investment (in training the worker) to another company once the worker left his position and found work elsewhere. In terms of income distribution, this mechanism was an obstacle to the formation of human capital in the labor market and did not favor the promotion of less skilled workers to better occupations, positions, and salaries.

The intervention and strong repression imposed by the government on unions between 1960 and 1970 also rendered perverse effects on income distribution, especially for workers in the less skilled occupation categories. It precluded the stabilization of labor demand in general and restricted wage demands and the determination of floor salaries that would follow gains in productivity in particular.

Tavares (1969) and Bacha (1975) add an additional hypothesis to these factors to explain the increase in wage differentials and inequality indices. According to these authors, managers and executives, and professionals in general, were in a position to determine for themselves better levels of remuneration during the period since a portion of their earnings was determined by company earnings that had increased significantly.[9]

Studies on the existence of internal labor markets in the Brazilian economy reinforce this argument and confirm the configuration of these markets in a sample of manufacturing and service firms in São Paulo (Barbosa, Morley, and Cacciamali de Souza 1976). According to these studies, it was a common practice in the human resources departments of these firms to fill vacancies by hiring their own workers.

Finally, three points must be added to the debate on the increasing inequality in income distribution during the 1960s and mid-1970s that were not emphasized in the literature. The first refers to an improvement in income distribution derived from an improvement in the distribution of wealth — in physical terms or in terms of human capital — and also the existence of political institutions with this same goal.[10] These elements, when not missing from the country's economic and political environment (as during the first five decades of this century), have more immediate populist interests than practical effect. In the present analysis, however, these elements did not constitute government priorities.

The second point relates to human capital theory that associates increases in individual human capital (qualification) to increases in labor productivity on an individual level that should result in wage increases for the individual. Four arguments are in place. First, the level of labor productivity in the production process, especially in the Fordist period, is an average, is global, and is dissociated completely from specific members of a given production team. Second, the average labor productivity level is influenced not only by the qualification level of a given worker but also by factors such as capital intensity and technology and management practices adopted by the firm. The third argument is that increases in labor productivity are not always reflected by increases in salaries — higher salaries being a necessary but insufficient condition for attaining better income distribution. A number of other factors interfere with and determine this process: the bargaining power involved in capital-labor relations, the practice of collective negotiations, institutions, and sociocultural aspects, as well as the macroeconomic conjuncture, among others. The fourth argument refers to the method used to capture the qualification variable through schooling that captures numerous other social, cultural, and class aspects not necessarily reflected in the job qualification variable.[11]

Finally, a third point that should be added to the debate is associated with the process of reproduction of social inequality itself, in general terms and in the case of Brazilian society in particular. One cannot overemphasize the fact that strong income inequality and other aspects of social discrimination play a major role in reproducing this inequality. It is the process of inequality that selects, informs, and opens up opportunities to place families and individuals from the medium and high strata at high levels in the formal educational system and in job positions requiring higher qualifications and ascensional profiles.[12]

## The Behavior Inequality Indices in the 1970s

Throughout the 1970s, the trend toward concentration of income distribution, albeit less severe than in the previous decade, would continue. The Gini coefficient calculated from census information increased from 0.565 in 1970 to 0.592 in 1980 (Tables 1 and 2). In contrast to the 1960s, medium and low income strata obtained real gains during the 1970s and especially after 1976, while those with higher incomes did not perform as well.

### Table 2
### Distribution of Income of the Economically Active Population (EAP) 1976–1989
(percent)

| Percentile | Appropriation of income | | | | | | |
|---|---|---|---|---|---|---|---|
|  | 1976 | 1979 | 1981 | 1983 | 1985 | 1986 | 1989 |
| 10 - | 1.0 | 0.9 | 1.0 | 1.0 | 0.9 | 1.0 | 0.65 |
| 30 - | 5.9 | 5.8 | 5.8 | 5.5 | 5.3 | 5.8 | 4.51 |
| 50 - | 13.5 | 13.9 | 14.2 | 13.2 | 13.1 | 13.5 | 10.94 |
| 30 + | 74.7 | 73.0 | 71.9 | 73.8 | 74.6 | 73.5 | 77.52 |
| 10 + | 50.4 | 46.8 | 45.3 | 46.9 | 47.7 | 47.5 | 52.23 |
| 1 + | 17.4 | 13.8 | 12.7 | 13.7 | 14.3 | 16.3 | 16.81 |
| Gini | 0.615 | 0.585 | 0.573 | 0.592 | 0.605 | 0.595 | 0.635 |

Source: IBGE, *PNAD*.

The improvement in distribution can be associated with factors such as the economic cycle, erosion of the wage policy implemented by the first military government, and the beginning of the reorganization of the union movement, especially in the Southeast of Brazil. It produced, among other things, increases in salaries, minimum wage levels defined in collective negotiations, and the convergence of wage differentials after the second half of the 1970s.[13]

## Table 3
## Real Changes in Average Income by Income Groups 1960–1986

| | Percentage changes in average income | | | | | | |
|---|---|---|---|---|---|---|---|
| Percentile | 1960-70 | 1970-80 | 1970-76 | 1976-80 | 1979-81 | 1981-83 | 1983-85 |
| 10 - | 8.6 | 50.5 | 25.2 | 20.2 | 2.8 | -8.1 | 4.5 |
| 30 - | 54.3 | 46.9 | 37.5 | 6.8 | -2.4 | -14.2 | 15.0 |
| following 40 | 41.0 | 38.5 | 28.4 | 7.8 | 3.1 | -16.4 | 17.5 |
| 30 + | 85.8 | 51.3 | 53.6 | -1.2 | -3.4 | -7.7 | 22.4 |
| 10 + | 101.4 | 53.0 | 59.5 | -4.0 | -5.2 | -6.8 | 23.1 |
| 1 + | INC | INC | INC | INC | -9.5 | -3.0 | 25.8 |
| Average | 71.4 | 48.5 | 47.2 | 9.2 | -1.9 | -10.0 | 21.1 |

INC = information not computed.

Notes: Information related to censuses is not fully compatible with the information obtained from *Pesquisa Nacional por Amostra de Domicílios, PNAD*. Data from PNAD for the period 1979 to 1989 are absolutely compatible.

Census information itself is not always compatible. Income data in 1960, for instance, were obtained in closed intervals, while for the other two years (1979 and 1989), open intervals were used. Moreover, the data collection in 1980 on the income variable was more extensive than in other years. Therefore, it is possible that this variable is underestimated in 1970 vis á vis 1980.

Sources: Primary data obtained from Bonelli and Sedlacek (1989, 18-20) and IBGE - *Censos Demográficos* and PNAD. Deflator: GPI-FGV.

Moreover, according to the concept of household income, information on income distribution indicated that the Gini coefficient remained essentially stable during the decade of the 1970s (Hoffmann and Kageyama 1985), due to an increase in the number of active persons per family, especially in the primary sector of the economy,[14] and a decrease in income inequality in the Southeast region.[15]

In light of this relatively optimistic picture for the beginning of the 1980s, several segments of academia and government began to surmise that the era of expressive increases in income concentration had ended. The expansion of employment through economic growth and relatively low inflation, together with the implementation of redistributive social policies and official rules of wage indexation also favoring redistribution of income, would suffice to reverse the trend of inequality in Brazil. Moreover, institutions during this period were moving toward the creation of a formal democratic regime. The belief, therefore, spread throughout the nation that the presence of a more progressive representation in the parliament and unions could secure the enforcement of these policies. The circumstances that unfolded during the 1980s, however, did not confirm these hypotheses.

## An Acceleration of Inequality in the 1980s

From a macroeconomic perspective, the 1980s were marked by high levels of instability, characterized at the beginning (1981-1983) by a deep recession and immediately followed by unusually short-run fluctuations. After 1986, there were alternating periods of moderate expansion and contraction of real GDP: between 1986 and 1987 and between 1988 and 1989, the real GDP expanded by 1.4 and 1.2 percent, respectively, and decreased by 2.2 between 1987 and 1989 (Table 4). Inflation rates, on the other hand, reached higher levels than ever in Brazil, and four attempts to stabilize the economy between 1981 and 1989 ended in failure. The prevailing instability of the period restricted economic policy options, especially those of a redistributive character.

### Table 4
## Real Gross Domestic Product Index and Annual Change in the Implicit Income Deflator 1980–1989

| Year | Real GDP | Implicit deflator |
|------|----------|-------------------|
| 1980 | 100.0 | 90 |
| 1981 | 93.5 | 107 |
| 1982 | 91.9 | 105 |
| 1983 | 86.8 | 140 |
| 1984 | 89.4 | 213 |
| 1985 | 94.4 | 232 |
| 1986 | 99.4 | 146 |
| 1987 | 100.8 | 204 |
| 1988 | 98.6 | 648 |
| 1989 | 99.8 | 1322 |

Source: IBGE, 1991. *Contas Consolidadas para a Nação.*

Federal expenditure cuts aimed at controlling the public deficit, especially those in social infrastructure, affected investment. Social tension and the redistributive conflict were exacerbated, and the state, which had conducted the development process, faced an unprecedented political and financial crisis. Because the crisis developed during the transition to a formal democratic regime, its consequences affected its identity, the rationality of its decision-making process, and the coherence of economic signals to the private sector.

The labor market made adjustments during the period through a combination of different mechanisms with varying degrees of intensity. Among the relatively less intensive mechanisms were a decrease in the employment growth rate, an increase in the open unemployment rate — including a relative increase in the number of family heads unemployed — and an increase in the participation of non-salaried and self-employed workers in the EAP. Among the more intensive mechanisms, the level of real earnings increased, especially for those in the lower income brackets, and a greater concentration in income distribution occurred.[16] The trend toward concentration during this period was astounding. In 1980, for instance, the Gini coefficient reached 0.635, which was 27.3 percent greater than in 1960 and about 12 percent greater than at the beginning of the 1980s.

At the beginning of the recession, the highest income brackets were affected more vigorously, forcing a drop in the inequality index. As the recession intensified, however, income concentration regained momentum, and disparity levels increased despite a government redistributive salary-indexation policy in effect from 1970 until 1985.[17]

The policy's failure was due mostly to a recessive environment and a high turnover of labor in the private sector. Faced with relatively low costs in discharging workers in 1988 and with a labor market favorable to employers, businesses replaced higher salaried workers with those willing to accept lower compensation.

Except for the period of the Cruzado Plan in 1986 that had favored modest income redistribution, economic recovery after 1984 increased inequality levels. Between 1983 and 1989, for example, the middle-income strata once again suffered losses in comparison to the higher income strata. It was apparent that higher income groups had a larger number of real possibilities and strategies to protect themselves from high inflation rates and from an unstable stagnant labor market.

# New Elements Introduced During the 1980s in the Debate on the Causes of Inequality

During the 1980s, other interpretations, as well as empirical evidence concerning the growing inequality of wages between and within occupations, surfaced in Brazil, focusing especially on the high salary differentials identified by Tavares (1969) more than 20 years earlier.

Labor income — salaries, wages, and remuneration to self-employed workers — constitutes approximately 87 percent of the total income reported in the annual household surveys (PNAD); around 65 percent of this income comes from wages.

Brazilian literature on wage differentials places special attention on five aspects of this problem: 1) discrimination in the labor market (when firms value the identical production qualifications of individuals through extra-market criteria), 2) diversification and segmentation of the labor market (when economic sectors or firms use different forms of evaluation for workers with identical qualifications), 3) the dynamics between the formal and informal sectors of the economy, 4) the perversity of human capital distribution as a source of inequality, and 5) the institutional structure of the labor market as the cause of inequalities.

Studies on discrimination in the labor market concentrate mostly on gender and race differentials, and the results are evidence of the existence of discrimination practices (Camargo and Serrano 1983, Lovell 1989, Porcaro 1988).

In reference to labor market differentiation and segmentation, the analyses examine the effects of the institutional aspects and heterogeneity of the production structure. In the first case, the studies focus on the wage differentials between registered and non-registered workers, between public and private employees (Cacciamali 1989a, Sedlacek et al. 1989, Cacciamali and Torres 1988, Macedo 1986), and among industrial sectors and regions (Kon 1989, Saboia 1989, Cacciamali 1989b, Cacciamali and Springer 1991). All of the studies show that wage differentials persist even when the studies control for variables of a general character, as well as personal characteristics (gender, age, education), a firm's attributes (size, sector, human resources practices), type of occupation, and level of qualification. Significantly, the intensity of the mobility process is vital in decreasing the impact of differentials on the distribution of wages obtained by the worker during his professional life; the impact should be much lower under circumstances of high mobility. Longitudinal studies, however, are scarce and incipient in Brazil; most cover only the 1980s, which is a relatively brief period for deriving conclusive results.

Studies related to the characteristics and dynamics of the formal and informal production sectors and labor markets also advanced significantly during the 1980s, not only conceptually but also empirically. With respect to conceptual aspects, two points should be emphasized: the recognition in the literature of distinct dynamics in determining levels of employment and income according to the insertion of the worker in the production process and labor market — whether registered or non-registered salaried worker or self-employed worker — and the incorporation of these categories into official statistics on employment and the labor market.[18] Among the most important rationalizations and empirical evidence on this theme that have made a significant contribution to an understanding of the topic, those related to specific mechanisms for determining the incomes of self-employed and salaried workers must be mentioned (Camargo 1989, Cacciamali 1989b). The income level of self-employed workers is determined in the goods and services market, while the income of salaried workers is determined in the labor market. The distinction between them has two important implications. The first refers to the pro-cycle average behavior of the two categories of labor income. The second relates to the possibility of certain self-employed workers securing a relatively higher average income than salaried workers since they are able to readjust their earnings more quickly than regular salaried workers.

The fourth set of themes in recent literature focuses on the acknowledgment of the inequity of the Brazilian educational system as a source of inequalities in income distribution. Education is unevenly distributed, especially in terms of quality. The level of educational services provided in rural areas in Brazil's less developed regions is very low. In addition, it should be noted that the share of federal government expenditures during the 1980s in education and culture decreased from 22.72 percent between 1979 and 1981 to 15.26 percent between 1982 and 1984 (Leal and Werlang 1991).

Furthermore, due to economic factors and the low quality of educational services, the drop-out rate is quite high, especially during the first four years of school. To avoid this, it would be necessary to restructure courses, offer additional training to teachers (mainly in elementary school), and increase their remuneration. The impact of this picture of deterioration can be seen by examining the EAP's level of education: approximately 17 percent of individuals surveyed have attended school less than one year, 37 percent have between one and four years of formal education, and 23 percent have more than nine years of education. Only 2.6 percent of the EAP have a college degree (IBGE 1988).

In terms of education, wage differentials among homogeneous groups are much higher in Brazil than in industrialized countries. In Brazil, education accounts for 40 percent of total inequality, while the age factor responds for only 10 to 15 percent (Almeida Reis and Barros 1989). Moreover, empirical studies show that the contribution of education to inequality in income distribution in Brazil is due to both the poor distribution of the variable among the labor force and the distribution of increases in levels of education (Lam and Levinson 1987, Almeida Reis and Barros 1989).

Finally, regarding the institutional aspects of the labor market, analyses have focused mainly on the structure of unions and the effects of labor law on the behavior of the labor market.

Brazilian unions were created in the early 1940s and have continued to exhibit corporative characteristics (Camargo and Amadeo 1991; Cacciamali 1992), among which are the monopoly of representation for workers and firms, the creation of the Labor Justice Department and its power of arbitration, and the rhetorical subordination of collective labor agreements to wage policy. Direct capital and labor negotiations are generally discouraged and have had at least three important impacts on macroeconomic conditions: they have contributed to the slow pace of adjustment in the labor market during periods of low growth and recession, they have caused greater disparity among prices and salaries, and they have limited the effects of anti-inflationary policies.

Additionally, Camargo and Amadeo (1991) demonstrated that this structure has permitted certain oligopolist sectors to provide real salary raises to their workers during the 1980s — a period characterized by high inflation — since these wage increases translated into higher consumer prices, subsequently restraining the effects of anti-inflationary policies. On the other hand, because these sectors were representative of strong unions, their workers received higher wage increases in comparison to workers in more competitive sectors, thereby inducing a higher differentiation in the labor market that caused greater disparity in salaries and extended the labor market's adjustment process.

The second institutional aspect, researched in greater depth in the 1990s, involves the composition of labor law as well as its participation in labor costs or the level of employment and income distribution. In Brazil, where the level of taxation on wages is very high — nearly 100 percent — demand for labor in the formal sector is reduced especially in periods of lower investment. Yet a greater differentiation in the labor market and further wage disparities are induced, creating jobs that require low qualifications and that are marginal to labor law. This serious phenomenon continued throughout the 1980s (Cacciamali 1991).

## Final Considerations

In the past 30 years, the theoretical debate and the empirical evidence on the growing inequality of income distribution in Brazil have intensified and have been enriched with new analytical elements. The debate on inequality fascinated social scientists and politicians during the 1960s and 1970s, especially because of the impacts and concrete implications of high growth without significant redistributive effects.

The period did not, however, worsen poverty in Brazil. Although higher income groups received higher income until the mid-1970s, all income strata obtained real gains. The situation has changed, however, in the past decade.

The 1980s were characterized by an excessive concentration of income along with an increase in the absolute number of poor people. In 1989, for instance, the poor represented 27.9 percent of the population residing in metropolitan areas. The political and economic aspects of inequality in income distribution had again become a priority on political party and economy policy agendas.

Two types of income deficiency are recognized: one is related to Brazil's social structure, and the other is generated by the nature of the labor market. The main arguments regarding the first aspect center on the unequal distribution of wealth — physical and human capital. Regarding the second aspect, restrictions are related to discrimination and segmentation of the labor market and to the weak institutional stimulus for the creation of good jobs that would permit human capital accumulation by the worker.

The distribution of physical capital in Brazil is highly uneven in both urban and rural areas. The country has one of the most concentrated and stable land tenure structures in the world. Census data (Censo Agropecuário 1980) reveal that only 1 percent of all rural properties are made up of more than 1,000 hectares, yet these holdings make up about 45 percent of the total area. Properties with less than 100 hectares represent 90 percent of the total number of properties; yet they constitute only 20 percent of the total area. Despite the fact that inequality indices of the South and Southeast are lower than other regions, all regions exhibit a similar distribution pattern.

In urban areas, the industrialization process that was carried out by the state after the 1950s, more intensively at the end of the 1960s, and throughout the 1970s caused the availability of technology to be highly differentiated across sectors and regions. The result was the highly heterogeneous structure of the production sector, with perverse implications for income distribution. In 1980, large industries represented about 3 percent of all production establishments, generating 38 percent of the jobs and producing approximately 70 percent of the total value added by the manufacturing sector. In contrast, the smallest 40 percent of businesses generated only 5 percent of jobs and value added in the manufacturing industry (IBGE 1980).

The disparity in the allocation of physical capital affects income distribution in two ways. First, it does not permit further homogeneous increases in labor productivity and wages. It does, however, reduce the possibility of generating more productive jobs and higher salaried jobs and, thus, over time, impacts on the accumulation of human capital by the worker.

Additionally, three points must be included that relate to the institutional aspect of the labor market. The first involves the structure of union-labor relations. As has been mentioned, the monopoly of representation — of both businesses and workers — in addition to concentrated political power impose serious obstacles on more open labor relations, adjustments in the labor market, and anti-inflationary policies. The second point refers to the creation of the Time Service Guarantee Fund (FGTS). Created in 1965 to introduce more flexibility into the Brazilian labor market and replacing the Stability Law that had granted job security to workers with more than ten years of service with the same company, this fund requires firms to deposit 8 percent of a worker's monthly wages into a trust fund in the worker's name. By law, this account is adjusted for inflation every quarter and yields 3 percent interest per year. Workers can withdraw their money only in the event of termination of employment without just cause, when purchasing a house, or upon retirement.

Since 1988, any worker whose position is terminated without just cause is entitled to an additional sum equal to 40 percent of his/her total fund, to be paid by the employer as a penalty for dismissal. Thus, the longer a worker stays with a company, the greater the penalty to the employer for terminating the job without just cause.

Such a mechanism encourages workers — especially those with poor qualifications and low salaries — to push for dismissal in order to receive, in the short run, a compensation that he/she would otherwise receive only upon retirement. In the case of a worker who has been fired without just cause after one or more years of service with the same company, the amount is equal to 3.4 times his/her minimum salary (ms) earned per month (where only 1.4 ms would originate from the FGTS). The company is encouraged, on the other hand, to utilize labor capacity to its maximum in the shortest period of time without offering any training, since in the case of job termination, the training costs would fall on the current employer with benefits received by the new employer.

Finally, the third point concerns labor market legislation. Taxes on wages considerably increase labor costs, deter the creation of good jobs, and negatively impact on income distribution. These taxes can be reduced, especially those related to the maintenance of the state and parastatal apparatus that support the union structure and the labor market bureaucracy in general. Moreover, labor legislation is not sufficiently flexible to allow other forms of remuneration aside from wages, such as productivity bonuses or profit sharing that effectively could stimulate greater labor productivity.

In summary, an improvement in income inequality indices in Brazil should be initiated by a set of consistent, long-run economic policies. Among policy priorities that were identified in this work, the following should be mentioned: public investment to improve the quality of basic education that will not only generate significant social benefits but will also exhibit the highest rates of return among all investments in education; adoption of redistributive measures (in terms of wealth) that could improve the allocation of capital per job and increase the average levels of labor productivity; and elimination of all elements in the current legislation restricting the creation of a large number of good jobs.

These topics do not exhaust the list of alternative economic policies that prioritize better distribution. These policy prescriptions cannot alleviate poverty in the short or even medium run, nor could they replace the government's traditional social programs. Nutritional, health, and housing programs, as well as programs that support the low productivity and low income informal sector, should not only be maintained but should also aim for greater efficiency and efficacy.

# Notes

1. The discussion on the inequality index is based on the concept of EAP with positive income. The Gini coefficient is a measure of inequality based on the distribution of income. A coefficient equal to one (1) indicates perfect inequality, and a coefficient equal to zero (0) indicates perfect equality.

2. This is the case, for instance, of the studies developed by Hoffmann and Duarte 1972, Hoffmann 1973, Fishlow 1972, and Bacha and Taylor 1978.

3. This is the case, among others, of the studies by Tavares 1969, Tavares and Serra 1979, Tavares and Souza 1979, and Oliveira 1977. These studies are more theoretically based, especially because of the difficulties in obtaining and handling this information.

4. Langoni based his work on the composition effects proposed by Kuznets in his 1955 work. According to Kuznets, the changes in the employment structure that occur in the first stages of economic development, primarily those between agriculture and industry and also among sectors with high and low productivity, generate higher income inequalities. Accordingly, the relationship between per capita income levels and concentration indices exhibits the shape of a parabola, concave to the origin.

5. Utilizing the variance of the logarithms, Langoni estimated that 35 percent of the change in the degree of inequality between 1960 and 1970 was due to the change in the educational structure of the labor force.

6. The first three arguments were defended by Hoffmann and Duarte 1972 and Hoffmann 1973, while the last one was espoused by Barbosa, Morley, and Cacciamali de Souza 1976.

7. The specialized Brazilian literature defines the formal sector of the economy as a set of economic activities organized in a capitalist manner, based on the use of salaried labor. This concept encompasses the activities of employers and employees of private and public sectors, as well as the direct administration of the state. The registered sector of the economy constitutes the set of activities that perform functions encompassed within the regulatory and institutional framework. Those are activities that, independently from their form of production organization, perform legal operations and are therefore registered with the respective public agencies, follow the legislation, pay taxes, and hire workers according to the law.

8. The Fundo de Garantia por Tempo de Serviço (FGTS) was created in 1966 to replace the law that established stability in the job for those with 10 or more years of service. Firms collect 8 percent of the monthly salary of workers and deposit these resources in a fund where the workers will eventually receive 3 percent interest per year plus the indexation for past inflation. This fund can be withdrawn when the worker is fired without just reason by the employer. Moreover, until October 1988, when dismissing the worker, the firm had to pay a fine of 10 percent of the total fund, an amount that could be withdrawn by the dismissed worker. After October 1988, the penalty was increased to 40 percent of the total fund. More information on this fund and other labor costs can be found later in the chapter as well as in Cacciamali 1992.

9. It is necessary to stress that individuals in these positions, in general, are better educated. This educational achievement is an additional element for explaining the results obtained by Langoni 1973.

10. Fishlow (1972) discusses the former of these themes in a superficial manner and adopts the variable position in the occupation — a variable also utilized by IBGE in its censuses — to measure the effect of wealth on income distribution.

11. A recent discussion on this theme may be found in Cacciamali and Springer de Freitas 1991.

12. Cacciamali (1985) explores this theme and shows empirical evidence for a representative sample in the city of São Paulo, analyzed according to social and occupational criteria. Groups of families whose heads hold a low-ranking job in the occupational hierarchy exhibit the highest number of members in the same occupational category as the head of the family.

13. A study by Lanzana (1986) deals with this theme.

14. The inequality increased more among the EAP from the primary sector, which represented about 30 percent of the total EAP in 1980. This was a movement in the opposite direction from the one observed in the 1970s, when the more expressive increases in inequality occurred in the urban areas. Certainly, this change is associated with the expansion of capitalist production processes and labor relations in agriculture and to the smaller number of persons without remuneration in this sector.

15. Likewise, the Gini coefficient expanded more in the Southeast and South regions, while in the following decade, the increase was more intense in the relatively less developed regions such as the Northeast, Center-West, and North. This result is coherent with the industrial expansion, stimulated by economic policy pursued by the federal administration and the growth of modern service sectors that assist production, commercialization, and all private and government social activities that took place in those regions during the 1970s.

16. A more detailed analysis on the structural changes and adjustments in the labor market during the 1980s may be found in Cacciamali 1991b and 1992, among other sources.

17. The wage policy adopted in this period was characterized by an adjustment mechanism that would benefit the lower wage strata. Initially, it contemplated groups with salaries below three minimum wages; later, the policy coverage was expanded to include salaries up to 15 minimum wages. This wage policy brought up problems with the administration of positions and salaries and faced strong resistance from business owners who wanted to maintain the prevailing occupational structure.

18. See Souza 1980; Cacciamali 1983, 1989a, and 1990; the special issue of *Estudos Econômicos*, 1989; the methodology reports produced by IBGE-PNAD and Pesquisa Mensal de Emprego- PM; the methodological documents published by the Pesquisa de Emprego e Desemprego- PED and developed in São Paulo's metropolitan area by SEADE.

# References

Albuquerque, R.C., and R. Vilella. 1990. *A Situação Social do Brasil: Balanço de Duas Décadas*. Rio de Janeiro: IPEA.

Almeida Reis, J.G., and R. Paes de Barros. 1989. *Desigualdade Salarial e Distribuição de Educação*. Discussion Paper no. 178. Rio de Janeiro: IPEA/INPES.

Amadeo, E.J., and J.M. Camargo. 1991. "Mercado de Trabalho e Dança Redistributiva." In *A Distribuição de Renda no Brasil*, eds. J. M. Camargo and F. Giambiagi. Rio de Janeiro: Paz e Terra.

Bacha, E. 1975. "Hierarquia e Remuneração Gerencial." In *A Controvérsia sobre a Distribuição de Renda e Desenvolvimento*, eds. R. Tollipan and A.C. Tinelli. Rio de Janeiro: Zahar.

Bacha, E., and L. Taylor. 1978. "Brazilian Income Distribution in the Sixties: Facts, Model, Results and Controversy." *Journal of Development Economics* 3.

Barbosa, M., S. Morley, and M.C. Cacciamali de Souza. 1976. *Evidências Sobre o Mercado Interno de Trabalho em um Processo de Crescimento Rápido*. Brasília: CNRH/IPEA. (Mimeo).

Bonelli, R., and G.L. Sedlacek. 1989. "Distribuição de Renda: Evolução no Último Quarto de Século." In *Mercado de Trabalho e Distribuição de Renda: Uma Coletânea*, eds. G.L. Sedlacek and R. Paes de Barros. Série Monografias no. 35. Rio de Janeiro: IPEA/INPES.

Cacciamali, M.C. 1982. *Um Estudo Sobre o Setor Informal Urbano e as Formas de Participação na Produção*. Ph.D. dissertation. Department of Economics, University of São Paulo. Published in 1983 by the IPE, São Paulo.

Cacciamali, M.C. 1985. *Emprego e Geração de Renda no Brasil (Ensaios)*. São Paulo: IPE/IPEA/BID.

Cacciamali, M.C. 1989a. "A Expansão do Mercado de Trabalho não Regulamentado e Setor Informal no Brasil." *Estudos Econômicos* 19 (special issue): 25-48.

Cacciamali, M.C. 1989b. "A Informalização Recente do Mercado de Trabalho no Brasil." *Literatura Econômica* ll(3).

Cacciamali, M.C. 1991a. "As Economias Informal e Submersa: Conceitos e Distribuição de Renda." In *A Distribuição de Renda no Brasil*, eds. J.M. Camargo and F. Giambiagi. Rio de Janeiro: Paz e Terra.

Cacciamali, M.C. 1991b. "O Ajustamento do Mercado de Trabalho Brasileiro na Década de 80." In *Reestruturação do Espaço Regional e Urbano no Brasil*, eds. L. Lavinas et al. São Paulo: Hucitec.

Cacciamali, M.C. 1992. "O Mercado Brasileiro na Década de 80: Mudanças Estruturais e na Regulação." In *Funcionamiento y Regulación del Mercado de Trabajo en America Latina*, ed. G. Marquez. Caracas: CINDE/IESA.

Cacciamali, M.C., and I. Torres. 1988. *Atividades Públicas e Privadas: Diferenças Salariais e Desempenho*. São Paulo: IPE.

Cacciamali, M.C., and P. Springer de Freitas. 1991. "From Human Capital Theory to Efficiency Wages." *Pesquisa e Planejamento Econômico* 21. Rio de Janeiro.

Camargo, J.M. 1989. "Informalização e Renda no Mercado de Trabalho." In *Mercado de Trabalho e Distribuição de Renda: Uma Coletânea*, eds. G.L. Sedlacek and R. Paes de Barros, Série Monografias, no. 35. Rio de Janeiro: IPEA/INPES.

Camargo, J.M., and F. Serrano. 1983. "Os Dois Mercados: Homens e Mulheres na Indústria Brasileira," *Revista Brasileira de Economia* 38. Rio de Janeiro.

Camargo, J.M., and E.J. Amadeo. 1991. "Labour Legislation and Institutional Aspects of the Brazilian Labour Market." *Reestructuración y Regulación Institucional del Mercado de Trabajo en América Latina*. Buenos Aires: International Institute for Labour Studies, July 2-5.

Castello Branco, R.C. 1979. *Crescimento Acelerado e o Mercado de Trabalho: A Experiência Brasileira*. Rio de Janeiro: Fundação Getúlio Vargas (FGV).

Fishlow, A. 1972. "Brazilian Size Distribution of Income." *American Economic Review* 42(2): 391-415.

Fishlow, A. 1973. "Distribuição de Renda no Brasil: Um Novo Exame." *Dados* 11.

Hoffmann, R. 1973. "Considerações Sobre a Evolução Recente da Distribuição de Renda no Brasil." *Revista de Administração de Empresas* 13(4): 7-17.

Hoffmann, R. 1989. "Evolução da Distribuição da Renda no Brasil, entre Pessoas e entre Famílias, 1979/86." In *Mercado de Trabalho e Distribuição de Renda: Uma Coletânea*, eds. G.L. Sedlacek and R. Paes de Barros. Série Monografias no. 35. Rio de Janeiro: IPEA/INPES.

Hoffmann, R., and J.C. Duarte. 1972. "A Distribuição da Renda no Brasil." *Revista de Administração de Empresas* 12(2): 46-66.

Hoffmann, R., and A. Kageyama. 1985. *A Distribuição da Renda no Brasil entre Famílias e entre Pessoas*. Discussion paper no. 4. São Paulo: IPE, University of São Paulo.

IBGE. 1960, 1965, 1970, 1975, 1980, 1985. *Censo Agropecuário*. Rio de Janeiro: IBGE.

IBGE. 1980. *Censo Econômico da Indústria*. Rio de Janeiro: IBGE.

IBGE. 1960, 1970, 1980, 1991. *Censos Demográficos*. Rio de Janeiro: IBGE.

IBGE. 1991. *Contas Consolidadas para a Nação*. Rio de Janeiro: IBGE.

IBGE. 1988. *Pesquisa Nacional por Amostra de Domicílios*. Rio de Janeiro: IBGE.

Kon, A. 1990. *Padrões Condicionantes da Estrutura Ocupacional Brasileira: Uma Abordagem Regional*. Ph.D. dissertation. Faculty of Economics, University of São Paulo.

Kuznets, S. 1955. "Economic Growth and Income Inequality." *American Economic Review* 45(1): 1-28.

Lam, D., and D. Levinson. 1987. *Age, Experience and Schooling: Decomposing Earnings Inequality in the US and Brazil*. Ann Arbor, Mich.: Population Studies Center, University of Michigan.

Langoni, C.G. 1973. *Distribuição de Renda e Desenvolvimento Econômico*. Rio de Janeiro: Expressão e Cultura.

Lanzana, A. 1986. *Diferenciais na Economia Brasileira: Uma Análise do Período 1960-86*. Ph.D. dissertation. Faculty of Economics, University of São Paulo.

Leal, C.I.S., and S. Werlang. 1991. "Educação e Distribuição de Renda no Brasil." In *Distribuição de Renda no Brasil*, eds. J.M. Camargo and F. Giambagi. Rio de Janeiro: Paz e Terra.

Lovell, P. 1989. *Racial Inequality and the Brazilian Labor Market.* Ph.D. dissertation, University of Florida.

Macedo, R. 1986. "Diferenciais de Salários entre Empresas Estatais e Privadas: Novos Resultados." *Estudos Econômicos* 16 (special issue): 21-43.

Oliveira, F. 1977. *A Economia da Dependência Imperfeita.* Rio de Janeiro: Graal.

Porcaro, R.M. 1988. "Desigualdade Racial e Segmentação no Mercado de Trabalho." *Cadernos de Cândido Mendes* 15: 171-207. Rio de Janeiro: Centro de Estudos Afro-Asiáticos.

Ramos, L., and J.G. de Almeida Reis. 1990. "Distribuição da Renda: Aspectos Teóricos e o Debate." In *Distribuição de Renda no Brasil*, eds. J.M. Camargo and F. Giambagi. Rio de Janeiro: Paz e Terra.

Saboia, J. 1990. "Política Salarial e Distribuição de Renda: 25 Anos de Desencontros." In *Distribuição de Renda no Brasil*, eds. J.M. Camargo and F. Giambagi. Rio de Janeiro: Paz e Terra.

Sedlacek, G. et al. 1989. *Segmentação e Mobilidade no Mercado de Trabalho Brasileiro: Uma Análise da Área Metropolitana de São Paulo.* Discussion paper no. 173. Rio de Janeiro: IPEA/INPES.

Souza, P.R. 1980. *Emprego e Salários em Economias Atrasadas.* Ph.D. dissertation. Economics Institute, State University of Campinas, São Paulo. (mimeo).

Souza, P.R., and P.E. Baltar. 1979. "Salário Mínimo e Taxa de Salários no Brasil." *Pesquisa e Planejamento Econômico* 9 (3): 629-659.

Tavares, M.C. 1969. *Características da Distribuição de Renda no Brasil.* Santiago, Chile: CEPAL/ILPES.

Tavares, M.C. 1986. *Acumulação de Capital e Industrialização no Brasil.* Second edition. Campinas, São Paulo: Editora da Universidade Estadual de Campinas (UNICAMP).

Taylor, L., and E. Bacha. 1976. "The Unequalizing Spiral: The First Growth Model for Belindia." *Quarterly Journal of Economics* 90(2): 197-218.

Tulipan, R., and A.C. Tinelli. 1975. *A Controvérsia Sobre a Distribuição de Renda no Brasil.* Rio de Janeiro: Zahar.

# ELEVEN

# Regional Disparities in Brazil

## Maria J.F. Willumsen

## Introduction

The development process in Brazil, as in many other large countries, has been marked by deep economic and social disparities. Despite the high levels of economic growth and structural changes in the Brazilian economy in recent decades, regional disparities have remained practically unchanged. The persistence of dramatic geographic differentiation with respect to population and income distribution, as well as the distribution of economic activities and technology, has been one of the most serious problems facing the Brazilian economy.

Although these inequalities have often been treated as independent phenomena and have been considered the causes of imbalances in Brazil's development, the approach in this chapter is to study them in light of the historical processes of recent decades and to examine how they may have affected the generation or perpetuation of spatial imbalances. The presumption is that it is impossible to understand the distributional patterns of economic and social variables without taking into account the historical background of Brazil's development and the socioeconomic transformations that determined its trajectory. Therefore, an analysis of spatial dynamics of production and distribution and of spatial inequalities requires an understanding of population dynamics, population characteristics, and the interfaces between the population and the production structures.

This chapter is organized into five major parts. In the first section, a brief background of the spatial organization of Brazil's territory is presented. The second section discusses the spatial distribution of the population and its characteristics. The third section analyzes the manifestation of regional disparities in terms of the distribution of productive activity and its composition, as well as the patterns of regional income distribution. Section four discusses the likelihood of a reversal of this polarization and the role of the state with respect to regional planning. Conclusions are presented in the last section.

# Spatial Organization of the Economy
## Geographic Division

As people organize themselves, the space in which they live is also organized. At each different cultural, political, and economic stage, a distinct spatial organization emerges, revealing the level of social organization. At a spatial level, this structure may become more or less integrated, either prompting or hindering the formation of sub-areas, named regions, each with unique characteristics that distinguish it from the other areas.

Brazil, which has already witnessed several regionalization schemes during its history, is divided into five regions: North, Northeast, Southeast, South, and Center-West.[1] The North region comprises seven states: Acre, Amapá, Amazonas, Pará, Rondônia, Roraima, and Tocantins. The Northeast region comprises Maranhão, Piauí, Ceará, Rio Grande do Norte, Paraíba, Pernambuco, Alagoas, Sergipe, Bahia, and the territory of Fernando de Noronha. The states of Minas Gerais, Espírito Santo, Rio de Janeiro, and São Paulo make up the Southeast region. The Center-West region includes the states of Goiás, Mato Grosso, Mato Grosso do Sul, and the Federal District (Brasília). The South region includes Paraná, Santa Catarina, and Rio Grande do Sul.

These regions, performing different roles in the inter-regional division of labor and production, make up the national productive matrix. Within this major production unit, other levels of regionalization exist. Almost all of them are the result of specific federal government programs. Among those regionalizations worth mentioning are the Polígono das Secas (formed by the states in the Northeast and the northern part of Minas Gerais), the Vale do Rio São Francisco (adjacent area to the São Francisco River), and the Legal Amazon (composed of the whole Amazon area and part of Maranhão, Mato Grosso, and Goiás).

## Brief Historical Background

Settlement of the Brazilian territory took place in two distinct phases. The first phase was characterized by the predominance of the external market, while the more recent phase has been led by the expansion and consolidation of the domestic market. During the first period, colonization was boosted by export activities, which concentrated Brazil's population along the coastal areas. The fortunes of this population were related closely to the success and failure of export activities. The external market essentially defined the fate of these regions: the exhaustion of one activity in a certain region would give birth to a new one in a different area. The stagnation of one region thus resulted in the emergence of a new region, characterizing a discontinuous settlement process. It was through this process that the primary export period, which so deeply affected the Brazilian economy, benefited different regions in different stages.

The sugarcane cycle of the sixteenth and seventeenth centuries favored the Northeast, a region that experienced the greatest capital accumulation during those centuries. The gold cycle of the eighteenth century brought economic dynamism to the state of Minas Gerais, creating important linkages with other regions to the South (Southeast and South). Coffee became the leading product of the nineteenth century, bringing the benefits of growth to Rio de Janeiro and, later, to São Paulo, where the activity finally established itself. Besides these well-known cycles, other cycles, such as the rubber and cocoa eras, should also be mentioned here. The rubber period developed in the Amazon region and extended from the third quarter of the nineteenth century to the first quarter of the twentieth century. At their apex, rubber exports were about half the size of coffee exports. The cocoa period in southern Bahia took place in the middle of the twentieth century when industrialization policies were already in force. Although not as powerful as previous export booms, its importance cannot be denied, as cocoa exports reached such high levels in the 1950s that cocoa became one of the country's main export products. With the exception of coffee, the historical transformations that benefited specific regions came to an end. The Southeast, which had already become the country's most dynamic region during the coffee boom, developed into Brazil's industrial production center.

After the exhaustion of the primary-products export cycle, Brazil began to search for new activities to replace those prevailing in the stagnated areas by focusing on the domestic market. During this period, cotton experienced significant growth and played an important role in minimizing the impacts of the crisis generated by the exhaustion of the sugarcane cycle in the Northeast. Together with cattle ranching, cotton was responsible for the colonization of the Northeast hinterland. A similar process took place in Minas Gerais, where cattle ranching replaced gold mining. In the North, however, no activity was introduced to replace rubber; only in recent decades have timber, tobacco, and food products begun to fill the role played by rubber in the regional economy.

Industrialization was launched immediately after World War I (1914-1918) and again after the Great Depression (1929). Industrialization was not only stimulated by these two events, which generated constant crises in the external sector, but also by the prosperity of the coffee sector. Industrialization exacerbated the asymmetry created by discontinuous export cycles by concentrating economic activity, which in turn has generated very distinct profiles in product and income distributions across regions. After 1930, industry became the most important sector of the Brazilian economy. Located in the Southeast region, São Paulo has been the nucleus of industrialization. At the same time that industry was being established, a process of regional articulation and integration, based on the domestic market, began to take shape. Industrialization, concentrated in the Southeast region, intensified this articulation. The increasing demand for industrial inputs created a domestic market of considerable size.

It was only in the second half of the 1950s, during the implementation and consolidation phase of heavy industry, that less industrialized regions such as the Northeast were incorporated into this process. This process was enhanced by the creation of infrastructure, especially transportation and communication, as well as by the stimulus created by fiscal and financial incentives to attract productive capital from more industrialized areas to less developed ones. In the Northeast, the incentives for industrialization resulted in the implementation of an industrial park, which predominantly focused on the production of textiles, apparel, food, and chemical products. A petrochemical industry was also established in the Camaçari Pole along with a chemical complex in Maceió.

The Center-West region began to develop only a few years later. Its growth originally was linked to São Paulo's growth. Only after 1960 was this region integrated definitively into the rest of the economy. The construction of a transportation network and the founding of the new capital, Brasília, induced the spread of agriculture to the interior of the country, whereas previously it had remained highly concentrated in the South region.

The integration of the North, motivated initially by strategic geopolitics, took place during the 1970s with the construction of important roads connecting the region with the rest of the country. Characterized by lower participation of capital from other regions, the development of this area occurred through different processes than the ones observed in the Northeast. On the one hand, the construction of the state-owned Carajás Iron Project, a complex of mining-railroad-harbor activities, was an attempt to integrate the region into the country's productive structure and leverage its comparative advantage in terms of natural resources.[2] The construction of two large aluminum plants, on the other hand, represented an effort to explore the region's international competitiveness. While foreign investment was concentrated in the aluminum sector, domestic private investment converged on the lumber sector. These sectors soon became important contributors to regional exports. The emergence of a small industrial center in Belém and an electro-electronic nucleus in Manaus were made possible by high participation of international capital that entered the country to take advantage of incentives offered those sectors by the government. In the area of non-industrial activities such as agriculture, generous incentives brought in a large inflow of productive and speculative capital in search of profits and appreciation of land values. However, the major part of the region is still a resource frontier for which expansion follows the classic model of frontier expansion and integration.

The South, which did not participate directly in the export cycles, constitutes a distinct case. Early in the eighteenth century, this area began to integrate with Minas Gerais and São Paulo and secured the status of the grain purveyor to the country.

At the same time that this macroregional articulation took place, producers and consumers interacted at an intraregional level, completing the articulation of the domestic market, which supplanted the external market that had prevailed since the colonial period.

This spatial organization created a configuration in which three large economic areas interact. The first, which can be called the resource frontier, corresponds to the North and part of the Center-West. Its total incorporation into the productive matrix is a matter of chance since development strategies depend more on the needs of capital accumulation on a world scale than on government plans detached from this reality. In this sense, the development of the Amazon region is subordinated more directly to the interests of mining enterprises than to the pursuits of local groups. Evidence of such a subordination already can be found in examining the social transformation experienced by the region in recent years. For instance, the construction of large hydropower plants and the creation of a modern center of capitalist production, mainly connected with the external sector, were determined by interests foreign to the region and not motivated by the needs of the local population. The local groups thus far have benefited very little from these investments.

The second area of Brazil's spatial economic configuration, encompassing the Northeast, a small portion of the Southeast (north of Minas Gerais and Espírito Santo), part of the Center-West (Goiás and part of Mato Grosso), and the North, is characterized by a low level of economic dynamism. It is a region that will be developed only after the economic potential of the Center-South region is exhausted. Before this process is completed, industrial and agricultural growth will be induced by the hegemonic region.

The third area is a mega-region encompassing the Center-South (Southeast, South, and part of Center-West) and is home to the country's economic hegemony. This region is the leader in economic terms and has two important economic centers — São Paulo and Rio de Janeiro. As the country's main market, it attracts significant population inflows, especially from the less dynamic Northeast region. The Center-South mega-region is characterized by a strong industrial base (mainly in the Southeast) and highly specialized agriculture (South and Center-West). In contrast to the Northeast, North, and Center-West regions, which were the target of explicit regional development policies, the historic processes that contributed to the consolidation of this dynamic economic center were characterized by sectoral economic policies that had privileged the area for massive investments since the 1920s. It is in this Center-South region that modern agriculture is practiced and high productivity is the norm. In addition to modern agriculture, this region hosts a significant portion of the national industrial park. Distributed along an important transportation network, it forms the important industrial area composed of the Rio-São Paulo wing along the Paraíba Valley, the São Paulo-Ribeirão Preto extension, areas of Belo Horizonte, Porto Alegre, and Curitiba, and the neighboring cities of Blumenau and Joinvile in the state of Santa Catarina. The concentration of equipment, new technology, and massive investments greatly transformed this enormous area, whose population enjoys the country's highest living standards.

## Spatial Distribution of Population and its Characteristics

As discussed above, the development of Brazil's territory occurred in a very asymmetrical way, resulting in an unequal population distribution across regions. Although the integration process is still under way, the most recent census information still reveals a very unequal population distribution. In contrast to the high concentration of population in the South and Northeast regions, the Center-West and the North regions have a low population density. Recent information also suggests a relative inertia in the medium-run spatial distribution, indicating that significant changes in the spatial distribution at the regional level would not be ensured even with the adoption of strict migration policies accompanied by radical changes in the political and economic systems (Martine and Garcia 1987). Table 1, which presents information on population distribution across time, shows that the population of the North increased between 1970 and 1980, corresponding to the expansion of job opportunities resulting from new gold mining activities, implementation of the Carajás Iron Project, and the construction of basic infrastructure such as roads and hydroelectric power plants. When the construction phase ended the following decade (1990), the population decreased in relative terms to lower levels than in 1960. The Northeast and the South regions experienced a small decrease in population between 1960 and 1990. The Northeast continues a three-decade trend, consolidating its status as a regional exporter of labor (Table 2). The South continues to exhibit a slight population loss, a trend that began in the last decade when a significant portion of the region's population, especially from rural areas, moved to the Center-West region. The Southeast exhibits a population increase after 1970, while the Center-West continues its upward trend as a result of migration from the South and other regions.

Table I
# Distribution of Resident Population
## 1960–1990
(in percentage)

| Region | | By Sex | | Total | By Area | |
|---|---|---|---|---|---|---|
| | | Male | Female | | Rural | Urban |
| North | 1960 | 1.86 | 1.79 | 3.65 | 2.28 | 1.37 |
| | 1970 | 2.06 | 1.92 | 3.87 | 2.12 | 1.75 |
| | 1980 | 2.51 | 2.43 | 4.94 | 2.39 | 2.55 |
| | 1990 | 1.65 | 1.77 | 3.42 | 1.47 | 1.95 |
| Northeast | 1960 | 15.50 | 16.15 | 31.65 | 20.92 | 10.73 |
| | 1970 | 14.73 | 15.45 | 30.18 | 17.56 | 12.62 |
| | 1980 | 14.32 | 14.94 | 29.26 | 14.5 | 14.76 |
| | 1990 | 14.30 | 14.97 | 29.27 | 11.96 | 17.31 |
| Southeast | 1960 | 21.95 | 21.76 | 43.71 | 18.79 | 24.92 |
| | 1970 | 21.32 | 21.47 | 42.79 | 11.69 | 31.10 |
| | 1980 | 21.62 | 21.85 | 43.47 | 7.47 | 36.00 |
| | 1990 | 21.87 | 22.77 | 44.64 | 5.09 | 39.55 |
| South | 1960 | 8.53 | 8.26 | 16.79 | 10.55 | 6.24 |
| | 1970 | 8.95 | 8.77 | 17.71 | 9.87 | 7.84 |
| | 1980 | 8.01 | 7.98 | 15.99 | 6.01 | 9.98 |
| | 1990 | 7.76 | 7.86 | 15.62 | 4.26 | 11.36 |
| Center-West | 1960 | 2.19 | 2.01 | 4.20 | 2.76 | 1.44 |
| | 1970 | 2.80 | 2.65 | 5.45 | 2.83 | 2.62 |
| | 1980 | 3.22 | 3.12 | 6.34 | 2.04 | 4.30 |
| | 1990 | 3.50 | 3.55 | 7.05 | 1.51 | 5.54 |
| Brazil | 1960 | 50.03 | 49.97 | 100.00 | 55.30 | 44.70 |
| | 1970 | 49.74 | 50.26 | 100.00 | 44.07 | 55.93 |
| | 1980 | 49.68 | 50.32 | 100.00 | 32.41 | 67.59 |
| | 1990 | 49.08 | 50.92 | 100.00 | 24.29 | 75.71 |

Sources: IBGE, *Anuário Estatístico do Brasil*, several years.

These distribution patterns are linked closely to migration movements that took place during the period under study. Table 2 exhibits data on interregional migration for 1990 and reveals some interesting features of the migration flows. The North and Center-West regions are characterized as recipients of migration flows, whereas the Northeast is an exporter of these flows. The Southeast, with its potential to generate employment, continues to experience a net population inflow. Finally, the South exhibits a more balanced migration movement, although it is beginning to exhibit a trend toward a higher outflow of people.

With respect to the distribution of population by sex, Table 1 reveals a greater balance. In almost every region, the male-female ratios are relatively balanced, but a slight predominance of the female population in the Northeast and of the male population in the North can be noticed. These phenomena are related surely to the migration movements mentioned above since the migrants leaving the Northeast and entering the North are almost always male.

## Table 2
## Interregional Migration
## 1990

| Region | TI | TE |
|---|---|---|
| North | 18.16 | 7.35 |
| Northeast | 6.49 | 19.46 |
| Southeast | 18.45 | 13.61 |
| South | 14.06 | 14.47 |
| Center-West | 35.14 | 13.20 |
| Brazil | 15.29 | 15.46 |

Sources: IBGE, *Anuário Estatístico do Brasil*, several years.
TI = rate of immigration
TE = rate of emigration

Finally, an analysis of the population distribution between rural and urban areas (Table 1) shows that the largest rural populations are found in the Northeast, followed by the North, the Center-West, and the South, respectively. In contrast, the Southeast has the largest urban population in the country. During the period under examination, the North, Northeast, and Center-West experienced increases in their rural populations, while the opposite occurred in the South and the Southeast.

In addition to the disequilibrium observed in the spatial distribution of population, there is also a disequilibrium in terms of social variables. In fact, the economic disparity is reflected in terms of social disparities because life expectancy, education, infant mortality, and other social indicators exhibit better performance in regions with higher levels of income. Table 3 presents a series of indices for 1990 that exemplify these inequalities: life expectancy at birth (LEB); literacy rate (LR), including persons of seven years of age and higher; infant mortality rate (IM) expressed per 1,000 births; and absolute poverty rate (AP). These indicators clearly reveal the profound social disparities among Brazil's regions. Life expectancy varies greatly across regions, with the Northeast exhibiting the lowest figures for that variable. The Northeast consistently has had the worst performance for each social indicator (Table 3), followed by the North and the Center-West. Except for the relatively high infant mortality rates in the Southeast, the South competes with this region for the highest position in social development. High rates of infant mortality are concentrated in Greater São Paulo, and this phenomenon is a common feature of large cities in developing countries where rapid urbanization has not yet been followed by sufficient social infrastructure. The situation in São Paulo has biased the whole Southeast region negatively with respect to this indicator.

### Table 3
## Social Disparities among Regions

| Region | LEB (age) | LR (%) | IM (per thousand) | AP (%) |
|---|---|---|---|---|
| North | 64.16 | 85.0 | 72.3 | 24.5 |
| Northeast | 51.57 | 60.7 | 121.4 | 51.2 |
| Southeast | 63.59 | 88.1 | 74.5 | 14.8 |
| South | 66.96 | 88.6 | 61.8 | 20.6 |
| Center-West | 64.70 | 82.0 | 70.3 | 24.7 |
| Brazil | 60.08 | 80.9 | 87.9 | 26.2 |

Sources: IBGE, *Anuário Estatístico do Brasil*, several years.
LEB = life expectancy at birth
LR = literacy rate
IM = infant mortality rate
AP = absolute poverty rate

Other studies also suggest that the pattern of social inequality not only persists over time but also is characterized by a higher concentration of poverty and lower living standards in the Northeast and North (Barros and Sawyer 1991). Table 4, which represents this inequality, shows that the unevenly distributed illiteracy rate is substantially higher in rural areas, especially the Northeast. The reason for the higher rate in the Northeast is that a very large percentage of its population lives in rural areas. The most intriguing aspect of these inequalities, however, is that the data presented do not indicate that this situation will reverse itself unless a specific education policy is implemented.

### Table 4
## Illiteracy Rate by Region
## 1990

| | Illiteracy Rate (%) | |
|---|---|---|
| Regions | Rural | Urban |
| North[1] | — | 14.3 |
| Northeast | 55.8 | 27.8 |
| Southeast | 23.9 | 9.1 |
| South | 15.9 | 8.7 |
| Center-West[2] | 31.3 | 12.8 |
| Brazil[3] | 37.8 | 13.5 |

Sources: IBGE: *Anuário Estatístico do Brasil*, several years; Demographic and Economic Census, several years; *Pesquisa Nacional de Amostragem Domiciliar (PNAD)*, several years.
Notes: 1. Excludes people from Tocantins. 2. Includes people from Tocantins. 3. Excludes people from the rural areas of Rondônia, Acre, Amazonas, Roraima, Pará, and Amapá.

A very similar pattern of uneven social development is observed in Table 5, where a high concentration of poverty in the Northeast and especially within the rural areas of the Northeast are revealed. Table 5 also reveals an important aspect of Brazil's poverty that is concealed in Table 3. Contrary to the trend shown by all other regions, poverty in the Southeast region is concentrated in urban areas, a phenomenon that is related also to the high urbanization of the Greater São Paulo area and an intense inflow of poor from other regions into cities in search of better job opportunities.

## Table 5
## Spatial Distribution of Total Population and Indigent Population, 1990
### (in percentage)

| Region | Total Population | Indigent Population | | |
|---|---|---|---|---|
| | | Urban | Rural | Total |
| North | 3.42 | 2.16 | — | 2.16 |
| Notheast | 29.27 | 22.54 | 32.03 | 54.57 |
| Southeast | 44.64 | 16.55 | 6.65 | 25.20 |
| South | 15.62 | 5.23 | 7.66 | 12.89 |
| Center-West | 7.05 | 2.84 | 2.34 | 5.18 |
| Brazil | 100.00 | 49.32 | 50.68 | 100.00 |

Sources: IBGE: *Anuário Estatístico do Brasil*, several years; *Demographic and Economic Census*, several years; *Pesquisa Nacional de Amostragem Domiciliar (PNAD)*, several years; IPEA, *Mapa da Fome: Subsídios à Formulação de uma Política de Segurança Alimentar*, 1993.

In short, it is possible to conclude that Brazil has a very perverse profile in terms of the distribution of social development, with the Northeast and North leading all other regions in terms of poverty, illiteracy, and infant mortality.

## Spatial Distribution of Economic Activities

The standard analysis of regional economic disparities usually is based on a study of the interregional distribution of total and per capita Gross Domestic Product (GDP). Despite well-known limitations this indicator poses in providing an accurate picture of social and economic welfare, undoubtedly it is closely related to the levels of production and consumption and usually is utilized as an indicator of the degree of economic development and living standards at a regional level. The next section's analysis has adopted the GDP as a proxy for economic development and concentrates on its sectoral composition across regions. The objective is to present an economic profile of Brazil's regions that resulted from the previously mentioned process of productive and commercial articulation.

## Regional Distribution of GDP

Historically, Brazil's production activities have been distributed unevenly across its territory. Table 6, which presents information on the distribution of GDP across regions, confirms the persistence of high imbalances in the spatial distribution of production during the last three decades (1960-1990). The analysis of data for this period testifies to the absolute leadership of the Southeast region in the generation of national GDP whose concentration reached its apex in the 1970s when the region alone was responsible for 65 percent of the national GDP. Since then, this trend has begun to reverse itself; the Southeast's participation in total GDP has decreased since the 1970s. The region's share of GDP fell 7 percent in 1990, reducing it to 58 percent of the national total.

A similar phenomenon has been occurring in the South region, although to a lesser extent. The South, as with the Southeast region, reached its highest share of national production in 1970 and, thereafter, became less important in generating national GDP. The North and the Center-West have increased their participation in national production with the North increasing its participation from 2 to 4 percent between 1960 and 1990. The Center-West, which only accounted for 2.4 percent in 1960, displayed dynamic growth by jumping to almost 9 percent of the national product by 1990.

The Northeast, which lost relative importance between 1960 and 1970, dropping from 14.1 to 12 percent of national GDP, maintained its share unchanged between 1970 and 1980 and increased it to 13.1 percent by 1990. The increase over the last decade, however, was not sufficient to bring the region back to its previous status, showing an absolute loss in terms of its share in total national production. Such a weak performance by the Northeast was somewhat unexpected in light of the fact that the region has received heavy government incentives to stimulate growth throughout these decades.

## Table 6
# Distribution of GDP among Regions
### (in percentage)

| Regions | 1960 | 1970 | 1980 | 1990 |
|---|---|---|---|---|
| North | 2.0 | 2.2 | 3.2 | 3.9 |
| Northeast | 14.1 | 12.0 | 12.2 | 13.1 |
| Southeast | 64.1 | 65.0 | 62.1 | 57.6 |
| South | 17.4 | 18.2 | 17.3 | 16.7 |
| Center-West | 2.4 | 2.6 | 5.2 | 8.7 |
| Brazil | 100.0 | 100.0 | 100.0 | 100.0 |

Sources: *Censos Demográficos*, 1960, 1970, 1980, 1991. National Accounts, FGV and IBGE.

The comparison between the spatial distribution of population (Table 1) and the distribution of economic activity (Table 6) shows yet another disequilibrium among regions. While the Southeast has nearly 45 percent of the country's population and produces 58 percent of the national GDP, the Northeast has approximately 30 percent of total population yet only accounts for 13 percent of the national product. The huge gap between the distribution of these two variables reveals that the disparity between the two regions goes beyond merely spatial distribution of productive activities. It also encompasses a large gap in terms of income distribution. Other regions, in contrast, exhibit a relative equilibrium between the spatial distribution of population and economic activities.

In general, one may conclude that the Southeast has suffered during the period in question as evidenced by a reduction in its relative share of the GDP, while other regions generally have increased their shares. With respect to this phenomenon, Andrade (1988) called attention to the fact that during the 1970s, less developed regions achieved higher levels of economic growth than more developed regions. This phenomenon seems to be confirmed by the data for 1990. Although the Southeast region still maintains its hegemony, it is clear that it suffered greater losses in terms of its share of GDP; the North and Center-West benefited most from the Southeast's losses. Although the trend seems to be clear, it is still too early to conclude that the predominance of the Southeast within the production structure is somehow threatened, despite relative losses in recent decades, the Southeast remains a very dynamic and vital area. The long-term trend will become more apparent only when the country resumes growth.

It is possible to infer, however, that there was a slight deconcentration of production activity in Brazil over the decades. In this respect, it is possible to identify a reduction in regional disparities. This phenomenon of deconcentration of economic activity has been pointed out already by several authors (Andrade 1988, Azzoni 1986, Buarque 1988, Diniz 1988, Martine and Garcia 1987, Guimarães Neto 1986) who claim that the so-called polarization reversal process" of economic activities in Brazilian territory is under way. According to some authors, this process may have begun in the 1950s (Pimes 1984), but only recently has it been established empirically.

It is beyond the scope of this chapter to discuss the determinants of such a trend toward production deconcentration. It is worth mentioning, however, that this process is partially the result of spatial reverberations of government policies, especially those based on the distribution of extensive financial and fiscal incentives.

What seems to be evident, however, is the changing profile of Brazil's regions, as the new Brazil grows toward the Center-West and the North. Nonetheless, the improved performance of these latter regions does not imply that their absolute position will be altered significantly in the next decade. As a matter of fact, if one projects regional and national growth rates of GDP and population to the year 2000, the result will be that the North, Center-West, and Northeast regions still will have lower total and per capita GDP levels than the national average.

To complete the analysis of the spatial distribution of economic activities, the sectoral composition of regional GDP must be examined. In order to do so, it is necessary to focus on the division of labor among the regions.

## Spatial Distribution of Productive Sectors

In addition to the changes in the spatial distribution of production, there have been profound changes in the interregional distribution of sectoral GDP in recent years. Table 7, which presents the distribution of sectoral regional GDP and its composition for the years 1970 and 1985, reveals that the sectoral distribution of GDP, as in the case of total GDP, is concentrated in the Southeast region, with the most significant concentration in industry. In 1970, almost 80 percent of industrial production was concentrated in the Southeast region but by 1985, the region's share of production of industrial goods had dropped to 65 percent. The Northeast region, in relative terms, increased its share of industrial production from 7 to 12 percent between 1970 and 1985, while all other regions benefited from the loss of production in the Southeast, although to a lesser extent.

The phenomenon of industrial concentration has been widely studied in Brazil. Largely determined by the effect of locational factors, which influence the cost of production and determine the spatial distribution of economic activities, this phenomenon is not new in the Brazilian economy. Transfer costs (especially transportation costs), the existence of external economies, and the presence of an "entrepreneurial atmosphere" are factors that have played a decisive role in location decisions. As the Southeast has been the center of industrial production since the beginning of industrialization, it is not surprising that it exhibits these factors that have induced industrial concentration. However, it is expected that as the other regions grow, they will also develop these advantages and attract new production plants.

Agriculture is the most evenly distributed sector across regions. In 1970, the Southeast and South regions shared the leadership of this sector at 34.2 and 33.4 of national production, respectively. The South's share of production declined in 1985. Despite the Southeast experiencing a small relative increase, it has lost competitiveness in comparison to the Center-West and North regions, where cattle ranching is an important activity.

The North and Center-West regions saw their shares of agricultural production substantially increased during the 1970-1985 period (from 4.1 to

6.6 percent and from 7.4 to 8.1 percent, respectively). However, these two regions still present the lowest share in the production of agricultural products.

The dynamism shown by the Center-West seems to be linked to an expansion of the agricultural frontier and the growth of capitalist production in the sector, the latter permitting a rational use of the savannah areas by farmers who migrated from areas with significant sectoral experience. Farmers from the South brought with them to the Center-West advanced technology developed in their home states. Brasília's consolidation is an equally important factor in the Center-West's development. It is expected that the growth of agriculture will be followed by an industrialization process in the coming years, as it has occurred in the South. In fact, the Central-West is witnessing such a trend, as demonstrated by the strong growth of the agroindustrial sector in the region. In the North, the situation is quite different. The growth of agriculture has been induced by certain industrial sectors, mineral and wood exploitation, and ranching. The existence of the Manaus Free Trade Zone and incentives given to attract electro-electronic industries were fundamental factors behind the region's development, as evidenced by the fast growth of those industries during the 1970-1985 period.

The Northeast decreased its participation in agricultural production from 20.9 percent in 1970 to 19 percent in 1985. Recurrent droughts continue to be the main factor hindering the growth of agricultural production. Taking into consideration the generous incentives offered to producers in the region, one would expect a better performance in agriculture, however.

The development of agriculture at the regional level exhibits a well-defined trend: the South has lost importance, while the frontier regions have expanded. The relative decline in the South and the relative gains in other regions are primarily a consequence of the exhaustion of new arable lands in the South and the expansion into previously uncultivated areas in frontier regions in other parts of the country. This has been true despite the fact that the most recent increases in agricultural production are the result of increased productivity of land already in use (Homem de Melo 1985).

The frontier regions (especially the Center-West) are beginning to account for larger shares of agricultural production for export and the domestic market. The same phenomenon was observed in the South in its early stages when agriculture was linked closely to the development of the industrial food complex in the Southeast. Agriculture has become more modernized in most regions. It has strengthened its relationship with the industrial sector gradually in terms of demand for modern inputs such as tractors and equipment that generate the so-called "backward linkages" as well as through the supply of inputs to the domestic and export food industry, generating the well-known "forward linkages."

## Table 7
# Sectoral Distribution and Composition of Regional GDP 1970 and 1985
### (in percentage)

| Sectors | North | Northeast | Southeast | South | Center-West | Total |
|---|---|---|---|---|---|---|
| Agriculture | | | | | | |
| 1970 | 4.1 | 20.9 | 34.2 | 33.4 | 7.4 | 100.0 |
| 1985 | 6.6 | 19.0 | 39.1 | 27.2 | 8.1 | 100.0 |
| Industry | | | | | | |
| 1970 | 1.1 | 7.0 | 79.1 | 11.9 | 0.9 | 100.0 |
| 1985 | 4.1 | 12.2 | 65.4 | 15.8 | 2.5 | 100.0 |
| Commerce | | | | | | |
| 1970 | 2.9 | 12.7 | 62.5 | 18.6 | 3.3 | 100.0 |
| 1985 | 4.6 | 16.8 | 53.8 | 19.1 | 5.5 | 100.0 |
| Transportation/Communications | | | | | | |
| 1970 | 2.2 | 11.1 | 67.0 | 15.8 | 3.9 | 100.0 |
| 1985 | 2.9 | 8.7 | 62.7 | 19.7 | 6.0 | 100.0 |
| Financial Services | | | | | | |
| 1970 | 1.3 | 8.6 | 70.4 | 12.1 | 7.6 | 100.0 |
| 1980 | 1.2 | 9.3 | 43.3 | 14.3 | 31.9 | 100.0 |
| Public Administration | | | | | | |
| 1970 | 2.9 | 14.7 | 60.8 | 14.3 | 7.3 | 100.0 |
| 1980 | 5.2 | 17.2 | 50.7 | 13.9 | 13.0 | 100.0 |
| Rent | | | | | | |
| 1970 | 2.2 | 12.5 | 66.8 | 14.7 | 3.8 | 100.0 |
| 1985 | 4.2 | 12.7 | 62.9 | 13.7 | 6.5 | 100.0 |
| Other Services | | | | | | |
| 1970 | 1.5 | 11.1 | 69.3 | 14.5 | 3.6 | 100.0 |
| 1985 | 3.3 | 12.5 | 62.1 | 14.7 | 7.4 | 100.0 |

Source: IBGE, National Accounts.

The introduction of new crops during the 1960s and 1970s, the surge of primary product exports, such as soybean and cacao, and an oil crisis that encouraged the substitution of alcohol for gasoline in Brazil were the main factors determining the new spatial division of production activities.

The Southeast maintained an obvious specialization in the production of industrial goods and services, gradually transferred agricultural production to other regions of the country, and since then has established effective forward and backward linkages with these other regions.

Taking a look at other sectors of production in Table 7, the same pattern of distribution can be observed. At the center of economic activities, the Southeast region lost importance over the 1970-1985 period mainly in the areas of commerce, transportation and communication, financial services, public administration, rent, and services in general; in other sectors, the trend is less obvious. The regions that benefited from the Southeast's losses were the North and Center-West, while the South and the Northeast exhibited a more stable pattern. The South lost a small share in the areas of public administration and rent, while it gained a small share of other sectors. The Northeast experienced a substantial decrease in transportation and communication while experiencing moderate increases in other sectors. The North and Center-West exhibited robust growth in all productive sectors. It should be noted that the tremendous growth (almost 320 percent) of the financial services in the Center-West was induced by agricultural growth.

## Income Distribution

One issue on which there is consensus among Brazilian economists is that the country has one of the most unequal income distributions in the world. This distribution, which has historical roots, results from the particular way Brazil has participated in industrial capitalism and from the differentiated ways of adopting technology by various sectors of the economy (Tavares and Serra 1972, Pinto 1982).

It is beyond the scope of this section to analyze this type of interpretation or to describe alternative interpretations of the factors that determined income concentration in Brazil.[3] Rather, the objective is to organize a body of information that permits a comparison of different distribution patterns across time and space. Once this inequality is determined, the intent is to evaluate existing degrees of regional disparities in terms of personal income.

Before the analysis can proceed, the quality of data and the methodology employed should be discussed. Basic data on the evolution of income distribution in Brazil and among its five regions were extracted from the 1960, 1970, 1980, and 1991 *Demographic Census*, as well as from the *National Household Survey* (*Pesquisa Nacional por Amostra de Domicílios* — PNAD) for the years 1983, 1986, 1987, 1988, and 1992. Although some methodological differences exist between the two sources, such divergences do not significantly alter the results, and therefore, comparisons in regional income distribution may be carried out without too many restrictions.

The first variable to be utilized in the study of personal income distribution at the regional level is the per capita regional gross domestic product (RGDP), expressed in Table 8 as a percentage of the average national GDP.

Consistent with the results obtained so far, the above-mentioned data also confirm the Southeast region's privileged position with respect to this variable. The Southeast followed by the South are the two areas with the highest average per capita incomes. However, the relative decline of the Southeast's per capita income over the years indicates a slight movement toward deconcentration of income across regions. The Southeast's population, with an average per capita income 49 percent higher than the national level in 1960, had declined 9 percent by 1990 to an amount that was still 40 percent higher than the national average. The South region, on the other hand, where per capita income was equivalent to the national average in 1960, experienced an increase to 10 percent above the national average by 1990. If the South continues this positive trend and the Southeast its relative negative trend, the overall profile of per capita income among regions could change, possibly resulting in the Southeast's loss of its position as the country's regional economic hegemony.

## Table 8
## Average Regional Income per Capita
## (Brazil = 100)
Percentage of the national average

| Regions | 1960 | 1970 | 1975 | 1980 | 1985 | 1990 |
|---|---|---|---|---|---|---|
| North | 55 | 58 | 50 | 66 | 69 | 55 |
| Northeast | 45 | 40 | 39 | 42 | 47 | 46 |
| Southeast | 149 | 152 | 148 | 143 | 133 | 140 |
| South | 98 | 96 | 109 | 108 | 116 | 110 |
| Center-West | * | 68 | 72 | 87 | 88 | 87 |

* Not available.
Sources: National Accounts, Fundação Getúlio Vargas, and IBGE, several years.

The Center-West and the North are next in terms of per capita income levels. Compared to the national average, the Center-West region experienced a relative increase in its per capita income over the years, although it is still below the national average. The North shows a similar pattern, exhibiting a relative increase in per capita income yet still well below the national average. The Northeast, on the other hand, has had the worst performance with per capita income less than half the national average. It was the only region to experience a relative decline in per capita income during the 1970-1975 period, and it is the only region whose per capita income at the end of three decades (1990) remained the same (1960). No indication of any improvement is apparent. The fact is that in 30 years, the Northeast was unable to boost its per capita income in relation to other regions. This low level of stagnation resulted not only from the apparently slow growth of regional output and income but also from the region's relatively higher population growth rates.

A final observation concerning Table 8 is that between 1985 and 1990, each region, with the exception of the Southeast, exhibited a slight reduction in its relative per capita income. Although this decline largely reflects the economic crisis of the 1980s, it is difficult to identify its specific causes. However, one could speculate that for a long period of time, the Southeast was able to maintain the same level of per capita income in spite of economic crises. It had a higher concentration of capital, and a large proportion of that income was generated outside the production sector.

Now that the per capita income profile has been examined at the regional level, it will be interesting to examine the manner in which this income is appropriated by different groups in the various regions. Table 9 shows the share of total national income captured by the poorest 40 percent of the Brazilian population in each region and also includes the total labor force (10 years of age and older) with positive income. The figures tend to overestimate the inequality, since earnings include only monetary incomes, making it particularly difficult to identify poverty in rural areas accurately. Despite this restriction, however, the data offer the possibility of observing personal income distribution inequalities at the regional level.

For instance, at the beginning of the 1960-1990 period, the Southeast and Center-West regions were the ones with the lowest share of income for the poorest 40 percent (12.3 and 14.8 percent, respectively), both of them below the 15.8 percent national average. The Northeast was very close to the national average, with the poorest 40 percent of its population acquiring 15.9 percent of total regional income in 1960. In the South and the North, the shares appropriated by the poorest 40 percent of the population were the highest in 1960 (17 and 18.8 percent, respectively), a phenomenon that also occurred in the following two decades (based on the 1970 and 1980 statistics). In 1990, the situation was completely different. The relative positions of the regions are reversed, with the Center-West becoming the only region where the income appropriation by the poorest 40 percent of the population was lower than the national level. In all the other regions, this portion of the population received a little more than the national average. The Southeast, for example, which had one of the worst income distributions of all the regions at the beginning of the period, exhibited the second best income distribution (behind the South) by 1990, according to this indicator. In the South, although the poorest 40 percent of the population received only 9.4 percent of the income in 1990, this was significantly higher than the national average of 7.9 percent and higher than any other region in Brazil.

One interesting aspect is that all regions experienced a serious deterioration in income distribution over the 30-year time period. In 1990, the poorest 40 percent of the population in each region received a smaller share of income than they did in 1960. Another interesting point about this distribution is that the reduction in the shares appropriated by the poorest population had different trends in each region, bringing the highest and lowest regional extremes closer to the national average. At the end of the period, all regions were very close to the national average, although overall, 50 percent below their shares at the beginning of the period.

## Table 9
# Share of Total Income Appropriated by the Poorest 40 Percent of Total Population 1960–1990
### (in percentage)

| Regions | 1960 | 1970 | 1980 | 1990 |
|---|---|---|---|---|
| North | 18.8 | 15.9 | 11.6 | 8.2 |
| Northeast | 15.9 | 13.5 | 10.6 | 8.4 |
| Southeast | 12.3 | 10.7 | 10.1 | 8.7 |
| South | 17.0 | 13.2 | 10.7 | 9.4 |
| Center-West | 14.8 | 13.0 | 9.1 | 7.8 |
| Brazil | 15.8 | 13.3 | 10.4 | 7.9 |

Sources:  IBGE: PNAD and Demographic Censuses, 1960, 1970, 1980, and 1990/1991.

In the case of the share of total income appropriated by the richest 10 percent of the population, the opposite trends have been observed. The high income bracket shows a significant increase in its share of income in comparison to a reduction in the shares of the poorest 40 percent of the population. Table 10 presents this information and confirms other data showing a persistent overall increase in income concentration in the country.

According to Table 10, at the beginning of the period studied (1960-1990), the Northeast, Center-West, and Southeast regions were the ones with the highest shares distributed to the richest 10 percent of the population (37.6, 36.4, and 36.3 percent, respectively). In addition, all these shares were well above the national average, which was approximately 34.6 percent. Once again, the Northeast is situated significantly above the national average, exhibiting the greatest disparity in the distribution of regional personal income. It is worth mentioning that the poorest 40 percent of this region have a lower share of income than in any other region's poorest population (Table 9). Table 10 substantiates the previous table's findings that the South and North regions have the lowest income disparities. Shares of income allotted to the richest 10 percent of the population (32.1 and 30.5, respectively) in these regions are the lowest in the country.

During the 1970s, distribution patterns exhibited in the previous decade were maintained, although a general increase in income concentration across the nation was observed, as Table 10 indicates. In the 1980s, the regional pattern of concentration changed, as well as the relative position of each region. In 1990, the changes that occurred in the previous decade are consolidated, and the pattern became consistent with changes in the allocation of income among the poorest 40 percent (Table 9). There was a reversal in the regional position with respect to the distribution of income: the Northeast, followed closely by the Center-West and North, continued to display the greatest income concentration in the highest income brackets. The Southeast and the South switched positions with each other and exhibited the lowest concentrations of income in the highest income bracket (46.3 and 45.8, respectively). These two regions were also the only ones with shares below the national average (48.7 percent). The reversal in the positions presented at the beginning of the period is indicative of an improvement in relative terms in the income distribution pattern of the Southeast and South.

## Table 10
## Share of Total Income Appropriated by the Richest 10 Percent of Population 1960–1990
(in percentage)

| Regions | 1960 | 1970 | 1980 | 1990 |
|---|---|---|---|---|
| North | 30.5 | 39.3 | 43.2 | 49.9 |
| Northeast | 37.6 | 44.7 | 49.6 | 52.5 |
| Southeast | 36.3 | 42.3 | 44.5 | 46.3 |
| South | 32.1 | 40.7 | 45.6 | 45.8 |
| Center-West | 36.4 | 44.1 | 49.6 | 50.5 |
| Brazil | 34.6 | 42.3 | 46.7 | 48.7 |

Sources: National Accounts, FGV and IBGE.

In absolute terms, as Table 10 demonstrates, income distribution deteriorated in all regions, with a clear trend toward a higher concentration in the higher income brackets. This phenomenon is highly consistent with the trend exhibited in Table 9 and indicates a clear reduction in the share of income allotted to the poorest 40 percent of the population. It is, therefore, apparent that a perverse process of income concentration was occurring at the regional level, while the share of income allotted to the lowest income brackets was decreasing, while the share of income distributed to the highest income brackets was increasing significantly, and the gap between the rich and poor widened in all regions. It should be noted as well that the gap between these shares was extremely large: on the average, the richest 10 percent appropriated 48.7 percent of the income, and the poorest 40 percent received only 7.9 percent of the income. A comparison of Tables 9 and 10 clearly reveals a trend toward greater income concentration. Unfortunately, the poorest regions (Northeast and North) were the ones that showed this trend more clearly. The South and the Southeast were the areas where the trend was weakest.

# Regional Disparities and Reversal Perspectives

The historical insertion of the Brazilian economy into the expansionary process of capitalist industrialization and the spatial reverberation of this process have generated an economy characterized by profound regional disparities. From 1960 to 1990, there was a visible process of spatial deconcentration of economic activity in the Southeast, accompanied by a strong concentration of income distribution in the less developed regions. The Southeast exhibited a clear trend toward the deconcentration of economic activity and income, still maintaining hegemony in the production of goods and services at the national level. The South exhibited relative stability during the period and was able to secure a position as the second most important area in the country in terms of production. It also displayed the best income distribution among all regions and almost certainly will become the region with the highest personal income. The Northeast exhibited a very interesting profile. With a high population concentration, it generated a small portion of the national product and had the most unequal income distribution. All the states in the Northeast remained stagnant, with the exception of the states of Maranhão, Piauí, Ceará, and Rio Grande do Norte, which exhibited positive growth rates. Benefiting from the relative decline suffered by the Southeast, the North and Center-West regions displayed the highest growth rates. Growth in the North was led by industry (in Manaus), mining, wood extraction, and cattle ranching, while growth in the Center-West was driven by the expansion of the agricultural frontier.

Consolidation of the deconcentration process that is under way is far from complete and depends on a number of factors. It is crucial that the federal government's fiscal and financial crisis be resolved. The state can then regain its planning capacity and create new mechanisms and instruments that promote a more balanced regional development. Mechanisms utilized by the government during the three decades of this study, however, have proved to be inefficient. New ways to promote development in less developed regions must be considered.

The creation of a more balanced growth, moreover, requires that the short-run type of planning adopted in past years be abandoned. The pursuit of economic stabilization during the 1980s, for example, gained priority to the detriment of the more structural problems of poverty, regional inequalities, and production deconcentration. The pursuit of short-run economic policies without any concern for their redistributive effects and potential impacts on other sectors has exacerbated structural problems in the Brazilian economy. New policies should focus on finding solutions to old structural problems such as the low level of education among the country's population and the lack of basic sanitation and preventive medicine in a large portion of the territory.

Only an educated and healthy population can contribute effectively to the balanced growth of the country.

In addition to rescuing the state's capacity to plan and to attack structural problems, it is also important to implement policies aimed explicitly at regional development. Historically, sectoral and general macroeconomic policies have ignored the existence of space and its implications, and consequently, policies have been applied uniformly across the territory with only minor adaptations that will influence the spatial mobility of factors. This spaceless character of most economic policies implies that the government envisions homogeneous effects occurring across regions that are presumed to be alike but that are, in reality, very distinct. However, when applied to heterogeneous economic and social spaces — typical of Brazil — these policies produce highly differential effects across regions.

International experience supports national policies' non-neutral character over the space. Moreover, Brazilian researchers have studied the effects of national policies on regional development. In 1984, the Superintendency for Northeast Development (Superintendência de Desenvolvimento do Nordeste — SUDENE), the most important regional development agency in Brazil, investigated the impact of macroeconomic policies on Brazil's regions. Focusing on several periods, the study concluded that national policies exert a strong influence on the spatial organization of production. Another study (Gomes 1987) analyzed the impact of the first years of the 1980 crisis on the country's regions and concluded that more developed regions such as the Southeast and South found it more difficult to adapt to the crisis and, therefore, suffered more than the peripheral regions during that period. This conclusion suggests that regions adjust differently in periods of crisis and that, in the Brazilian case, the more developed regions faced more difficulties in adapting to the new environment.

Moreover, government planning in Brazil has followed the well-known "top-down approach" that presumes the existence of so-called spillover effects. Accordingly, the strength of some key sectors is utilized as an engine of growth, which is based on the assumption that most of the effects will spread to other sectors and geographic areas. These effects do not always take place, however. For them to do so, it is necessary for activities to bear a high degree of dynamism and a substantial degree of linkage with other sectors, thereby preventing the emergence of economic enclaves. Moreover, in addition to the importance of the dynamic nature of the sector under consideration, it is crucial that neighboring regions be ready for development (Haddad 1988, 138-142).

The negligence shown toward regional planning in Brazil is evidenced by the absence of a multiregional macroeconomic model capable of advancing an evaluation of the spatial impacts of alternative macroeconomic policies.

Since the regions, as previously discussed, are different in terms of economic and social structures, the consequences of national policies will be different over the economic space (Willumsen and Dutt 1991). Therefore, it is fundamental that the government evaluate beforehand the likely impacts of such policies so that their decision regarding the adoption of alternative policies is consistent with the objective being pursued.

Keeping these considerations in mind, the prospects for a reversal of the process of income and production concentration are not encouraging. A reduction in the gaps between regions in terms of production growth seems to be more closely related to the decline in the national economy than to the result of regional economic dynamism. Thus, it seems more reasonable to expect that, in the absence of any mechanism that will compensate for regional disparities, these inequalities may well increase as the country resumes growth, further intensifying the concentration in more advanced areas. The advantages of location, important for attracting new projects, are still more concentrated in industrialized than in peripheral regions. Due to the small size of consumer markets in Brazil's peripheral regions, attracting investment projects for the domestic market in these regions is difficult. The prospects for an autonomous process of production deconcentration do not seem to be very encouraging. However, it is hoped that the state may eventually rescue its planning capacity and use it advantageously, especially with respect to long-term goals.

## Conclusion

The information in this paper reveals that regional disparities in Brazil not only persisted during the period of study but also intensified. Deconcentration of economic activity in the Southeast region, observed in past decades, benefited the less developed areas of the Center-West and North. This deconcentration, however, seems to be more the result of a slackness in national economic growth than of regional economic dynamism. Therefore, it seems more plausible to expect that, without any mechanism to compensate or eliminate structural imbalances, regional disparities will increase when growth is resumed.

The elimination, or alleviation, of regional inequalities depends on the completion and consolidation of the deconcentration process in course. It depends also on the presence of long-term planning aimed at solving structural problems that can place the country in a position to grow in a balanced manner. However, for this to happen, it is crucial that the country rescue its planning capacity and define a development project that takes into account prevailing inequalities and aims at regional integration within the context of greater symmetrical growth.

# Notes

1. This division was established by the IBGE (Brazilian Statistical Bureau) and followed the geo-economic criteria.

2. Although the Carajás project was focused originally on the international market, a minor focus on the regional economy was also present. This concern became evident with the creation, in the 1980s, of the Carajás Program; its main objective was the planning of the region's development.

3. The debate on income distribution in Brazil dates from the early 1970s. The works of Langoni 1973, Macedo and Garcia 1978, Souza and Baltar 1979, Macedo 1981, Drobny and Wells 1983, Ocio 1986, Saboia 1985, Bonelli and Sedlacek 1988, Reis 1989, and Camargo and Giambiagi 1991 offer excellent views on the evolution of debates around the distributive question in Brazil.

# References

Andrade, Manuel C. de. 1988. *O Nordeste e a Questão Regional.* São Paulo: Editora Ática.

Azzoni, Carlos R. 1986. *Indústria e Reversão da Polarização no Brazil.* São Paulo: Instituto de Pesquisas Econômicas (IPE).

Barros, Reinaldo P., and D. Sawyer. 1991. *Unequal Opportunity to Survive, Education and Regional Disparities in Brazil.* New Haven, Conn.: Yale University Press.

Bonelli, Regis, and G. Sedlacek. 1988. "Distribuição de Renda: Evolução no Último Quarto de Século." In *Mercado de Trabalho e Distribuição de Renda: uma Coletânea,* eds. R.P. Barros and G. Sedlacek. Série Monográfica, no. 35. Rio de Janeiro: INPES/IPEA.

Buarque, Sérgio C. 1988. "O Estado no Processo de Integração e Desagregação no Nordeste." In *Anais do VII Encontro Nacional de Estudos Populacionais.* Olinda: ANPEC.

Camargo, José M., and F. Giambiagi. 1991. *Distribuição de Renda no Brasil.* São Paulo: Paz e Terra.

Cano, Wilson. 1977. *Raízes da Concentração Industrial no Brasil.* São Paulo: Difel.

Diniz, Clélio C. 1988. "O Nordeste e o Contexto Nacional." *Anais do VII Encontro Nacional de Estudos Populacionais.* Olinda.

Drobny, A., and J. Wells. 1983. "Salário Mínimo e Distribuição de Renda no Brasil: Uma análise do Setor de Construção Civil." *Pesquisa e Planejamento Econômico* 13(2).

FGV and Instituto Brasileiro de Geografia e Estatística (IBGE). National Accounts.

Gomes, G.M. 1987. "Da Recessão de 1981-1983 aos Impactos do Plano Cruzado no Brasil e no Nordeste: Um Alerta para o Presente." *Boletim Sócio-Econômico do Nordeste* 1(1).

Guimarães Neto, L. 1986. *Nordeste: Da Articulação Comercial à Integração Econômica.* Campinas, mimeo.

Haddad, Paulo. 1988. "A Economia Regional no Brasil: Velhas Dimensões, Novas Perspectivas." *Anais do XVI Encontro Nacional de Economia,* v. 1. Belo Horizonte: ANPEC.

Homem de Melo, Fernando. 1985. *Prioridade Agrícola: Sucesso ou Fracasso?* São Paulo: Livraria Pioneira Editora.

Homem de Melo, Fernando. 1982. "Inovações Tecnológicas e Efeitos Distributivos: O Caso de Economia Semi-Aberta." *Revista Brasileira de Economia* 36(4).

IBGE. 1960, 1970, 1980, 1990/1991. *Anuário Estatístico do Brasil.* Rio de Janeiro: IBGE.

IBGE. 1960, 1970, 1980, 1990, 1991. *Censos Demográficos.* Rio de Janeiro: IBGE.

IBGE. 1983, 1986, 1987, 1988, 1992. *Pesquisa Nacional de Amostragen Domiciliar (PNAD).* Rio de Janeiro: IBGE.

IPEA. 1993. *Mapa da Fome: Subsídios à Formulação de uma Política de Segurança Alimentar.* Rio de Janeiro: IBGE.

Langoni, Carlos. 1973. *Distribuição de Renda e Desenvolvimento Econômico no Brasil.* Rio de Janeiro: Expressão e Cultura.

Lessa, Carlos. 1975. *Quinze Anos de Política Econômica.* São Paulo: Brasiliense.

Macedo, Roberto B. 1981. "Salário Mínimo e Distribuição de Renda no Brasil." *Estudos Econômicos* 11(1).

Macedo, Roberto B., and M.E. Garcia. 1978. "Observações sobre a Política Brasileira de Salário Mínimo." Trabalho para Discussão n. 27. São Paulo: Instituto de Pesquisas Econômicas, Universidade de São Paulo.

Martine, George, and R. Garcia, eds. 1987. *Os Impactos Sociais da Modernização Agrícola.* São Paulo: Caetés/Hucitec.

Ocio, D.Z. 1986. "Salários e Política Salarial." *Revista de Economia Política* 6(2).

Oliveira, Francisco. 1977. "Mudança na Divisão Inter-regional do Trabalho no Brasil." *A Economia da Dependência Imperfeita.* Rio de Janeiro: Graal.

PIMES, Universidade Federal de Pernambuco. 1984. *Desigualdades Regionais do Desenvolvimento Brasileiro: a Política de Desenvolvimento Regional.* v. 14. Recife: Superintendência de Desenvolvimento do Nordeste (SUDENE).

Pereira, Luiz Carlos B. 1988. *Economia Brasileira: Uma Introdução Crítica.* São Paulo: Brasiliense.

Pinto, A. 1982. "Concentración del Progreso Técnico y de sus Fructos en el Desarrollo Latinoamericano," *Trimiestre Econômico* 145.

Reis, J.G. 1989. "Salário Mínimo e Distribuição de Renda." *Perspectivas da Economia Brasileira-1989.* Rio de Janeiro: IPEA/INPES.

Saboia, J. 1985. "A Controvérsia sobre o Salário Mínimo e a Taxa de Salários na Economia Brasileira: Novas Evidências." *Revista de Economia Política* 5(2).

Senado Nacional, Comissão Especial Mista. 1993. *Desequilíbrio Econômico Inter-regional Brasileiro*, v. 1-3. Brasília, D.F.: Congresso Nacional.

Secretaria de Indústria e Comércio do Estado de São Paulo. 1988. *A Interiorização da Indústria no Estado de São Paulo.* São Paulo.

Souza, H. 1979. *Estado e Desenvolvimento Capitalista no Brasil.* Rio de Janeiro: Paz e Terra.

Souza, P.E., and P.E. Baltar. 1979. "Salário Mínimo e Taxa de Salários no Brasil." *Pesquisa e Planejamento Econômico* 9(3).

SUDENE. 1984. *Desigualdades Regionais no Desenvolvimento Brasileiro.* Recife: SUDENE.

Tavares, Maria C., and J. Serra. 1972. "Além da Estagnação." In *Da Substituição de Importações ao Capitalismo Financeiro: Ensaio sobre a Economia Brasileira*, ed. Maria C. Tavares. São Paulo: Editora Zahar.

Villela, Aníbal, and W. Suzigan. 1973. *Política de Governo e Crescimento da Economia Brasileira.* Rio de Janeiro: IPEA.

Willumsen, Maria J.F., and A. Dutt. 1991. "Café, Cacau e Crescimento no Brasil." *Revista de Economia Política* 11(3).

# Contributors

**Fábio Barbosa** is Assistant to Brazil's Executive Director at the World Bank. Prior to this, he was an Economic Advisor to the Minister of Industry and Commerce (1984-1985) and a Researcher at the Institute of Applied Economics Research (Instituto de Pesquisa Econômica Aplicada, IPEA) (1987-1992). From May 1991 to October 1992, he held the positions of Coordinator of Fiscal Policy and Special Secretary of Economic Policy in the Finance Ministry. Among various works, he co-authored *O Déficit do Setor Público e a Política Fiscal no Brasil, 1980-1988* (1991).

**Maria Cristina Cacciamali** received her Ph.D. in economics from the University of São Paulo. She was a post-doctoral fellow at the Massachusetts Institute of Technology (MIT). She was also a Visiting Professor at the University of Porto (Portugal) and University of New Mexico (United States). Currently, she is a Professor at the University of São Paulo, teaching labor economics and economic development at graduate and undergraduate levels in the School of Economics and Administration (Faculdade de Economia e Administração, FEA) and in the Masters Program for Latin American Integration. She is also a Senior Researcher at the Institute of Economic Research Foundation (Fundação Instituto de Pesquisas Econômicas, FIPE). In addition to numerous publications in books and academic journals, she has written *Um Estudo Sobre o Setor Informal Urbano e as Formas de Participação na Produção* (1983).

**José Paulo Zeetano Chahad** received his Ph.D. from the University of São Paulo and was a post-doctoral fellow at Boston University. During his academic career, he held the positions of Director of Courses at the Institute of Economic Research Foundation (Fundação Instituto de Pesquisas Econômicas, FIPE), Vice President of the Brazilian Economic Association (Ordem dos Economistas do Brasil), Executive Secretary of the Brazilian Econometrics Society (Sociedade Brasileira de Econometria), and Vice President of the Brazilian Association for Labor Studies (Associação Brasileira de Estudos do Trabalho). He was also the National Adjunct Secretary at the

Brazilian Labor Ministry. He is currently a Professor in the Department of Economics in the School of Economics and Administration (Faculdade de Economia e Administração, FEA), University of São Paulo, and Senior Researcher at the Institute of Economic Research Foundation (Fundação Instituto de Pesquisas Econômicas, FIPE). His publications include *Seguro-Desemprego: Lições da História, Aspectos Teóricos e Perspectivas para o Brasil* (1987), *Crise e Infância no Brasil: O Impacto das Políticas de Ajustamento Econômico* (1988), and numerous articles in books and academic journals.

**Hélio Nogueira da Cruz** received his Ph.D. from the University of São Paulo. From August 1977 to October 1978, he was a post-doctoral fellow in the Economic Growth Center at Yale University. He chaired the Department of Economics at the University of São Paulo and held the position of General Coordinator of the University of São Paulo (CORDAGE). Presently, he is a Professor in the School of Economics and Administration (Faculdade de Economia e Administração, FEA), University of São Paulo, and a Senior Researcher at the Institute of Economic Research Foundation (Fundação Instituto de Pesquisas Econômicas, FIPE). His publications include several chapters in books and various articles in academic journals.

**Eduardo Giannetti da Fonseca** received his Ph.D. in economics from Cambridge University in 1987. He is a Professor of the history of economic thought at graduate and undergraduate levels in the School of Economics and Administration (Faculdade de Economia e Administração, FEA) at the University of São Paulo and a Researcher for the Fernand Braudel Institute (Instituto Fernando Braudel de Economia Mundial). In 1993 he occupied the Joan Robinson Memorial Lectureship as a Visiting Professor at Cambridge University. His many publications include *Beliefs in Action: Economic Philosophy and Social Change* (1991); *Ética e Inflação* (1993); and various articles in academic journals.

**Carlos Alberto Longo** received his Ph.D. from Rice University in 1978. He was awarded the "Haralambos Simeonides" prize in 1984 from the National Association of Centers for Post Graduate Education in Economics (Associação Nacional de Centros de Pós Graduação em Economia, ANPEC). Currently, he is President of the International Academy of Law and Economics. Among various publications in books and academic journals, he has written "Brazil: Monetary and Financial Systems," in *The New Palgrave Dictionary of Money and Finance* (1993).

**Roberto Macedo** received his Ph.D. from Harvard University in 1974. He was awarded the Gastão Vidigal prize and the Shell Brazil Oil (Shell Brasil Petróleo) prize in 1967. In 1985 he received the prestigious Guggenheim

Fellowship. He was a Visiting Professor at Cambridge University (1980), Florida International University (1985), and the University of Kobe, Japan (1989). At the University of São Paulo, he was Chairperson of the Economics Department, Dean of the School of Economics, and Director of the Institute of Economic Research Foundation (Fundação Instituto de Pesquisas Econômicas, FIPE). He was President of the Brazilian Economics Association (Ordem dos Economistas do Brasil), a committee member and Secretary of the Latin American Econometrics Society, and a member of the editorial board of the prestigious Brazilian newspaper *Folha de São Paulo*. He served as a Consultant to several international institutions and was the Special Secretary of Economic Policy in the Brazilian Finance Ministry between May 1991 and October 1992. His publications include several reports, articles in books and academic journals, and the following books: *Distribuição Funcional na Indústria de Transformação: Aspectos da Parcela Salarial* (1980); *Os Salários na Teoria Econômica* (1982); *Os Salários nas Empresas Estatais* (1985); *FGTS and Rotatividade* (1985, co-author); and *Sair da Crise* (1988, co-author). Currently, he is a Professor at the School of Economics and Administration (Faculdade de Economia e Administração, FEA), University of São Paulo, and a Senior Researcher at the Institute of Economic Research Foundation (Fundação Instituto de Pesquisas Econômicas, FIPE) and at the Fernand Braudel Institute for International Economics (Instituto Fernand Braudel de Economia Mundial).

**Fernando Homem de Melo** received his Ph.D. in economics from the University of North Carolina in 1973. He was President of the Institute of Economic Research Foundation (Fundação Instituto de Pesquisas Econômicas, FIPE) between 1985 and 1989. During his academic career, he received several awards: among them, the "Frederico de Menezes Veiga" prize in 1982, awarded by the Brazilian Enterprise for Agricultural Research (Empresa Brasileira de Pesquisa Agropecuária); the "Haralambos Simeonides" prize; and the Moinho Santista prize in 1988 for outstanding research in rural economics. Currently, he is a Professor of economics in the School of Economics and Administration (Faculdade de Economia e Administração, FEA) at the University of São Paulo and a Senior Researcher at the Institute of Economic Research Foundation (Fundação Instituto de Pesquisas Econômicas, FIPE). His publications include *Proálcool, Energia e Transportes* (1981); *O Problema Alimentar no Brasil* (1983); *Solução Energética e a Economia Brasileira* (1984); and *Prioridade Agrícola: Sucesso ou Fracasso* (1985).

**Eli Roberto Pelin** received his Ph.D. in economics from the University of São Paulo (Universidade de São Paulo), with a specialization in energy economics. He held a post-doctoral position at the University College in

London (1986-1987), where he developed research on international prices of petroleum and synthetic fuels — "Preços Internacionais do Petróleo e os Combustíveis Sintéticos." He occupied the post of Executive Secretary in the Institute of Economic Research Foundation (Fundação Instituto de Pesquisas Econômicas, FIPE) from 1992 to 1993. Among other works, he has authored the following: *As Soluções Energéticas e a Economia Brasileira* (1984, co-author); *Avaliação Econômica do Álcool Hidratado Carburante a Curto e Médio Prazos* (1985); *Efeitos Multiplicadores dos Investimentos Públicos no Estado de São Paulo* (1993, co-author).

**Simão Davi Silber** received his Ph.D. from Yale University. He was the Research Coordinator at the Institute of Economic Research Foundation (Fundação Instituto de Pesquisas Econômicas, FIPE), University of São Paulo. Currently, he is an Associate Professor in the School of Economics and Administration (Faculdade de Economia e Administração, FEA) at the University of São Paulo and a Senior Researcher at the Institute of Economic Research Foundation (Fundação Instituto de Pesquisas Econômicas, FIPE). His publications include several articles in books and academic journals and a book entitled *Livre para Crescer: Proposta para um Brasil Moderno* (1990).

**Marcos Eugênio da Silva** received his Ph.D. from the University of São Paulo. He was a post-doctoral fellow at the University of California at Berkeley from 1989 to 1990. He is currently an Assistant Professor in the School of Economics and Administration (Faculdade de Economia e Administração, FEA), University of São Paulo, and a Senior Researcher at the Institute of Economic Research Foundation (Fundação Instituto de Pesquisas Econômicas, FIPE). Additionally, he has authored various articles in academic journals.

**Maria J.F. Willumsen** received her Ph.D. from Cornell University in 1984. She was a Visiting Professor at the Universidad Autónoma de Honduras, the Universidad Autónoma de Nicaragua, and the Federal University of Ceará, and served as a Consultant to the Institute of Economic Research Foundation (Fundação Instituto de Pesquisas Econômicas, FIPE). Currently, she is Associate Professor of economics at Florida International University and a member of the Executive Council of the Southern Regional Science Association (1991-1994). Her publications include *The Social Accounting Matrix as a Tool for Policy Analysis: the Case of Brazil* (1984); *Efeitos Multiplicadores dos Investimentos Públicos no Estado de São Paulo* (1993, co-author); *Matriz de Contabilidade Social para o Estado do Ceará* (1993, co-author); and several articles in books and academic journals.

Alvaro Antônio Zini, Jr., received his Ph.D. from Cornell University in 1988. He was awarded the BNDES (Banco Nacional de Desenvolvimento Econômico e Social) prize for the best master's thesis (1985) and the "American Express for Latin America" award for the best article on international finance (1988). He has also received the "Haralambos Simeonides" prize, which is awarded by the National Association of Post Graduate Education in Economics (Associação Nacional de Centros de Pós Graduação em Economia, ANPEC). He is currently a Professor of international economics and economics of Latin America in the School of Economics and Administration (Faculdade de Economia e Administração, FEA) at the University of São Paulo. His publications include *Taxa de Câmbio e Política Cambial no Brasil* (1993), *The Market and the State in Economic Development in the 1990s* (1992), and several articles in academic journals.

# Index

## A